In the Potter's Kitchen

Handmade Pots for Home-Cooked Recipes

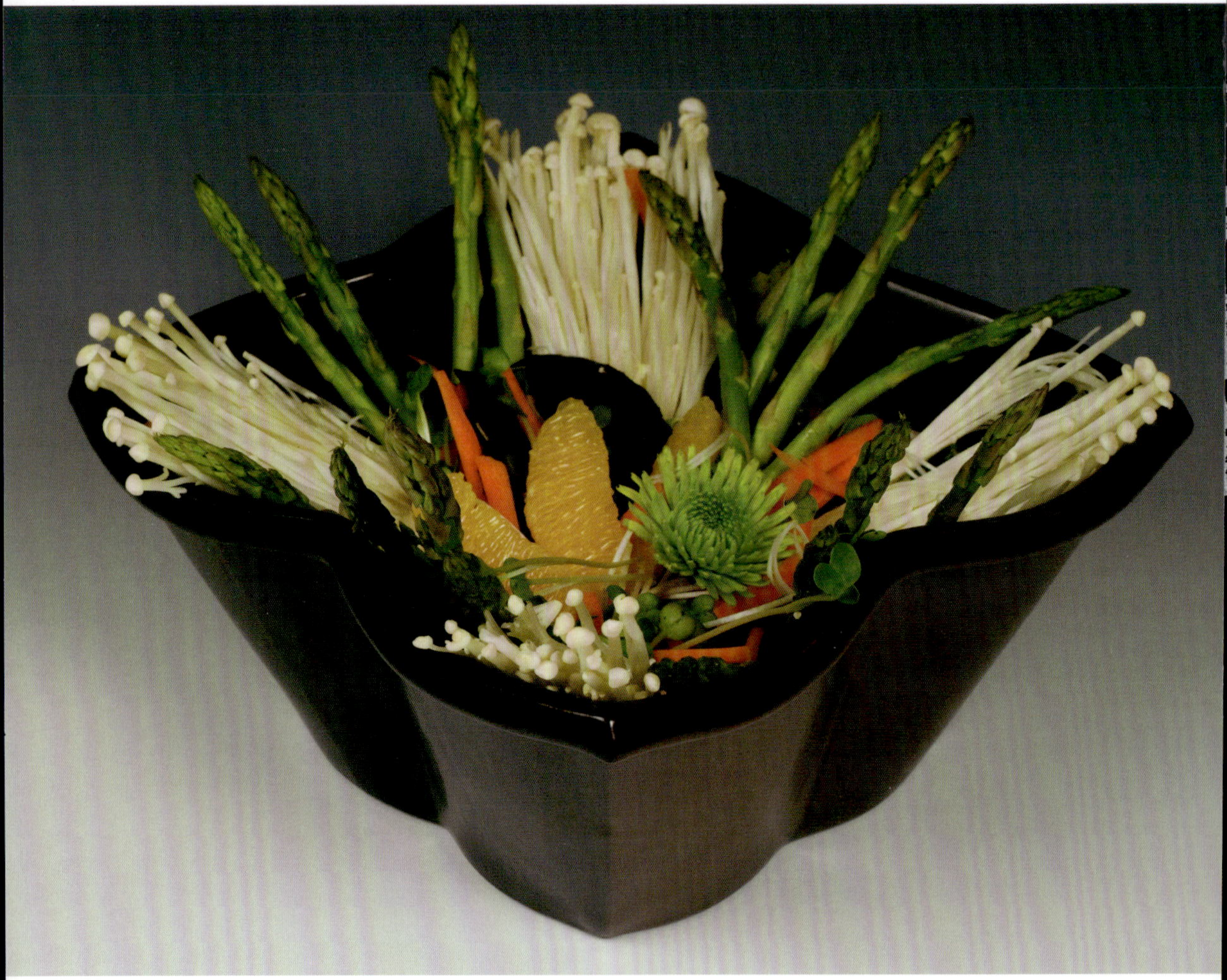

In the Potter's Kitchen

Handmade Pots for Home-Cooked Recipes

Sumi von Dassow

Published by
The American Ceramic Society
600 Cleveland Avenue, Suite 210
Westerville, Ohio 43082 USA

The American Ceramic Society
600 N. Cleveland Ave., Suite 210
Westerville, OH 43082

ISBN: 978-1-57498-329-6 (Paperback)

ISBN: 978-1-57498-570-2 (PDF)

Publisher: Charles Spahr, Executive Director, The American Ceramic Society.

Art Book Program Manager: Bill Jones

eBook Manager: Steven L. Hecker

Series Design: Melissa Bury

Graphic Production: Pamela S. Woodworth

Cover image: *Bean Pots in the Kitchen* Greg Hardy; top: Onggi jars by Adam Field; back cover top: Clay Coyote flameware tagine, *photo by Emily Swanter*; bottom: Onggi jars by Adam Field.

Frontispiece: Salad of greens, asparagus stalks, orange wedges and enoki mushrooms tasty miso dressing in a quatrefoil bowl by Julie Timm. Photo by Robert Paul.

Printed in China

Table of Contents

Foreword

In the 21st century we see a powerful movement toward buying local, organic and sustainably produced food products. More and more consumers are voting with their dollars to support family farmers instead of agribusiness. Every year we hear news reports of food-borne illnesses claiming hundreds of lives and causing costly recalls of incredible quantities of food, and these stories make some consumers think twice about buying mass-marketed food. When we shop at a grocery store we often have no way of knowing where and how the food we buy was produced. When we shop at a farm stand or farmer's market, we can meet the farmers and talk to them about their practices—maybe we can visit the farm and pick our own produce. There's a term for these consumers—*locavores*—people who prefer to consume locally produced food. More and more restaurants cater to locavores, and farmers' markets do a booming business all summer long.

At the farmer's market, alongside the fruits and veggies you'll often see potters selling their wares. After all, if you're going to shell out top dollar for farm-fresh produce and grass-fed beef, why take them home and cook them in mass-produced pottery made halfway around the world? Your local potter may even create pots specifically for some local specialty, and she will be happy to share with you her tips and recipes to get the most out of both your new pottery and your produce. Potters are often passionate and talented cooks who make pots to fulfill their own needs as cooks. Perhaps you've had the experience of purchasing a factory-made teapot or pitcher that looks elegant but slops its contents all over the table when you try to pour; or perhaps a mug with a cute silk-screened decoration that fits uncomfortably in your hand. Potters strive everyday to make their work not only beautiful but supremely useful, and they test their own work in their own kitchens.

I've spent decades discussing food, recipes and cooking with fellow potters, and I've come to realize that people who are drawn to making functional pottery tend to share a love of food, cooking and company. A potter who wants to try a new cooking technique may first make the pot for it and work to perfect both the recipe and the pot in the learning process. I've been to countless potters' potlucks and marveled at the variety of lovingly home-cooked dishes presented in lovingly handmade pots. I always tell my friends, if you're ever invited to dinner at a potter's home, go with an appetite.

Of course the marriage of food and pottery is hardly new—it's an age-old relationship that's been somewhat forgotten in the industrial era. The Moroccan tagine, the Pueblo bean pot, the Japanese donabe pot (not to mention the teapot and teabowls that serve such a central role in the Japanese tea ceremony), are all pottery forms that have evolved alongside local foods and recipes. In the European tradition there are countless vessel forms made by the thousands in factories that once were a staple of the potter's craft. Other forms have fallen by the wayside as home cooking declines, and are hard to find. When you think of baking dishes, loaf pans, pie pans, custard cups, and coffee pots, you're likely to envision mass marketed versions, even though until the industrial era, potters had to keep busy making these things. And could you even find such erstwhile kitchen essentials as a sturdy bread bowl big enough to mix up dough for the week's baking, or a French butter crock to keep butter cool without refrigeration, or a sauerkraut crock to preserve fall's bounty of cabbages? Perhaps not in Wal-Mart—but your local potter/cook may make one.

This book comes out of my own love of both cooking and pottery, and my desire to share both passions with as many people as possible. It's my hope that both potters and cooks will appreciate the contents. Potters will find new styles of pots that may appeal to customers, as well as recipes to inspire customers to use them. Cooks will find well-tested recipes suited to cooking and serving in hand-made pots. If you're in both groups—happy potting and bon appetit!

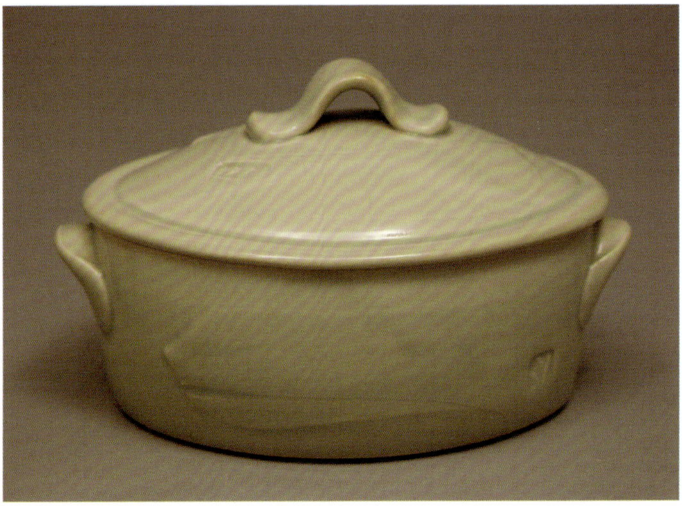

Porcelain potato baker by Robin Furuta, 6 inches in length, wheel-thrown and altered porcelain with celadon glaze. The translucent celadon glaze is perfect for showing off the whiteness of porcelain and subtle surface texture. Cone 10 reduction. Made for baking one potato! *Photo by Sumi von Dassow*

Introduction

Just as insects evolved alongside flowering plants, so did pottery and cooking evolve together. The first humans to learn to use fire may have done so for warmth at night, or to keep safe from predators, but they quickly learned that food cooked on the fire was tastier and easier to eat than raw food. And it must have been in the process of cooking food that people first discovered that clay hardens when exposed to fire. Perhaps a basket lined with mud to seal the pores was left too close to the fire and burned away leaving a fired clay pot. Perhaps someone noticed the hardened walls of a pit used to bake meat or roots—or maybe people simply noticed that the ground on which the fire was built became hard and impervious to water. Imagine the difference it must have made when the first potter began to cook in his first pots! Putting food in a pot on the fire was so much quicker than digging a pit and filling it with hot rocks, lining it with leaves, and leaving food inside to roast; easier than holding food over the fire on a stick, which makes it hard to do anything else with your hands while the food is cooking; and much less tedious than heating water inside a gourd by dropping hot rocks in.

The invention of pottery made it possible for people to eat many highly nutritious plant foods that aren't usable raw. Consider, for example, beans, which are highly nutritious, lightweight and easy to transport, and keep forever. Various kinds of beans are staple foods in traditional societies around the world, but they must be soaked in water for hours and then boiled for hours more before they can be chewed and digested. Consequently, pots for cooking beans are ubiquitous throughout the world. As important as legumes is the entire family of grains—rice, wheat, corn, and all the others—which also must be soaked and boiled, and so we have an entire family of traditional pots for cooking grains. Another such food comes from the oak tree. Native American learned that, although acorns have toxic amounts of tannins when raw, they could be used as a dietary staple once they were soaked and cooked.

Even foods that can be eaten raw are more nutritious and easier to eat when lightly cooked (not charred over a hot fire, but steamed in a pot of water). A whole armful of raw spinach that would take an hour to chew, cooks down to a few soft spoonfuls;

nutritionists tell us the lycopene in tomatoes is more usable when tomatoes are cooked; and potatoes, squash, and parsnips are hard to chew and slow to digest raw, but soft enough for a toothless baby or elder to swallow when cooked. So cooking renders some plant foods edible that would be inedible raw, while other foods are simply easier to eat or more nutritious when cooked. And when foods are easier to eat and more nutritious, people can spend more time doing other things besides chewing. Some people can be planting and cultivating crops, some can be making clay pots, and others can spend the day hunting, knowing that even if unsuccessful, there will be a nutritious meal the exhausted hunters can eat quickly upon their return.

If the hunter is successful, cooking will make his catch more usable. For even meats, which are perfectly nutritious raw, are much more digestible and easier to eat when cooked. Imagine trying to chew a piece of the haunch of an animal that has spent its life running—you could tire your jaws out chewing for hours and not get much of it down. Great apes spend their lives chewing vegetation, and they do not eat much meat because they can't get enough calories from raw meat to justify the chewing it takes. There are ways of cooking meat without pottery, which must have been invented almost as soon as humans tamed fire. An individual cut of meat can be roasted on a stick over a fire; a moderate-sized animal can be suspended whole over a fire; and a large animal can be roasted whole in a pit. But consider that tough haunch of antelope or elk—holding it over the fire on a stick wouldn't soften it much, but simmering it over the fire for hours in a pot of water would make it fall apart. Add some beans and grains, and some tubers, roots or leaves, and voilà, you have a nutritionally balanced feast! Civilization is born! Humans could settle down to cultivate plants and domesticate animals, and to make the pots, tools, fences, ropes and harnesses they need in these endeavors—all because their food could be cooked in clay pots. Agriculture, art and architecture arose and flourished, all because of the love triangle of fire, clay, and food.

Of course pottery didn't appear as soon as humans tamed fire. Historians do not agree on an exact timeline for when humans began using fire and cooking, but apparently the use of fire to prepare food is at least 40,000 years old. Grains and roots were ground and baked on hot stones by Paleolithic hunter-gatherers by about 30,000 years ago. The first known clay cooking pots are Jomon pottery from Japan, dating back to some 13,000 years ago, used by hunter-gatherer cultures. In other parts of the world, the shift to agriculture arose before pottery was fully developed—food was cooked in stone vessels or in vessels made from lime and ash built up around baskets. Interestingly, life expectancies dropped in this interim period of the early Neolithic, when people began to cultivate grains and legumes but didn't yet have the equipment or knowledge to prepare them for maximum nutrition. But pottery quickly developed and spread, becoming common throughout the world by 5,000 years ago.

Many traditional cooking pots designed for use directly on a fire are earthenware, typically unglazed. Earthenware is fired to a low temperature (1400°F to 1800°F—or 760 to 982°C) and is porous and relatively fragile. The low-firing temperature and lack of glaze means the pots are economical to produce, even if they don't last long. It also means the clay can withstand a direct flame without shattering. Food cooked in a porous unglazed pot flavors, and is flavored by, the clay. If the pot is soaked in water before use, the food is moistened in the cooking process. If not, moisture is drawn out of the food through the body of the pot, to evaporate as steam while the pot is on the

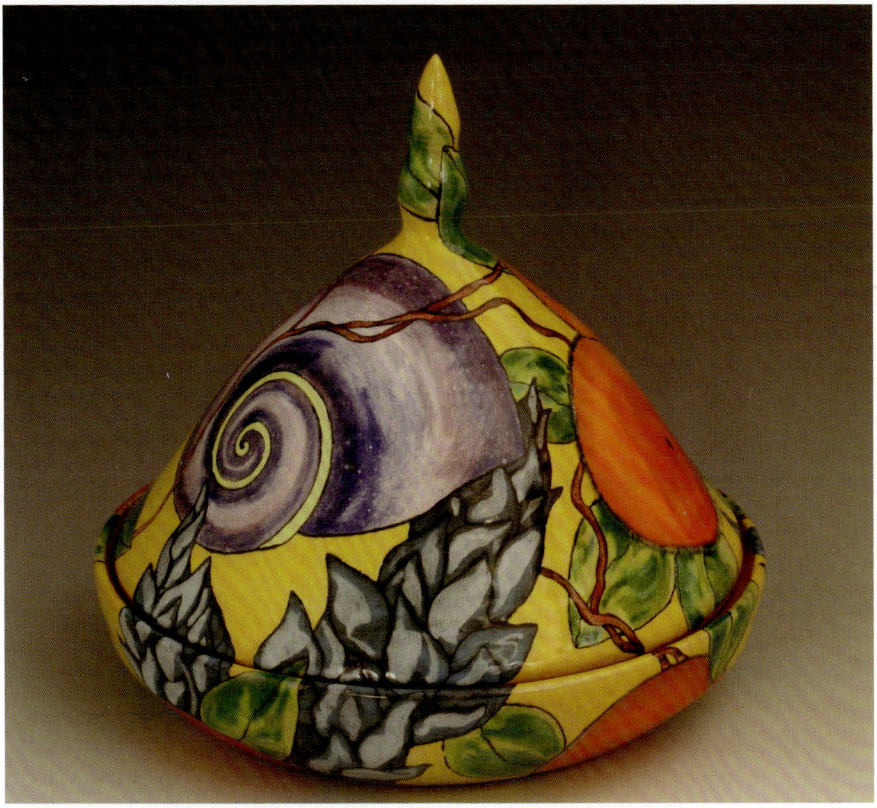

Yellow Garden Tagine, glazed terra cotta, 10 inches in height, by Farraday Newsome. This is a splendid example of earthenware with majolica decoration. The bright sunny colors and exuberant decoration are indicative of glazed earthenware. *Photo by Farraday Newsome*

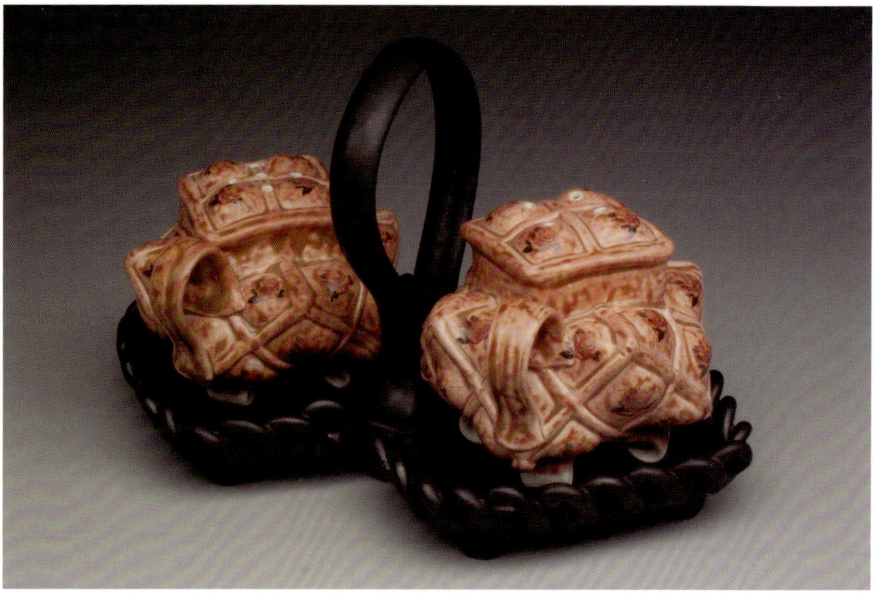

Pink Rose Salt and Pepper Set by Margaret Bohls, 8½ inches in length, slab-built, porcelain and earthenware (tray), cone 9 and cone 04 electric fired. *Photo by Margaret Bohls*

fire. Earthenware cooking pots are used all over the world and include the Moroccan tagine, the Japanese donabe, the Indian chatti, the Mexican olla, the Philippine palayok, the Chinese hot-pot, and the German Römertopf.

Traditional earthenware cooking pots in use today include ware for the stovetop and for the oven. Micaceous clay bean pots made by Pueblo Indians in the American Southwest, the chatti, used in India to make curried fish, and the donabe pot are stovetop pots. Tagines, necessary for all varieties of Moroccan foods, can be used on the stovetop and in the oven. The Römertopf, commonly used for cooking chickens, are covered pots for use in the oven.

The development of glazed stoneware cooking pots had to await the development of stoves with ovens. In a way, cooking in a stoneware pot inside an oven mimics on a smaller scale the ancient technique of cooking food in a pit lined with leaves and filled with hot coals or stones. Stoneware cooking pots have the advantage of being non-porous so wet foods can be contained in them without leaking through, but the corresponding disadvantage of being generally unsuited to cooking directly on a fire or hot stovetop. Typical European forms such as the casserole dish, loaf pan, baking pan, pie dish, and an unending catalog of other forms, must be placed in an oven isolated from a direct flame.

There are some traditional pottery forms that are not designed strictly for cooking, but were at one time integral to the preparation or storage of certain foods. Butter is no longer churned by hand, but when it was, it was done in a stoneware vessel—and before refrigeration became common, butter was stored in a French butter crock, designed to keep butter cool but spreadable above a layer of ice. It's still a nice way to keep your butter if you like to use it throughout the day. Another pot that is now hard to find is the sauerkraut crock, once indispensable for preserving large quantities of cabbage without refrigeration. If you want to make sauerkraut in the traditional manner, you can scrounge around for a suitable-sized bucket or canister, but a proper stoneware crock works better.

Some potters do make stoneware that can be used directly on a hot stovetop. This ware is called flameware, and it's technically challenging to make. The clay and glaze must be carefully formulated, and the temperature, environment, and speed of the firing must be carefully controlled, or the pots may fail disastrously in use. This type of ware benefits from modern technology, and the potter who wishes to make flameware can now put her clay through rigorous testing in labs before marketing it.

All this profusion of pottery means it's more fun than ever to cook and serve food. You can make a meal in traditional earthenware pots today, in stoneware

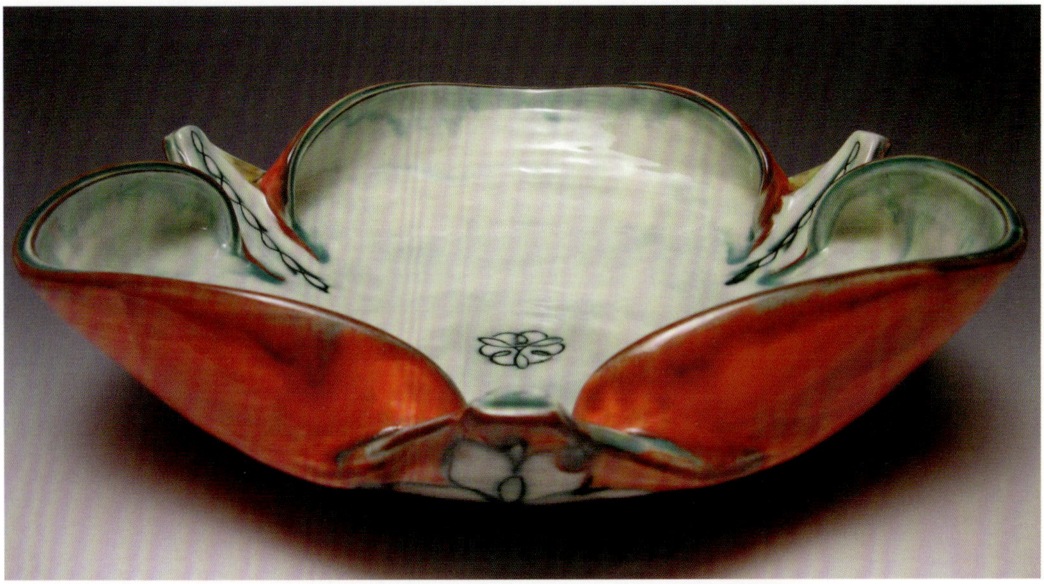

Trillium Bowl by Joan Bruneau, 18 inches in diameter, wheel thrown and assembled earthenware with slip, sgraffito decoration and polychrome glazes. Bruneau made this dish to serve lobster and to collect the shells. *Photo by Joan Bruneau*

tomorrow, and in flameware the next day. You can use the same ingredients in very different recipes based on the kind of pot you want to cook in. You have available all the technology developed in the thirteen millennia since humans began cooking in clay. It's equally fun to be a functional potter with a whole world of forms to try, so many kinds of clay to work with, and no end to the variety of forming and finishing techniques to explore.

The Wares and Recipes

Once you've made or bought your pot, what can you do with it? Any kind of food can be cooked, served, stored, and eaten on or in a clay pot. There is a pot for every purpose, including many traditional forms that have been made and used for thousands of years. There's no reason to hesitate to use pottery to cook and serve all the foods you love. Ask the potter or refer to chapter one of this book to be sure you know what kind of uses your new pot is suited for.

Chapters 4 through 9 of this book are organized according to how you will use your pot, rather than the type of clay it is made from. Ovenware is commonly made from stoneware, but all kinds of clay can be used to cook in the oven. Ovenware includes casserole dishes; rectangular, square, or round baking dishes for lasagna, brownies, breads or pies; many kinds of pots for roasting or braising meats; and special purpose bakers for apples, Brie, garlic, or other foods. Of course many cooks prefer to save time and energy by cooking in a microwave oven, and many of the forms that can be used in a standard oven can also be used in a microwave.

Ware for use on the stove top is much less common in the developed world than ovenware, although in many parts of the world all pottery is used directly on a fire. Placing a pot directly on a burner or over a flame is much harder on the clay than heating it in an oven. Although there are many traditional ethnic forms that are used for stovetop cooking, in the United States craft potters typically avoid making stovetop ware unless they work with flameware or micaceous clay. The best bean pots in the world may be micaceous clay bean pots, or *ollas*, made in the Southwestern United States. These pots may sell for hundreds of dollars. Still harder to find is ware for use on a grill or campfire, although there are many interesting historic forms that could be re-invented by an enterprising studio potter.

Any pottery collector will find a wide variety of serving ware made from all types of clay. Pitchers, gravy boats, platters, chip and dip sets, cake stands, and, of course, bowls, are made by every potter. While there are plenty of uses for generic platters and bowls, potters can be incredibly creative in coming up with special serving dishes. Any potter who cooks will come up with a dish in which to serve a favorite food. If you like artichokes, you might make a set of bowls for serving artichokes and collecting the leaves. A potter who attends a lot of picnics might make insulated pots for keeping foods hot or cold, or dishes designed to keep cold salads on ice.

Other forms are made for preparing and storing foods. Some still-popular items hark back hundreds of years, such as French butter crocks, sauerkraut crocks, batter bowls, and the mortar and pestle for grinding spices. Here, too, there is plenty of room for an individual potter's ingenuity, and for delving into history for forgotten useful forms.

You can approach these chapters of the book in a variety of ways. You can look for recipes that suit your pots or ones that take advantage of local or seasonal ingredients, or you can look for pottery forms you might like to try for favorite dishes. If you're a potter, you might want to look for new items to try making, or for recipes that will work in forms you enjoy making. Whether you're a pottery maker or a pottery collector, these chapters offer many ways you can further your enjoyment of pottery.

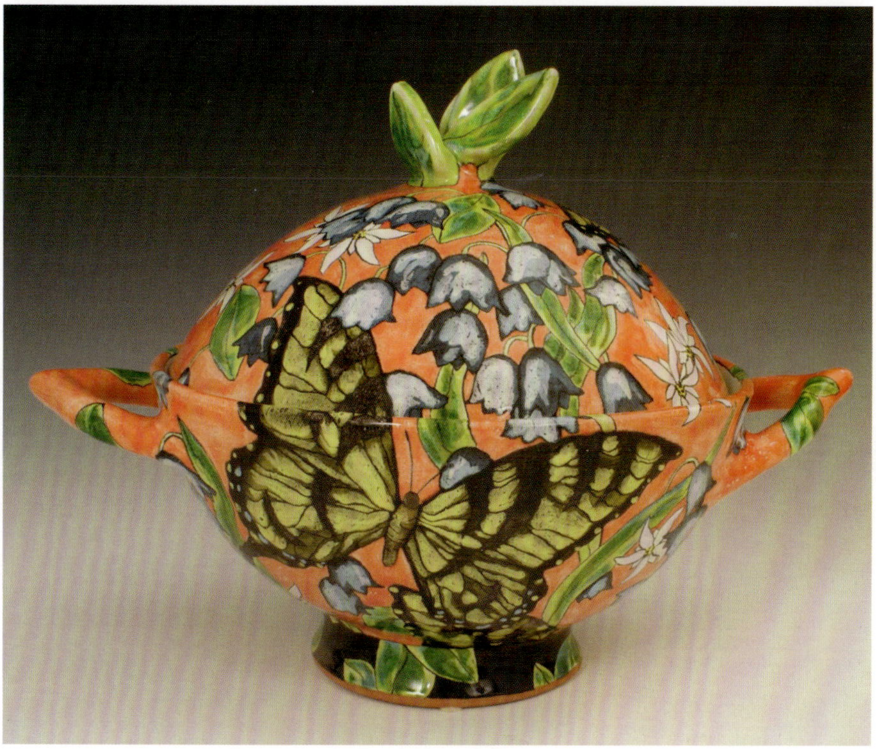

Coral Tureen with Butterflies and Bluebells by Farraday Newsome, 15 inches in height, glazeed terra cotta. The bright colors are typical of low-fire majolica ware. Farraday carefully seals the underside of her earthenware serving pieces with glaze to make sure they won't leak.
Photo by Farraday Newsome

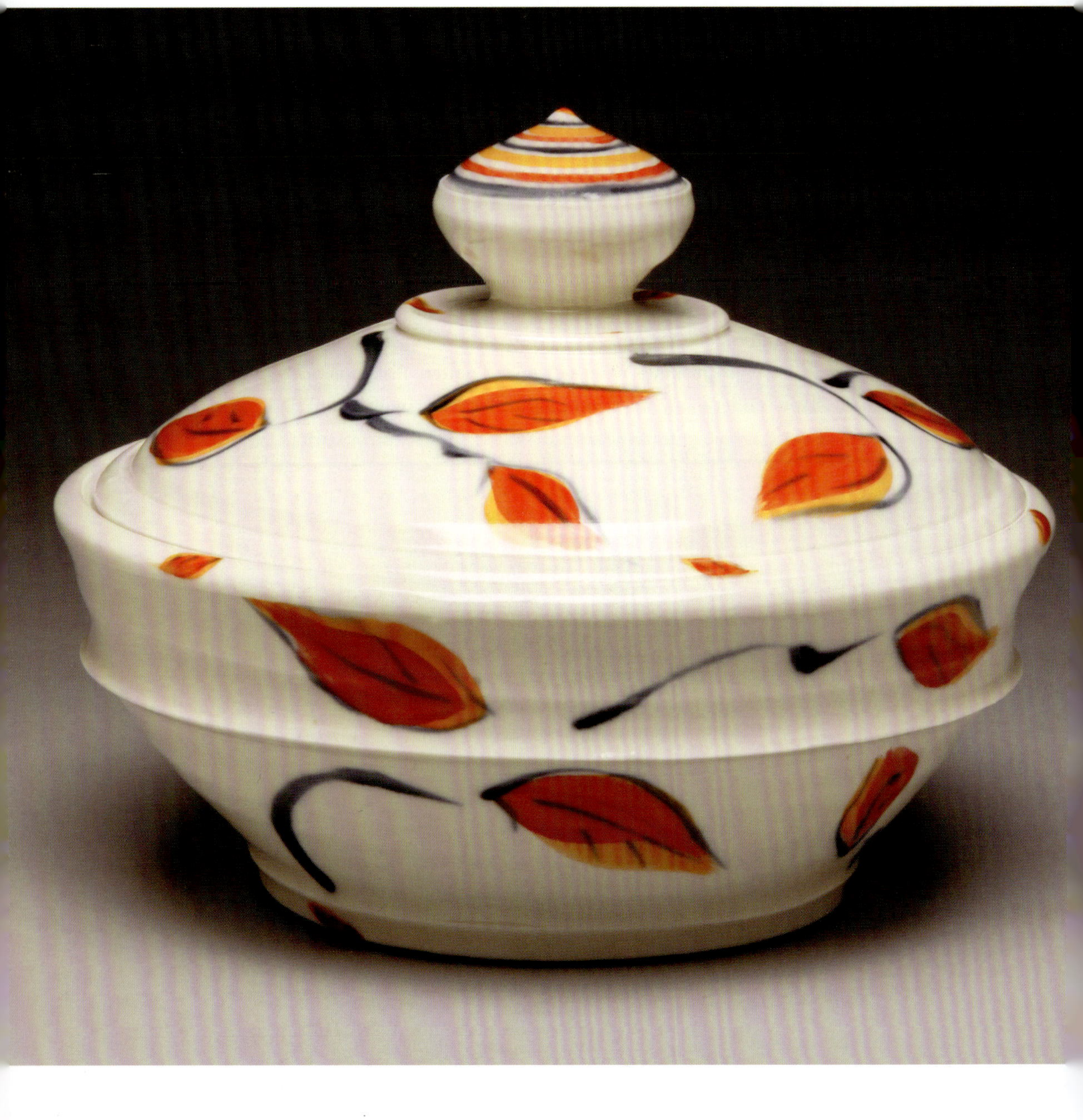

CHAPTER 1

Types of Clay

The first thing to think about when you're deciding what kind of clay to use, or what kind of pottery to buy, will be what kind of cooking you want to do in your pot. Do you want to cook casseroles in the oven or soup on the stovetop? Do you want to roast a chicken or bake a lasagna? If you refer to the chart below you'll see that earthenware, stoneware, porcelain and flameware are suitable for different types of cooking.

How can a piece of pottery be used?

	Microwave	Oven	Stovetop	Dishwasher
Stoneware	Yes	Yes	No	Yes
Porcelain	Yes	Yes	No	Yes
Glazed Earthenware	No	Yes	Maybe	Maybe
Unglazed Earthenware	No	Yes	Maybe	No
Flameware	Yes	Yes	Yes	Yes

What Is Stoneware and Porcelain?

Stoneware is pottery that's been fired to a high enough temperature to vitrify it. This means it's not porous and will not absorb moisture or "leak" when liquid is left in it. Usually this means it's fired to 2200°F (1093°C) or higher. Stoneware should have an absorbency rate of around 3–4%. Porcelain is very smooth and white and is even more vitrified and less absorbent than stoneware, with an absorbency rate of around 1%. Most porcelain is fired to a temperature of 2300°F (1260°C) or higher. Since properly vitrified stoneware and porcelain will not absorb moisture, they can be washed in a dishwasher without absorbing water and detergent. Because they will not absorb moisture, they won't get hot in a microwave oven. Stoneware and porcelain will break if heated unevenly, so these pots cannot be used on a stovetop. A stoneware or porcelain baking dish should be filled completely with food so that it heats evenly, whether you're using it in a conventional oven or a microwave oven. If a stoneware or porcelain baking dish is not completely full of food, it will heat unevenly and may crack. The spot where the food is will heat up slowly as the food heats, while the rest of the clay will heat quickly. This means that a standing roast or a chicken should not

Porcelain casserole dish by Sarah Jaeger, 8 inches in height, wheel-thrown with overglaze decoration and fired in gas oxidation to cone 10. *Photo by Tom Ferris*

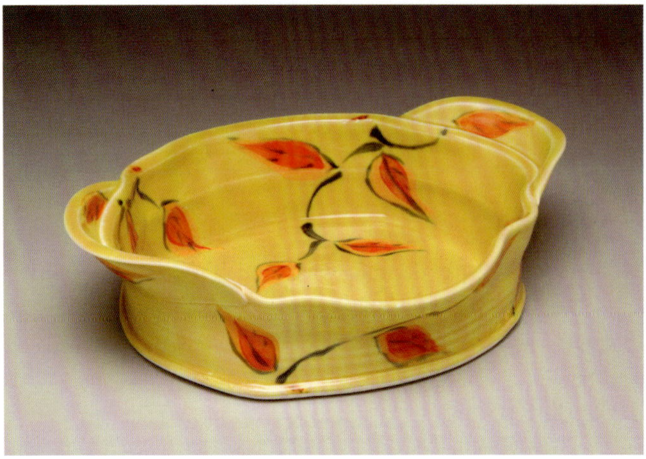

Porcelain baking dish by Sarah Jaeger, 14 inches in length, gas oxidation fired to cone 10. *Photo by Tom Ferris*

be roasted in a stoneware dish unless it's surrounded with vegetables and liquid so the entire baking dish is filled.

What Is Earthenware?

Earthenware is pottery that has been fired to a lower temperature than stoneware, and it's not vitrified, meaning it's porous and will absorb moisture. This does not necessarily mean that earthenware is more fragile than stoneware, just that it must be used differently. Earthenware may be glazed or unglazed, but even if it's glazed, the clay can absorb moisture. Consequently it will absorb water and detergent if it's washed in a dishwasher, although if it's glazed completely it may be acceptable to wash it in a dishwasher. Once earthenware pottery has been in use long enough to absorb moisture, it will get hot when used in a microwave oven due to the moisture in the clay. This would tend to cause a glaze to craze quickly, and maybe even lose its adhesion to the pot. Therefore, glazed earthenware should not be used in a microwave oven. Earthenware can be used in the oven and some kinds of earthenware can be used on the stovetop. If cooking on electric burners or a flat-top stove, use a diffuser under it to protect it from direct contact with a hot burner, and turn the heat up slowly. Unglazed earthenware baking dishes are typically soaked in water before they're used so that the food steams during the first part of the baking process. This allows the pot to heat up slowly as the food begins to cook, so something like a whole chicken or a standing roast can safely be roasted in a soaked earthenware pot. Some cooks even use unglazed earthenware in the microwave oven in this same way, soaking it first. This is hardly traditional but it can be done. Micaceous clay is a special kind of earthenware used in New Mexico to make very durable high-end cookware for stovetop and oven use. It contains a large amount of mica, which makes the clay sparkle beautifully but also makes it very strong and resistant to thermal shock.

What Is Flameware?

Flameware is a relatively modern product that relies on modern testing technology to ensure that each piece is correctly formulated and fired. It's made from specially formulated clay that can withstand the thermal shock of heating directly on a stovetop, and can also be used in the oven or microwave. Flameware absorbs no water at all. While flameware is very versatile, potters who work with this kind of clay must be diligent about testing their ware, so it's not commonly made. Only a few clay manufacturers make "flameware" clay. For most potters, it must be custom-made, and only a very experienced and committed potter will want to try to make this kind of ware. If you want to make flameware, you'll have to research clay recipes and materials and contract with your supplier to make it for you. The liability if the clay fails in use is too great, and ceramic materials are too variable for most suppliers to want to take on the risk of making flameware clay. If you want to work with it, you'll have to perform careful tests on every batch of clay and every kiln load of pots.

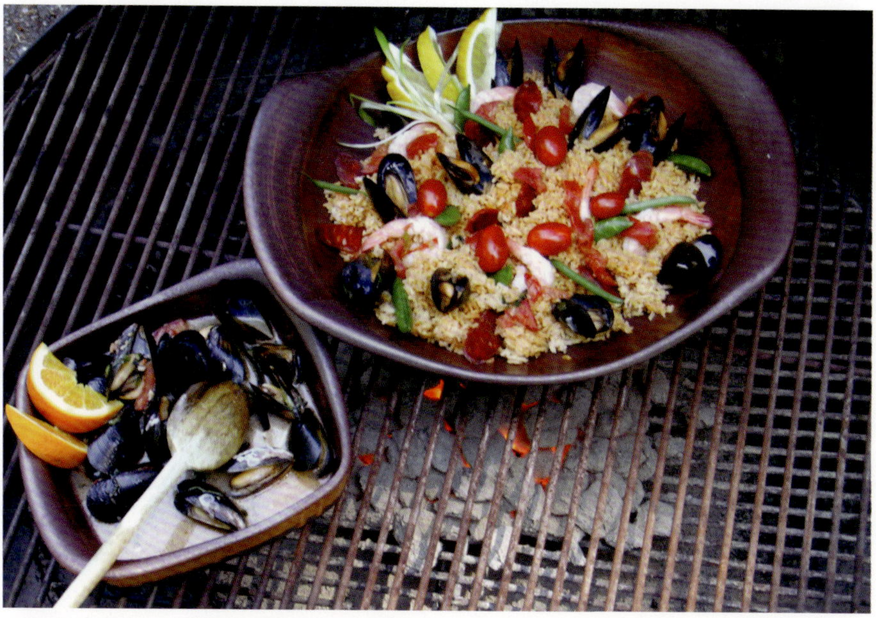

Flameware by Robbie Lobell. Paella pot and square baker on grill. The shape of the foot of a flameware pot must match the shape of the heat source. Therefore, the round paella pot can go on the grill or the stovetop or in the oven, while the square baker can go on the grill or in the oven but not directly on a burner. *Photo by Gina O. Burrill*

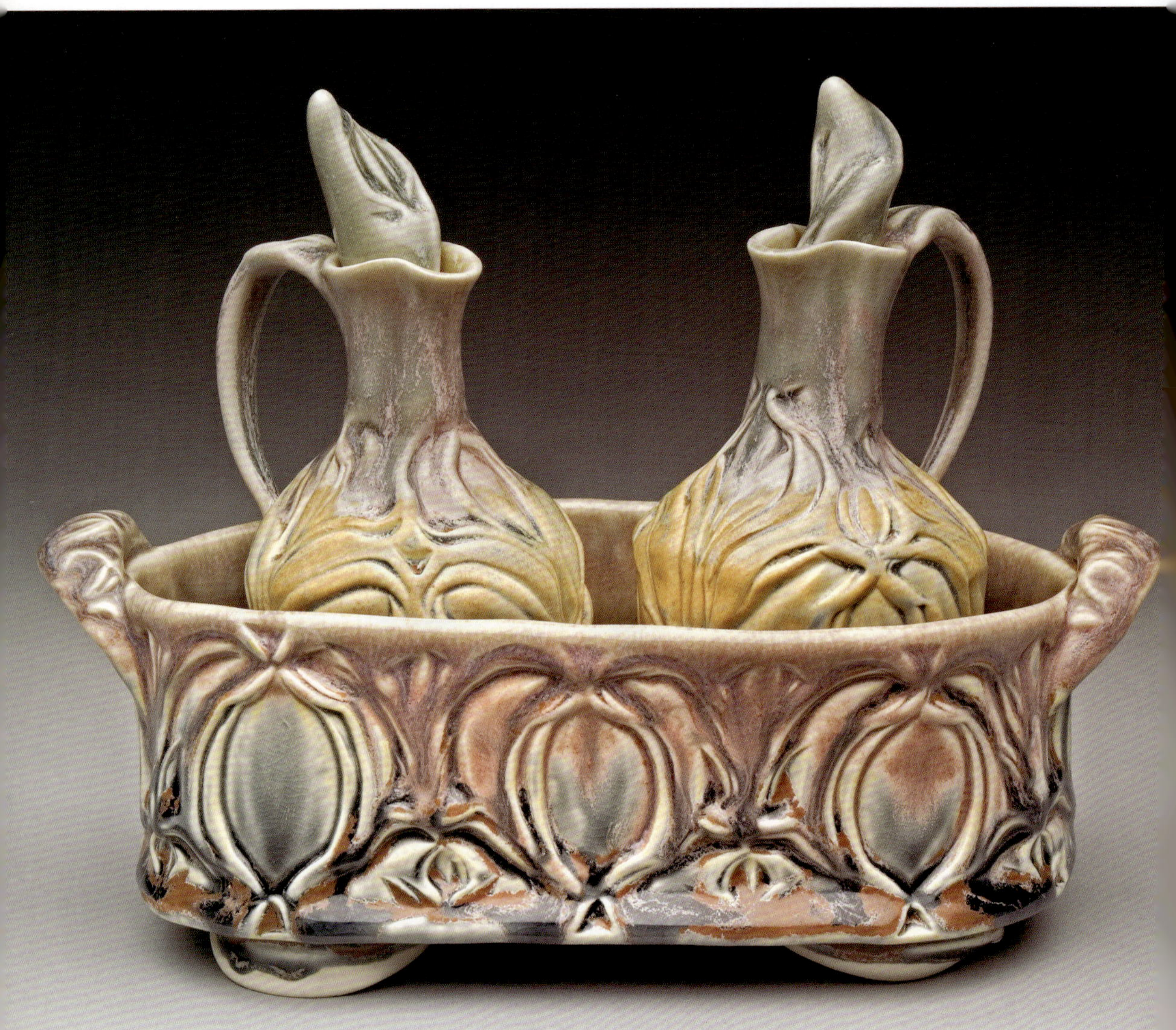

CHAPTER 2

Advice for the Potter

How Do I Decide What Kind of Clay to Use?

Presuming you're going to be buying clay at your local ceramic supplier, you can choose from earthenware or stoneware; and in the stoneware category, most suppliers sell clays designed to mature from cone 5/6 up to cone 10. You can choose your clay based on what kind of cookware you want to make, or based on your choice of glazes and glaze firing temperature. So, let's consider briefly the pros and cons of the different types of clay.

Earthenware offers the potter the obvious advantage of requiring less energy and fuel because it's fired to a lower temperature than stoneware. Unglazed earthenware only requires one firing to a relatively low temperature around cone 04 to 06, meaning it's the most efficient and cost-effective type of cookware to make. If your pottery requires no glaze, you save the time of applying glaze, you save money not buying glazes or glaze materials, and you save fuel and wear and tear on your kiln. Furthermore, you don't have to worry about issues such as glaze fit and whether your glaze is "food safe," although an unglazed pot is harder to clean and will absorb food odors. If used properly, earthenware is just as sturdy as stoneware—possibly even more durable and resistant to heat shock. Unglazed earthenware can even be used to make ware for cooking on the stovetop, although it must be used very carefully and may not last very long subjected to this kind of uneven heating.

Though earthenware is a fine choice for many types of cooking, the average American is probably more familiar with stoneware for cooking and baking. Likewise, although in many ways it's highly practical to make and use unglazed ware, most Americans assume pottery must be glazed to be useful, and many cooks are uncomfortable with the idea of pottery that can't be washed with soap or put in the dishwasher. You might really enjoy cooking in unglazed earthenware, but if you make this kind of ware for sale, you might have a harder job convincing buyers to bite. Of course, if you enjoy glazing and decorating, this type of pottery won't be very satisfying to make, either.

A special category of unglazed earthenware clay is micaceous clay. This clay is not widely available outside of New Mexico, where it's traditional and highly prized, but it can be shipped from suppliers in that state. If you're interested in making unglazed

Cruet set, 3½ inches in height, by Lora Rust, altered and handbuilt porcelain, fired to cone 6 oxidation. The decoration on Rust's work is neither impressed nor carved, but formed in the wet clay with handmade wooden tools. Photo by Walker Montgomery

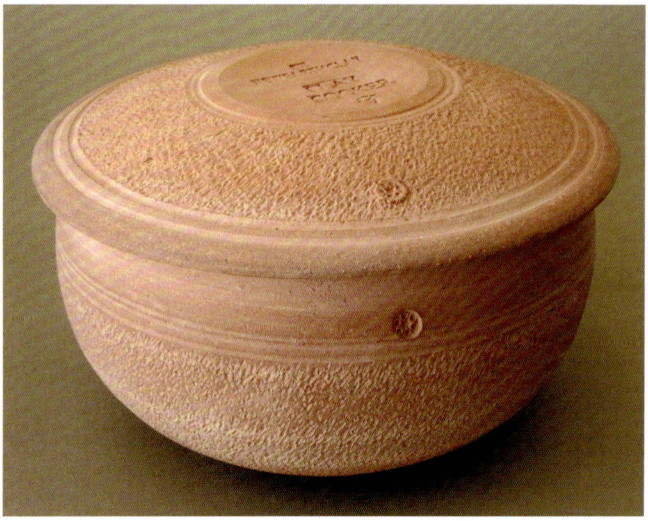

3½ quart clay cooker by Bill Robbins, 10 inches in diameter, wheel-thrown red brick clay with added grog, unglazed, reduction fired to cone 04.

earthenware, this kind of clay might be worth investigating. It has a very high resistance to thermal shock, and the clay itself is quite beautiful. It's typically used to make pots for cooking on the stovetop, which most other kinds of clay cannot withstand. Well-made micaceous clay cooking pots are very expensive and aficionados say they give a special flavor to food cooked in them due to the mineral content. Traditionally these pots are fired in open bonfires to very low temperatures, picking up beautiful markings from smoke in the process.

Glazed earthenware is still porous—you can't count on glaze to seal the porous clay because even if it's watertight when it comes out of the kiln, the clay will absorb water through the unglazed foot. Eventually this causes the glaze to develop fine cracks, called crazing, which will let water through. It also may be more fragile than stoneware, but to most Americans it looks more like what they expect pottery to look like, so your sales job may be easier. You'll still have to warn users not to put the ware in the microwave, and you might want to discourage washing it in the dishwasher. If you're not careful, your pottery might leak and leave a wet patch on the tabletop. Despite these cautions, it's quite possible to make completely functional ovenware and serving dishes from glazed earthenware. Your firing costs will be lower than for stoneware, since you'll be firing to the cone 06–04 range, and you'll have a wide range of glaze colors to choose from. If you like to decorate and you like bright colors, you might prefer to make glazed earthenware. If you want to avoid mixing your own glazes, there are many reliable commercial glazes in the earthenware temperature range. However, you'll have to be aware of the issue of lead in your glazes; although most commercial glazes are supposed to be safe when fired according to the directions on the label, you may want to steer clear of commercial glazes that contain lead.

Stoneware is probably the most familiar type of pottery cookware for most Americans. Though most non-potters won't necessarily understand the difference between glazed earthenware and glazed stoneware, pottery buyers will probably assume they can use a piece of pottery in the oven and the microwave and wash it in the dishwasher. In fact, you'll have to make sure your customers don't assume they can use your stoneware just like they might use metal cookware. Properly vitrified stoneware is easy to keep clean and sanitary, but it must be used with care or it may suffer thermal shock and break in use. Stoneware cookware must be filled with food and placed in a cool oven, and it can't be used on the stovetop. A casserole dish or lasagna pan will last years if it's used for casseroles and lasagna; but if you repeatedly cook a whole chicken in a stoneware baking dish, the cold meat sitting in the middle of the dish creates a cold spot in the center, which may cause it to eventually crack due to uneven heating.

One big advantage to working with stoneware is that high-temperature glazes are easier and cheaper to formulate and often easier to apply. You can be sure there's no lead

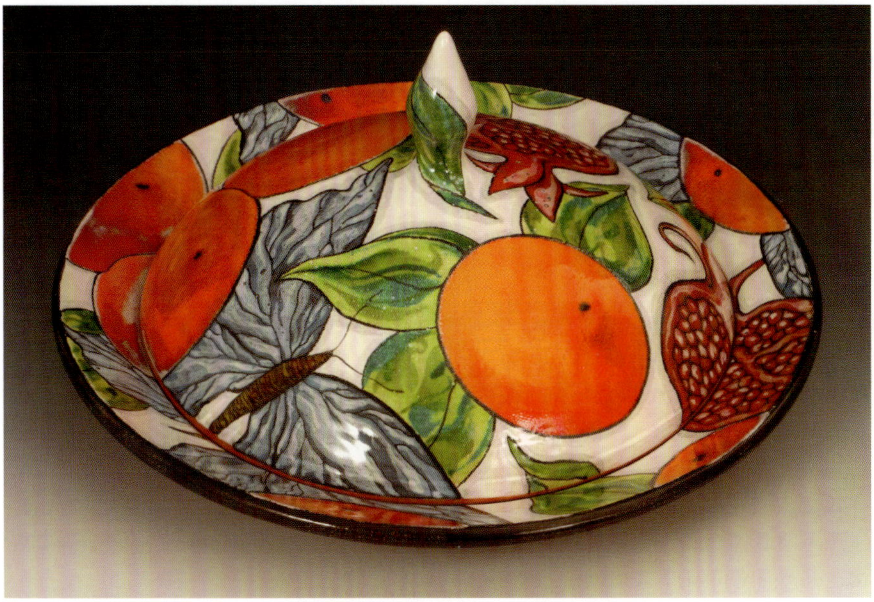

Covered Platter with Pomegranates, Butterflies, and Oranges by Farraday Newsome, glazed terra cotta, 13½ inches in diameter. If you enjoy painting and decorating, you might find it most satisfying to work in earthenware. At lower earthenware temperatures it's possible to achieve a wide range of vibrant colors. *Photo by Farraday Newsome*

in your glazes because lead is only useful at low temperatures. Many beautiful glaze colors can be achieved with iron oxide alone, and the more toxic colorants can create brilliant colors even when used in very tiny amounts. The stoneware range offers you two basic temperature choices, cone 6 or cone 10. Although some people fire at temperatures in between, most commercial clays are formulated for one of these two ranges. You also have your choice of kiln types—and your clay choice may well be guided by the kiln you have access to. If you only have an electric kiln, you'll probably be firing at cone 5 or 6. Many beautiful, bright, and reliable glazes are possible in electric kilns at this temperature, and if you don't want to mix your own glazes, there are more and more attractive commercial glazes available for this type of firing.

If you have a gas or wood kiln available, you may be able to fire to either cone 6 or cone 10 or beyond. If you're working with porcelain, you might need to get to cone 10 to mature the clay. Firing to cone 10 doesn't necessarily make your stoneware any "better" for cooking, but glaze formulas are simpler and some glaze effects are possible only at higher temperatures. Of course the higher firing temperature means higher fuel costs. If you feel that glazes fired in the "reducing," or oxygen-deprived, atmosphere of a gas or wood kiln are richer and more aesthetically pleasing than glazes fired in the neutral or oxygen-rich atmosphere of an electric kiln, then you probably want to make stoneware cooking pots.

Whichever clay you choose to use, it's important to make cookware that suits your clay. Flameware is the most versatile type of clay, and when properly formulated, it can be used on the stove-top, in the oven, in the microwave, on the grill, and even taken directly from the freezer into the oven; but the burden of making the clay and testing it properly is too great for most potters. If you choose stoneware, make pots for the microwave and the oven. If you choose earthenware, make pots for the oven and the stovetop. And make sure anyone who uses your pots has instructions for using them safely.

How Do I Test My Ware?

If you want to make cookware for sale—or even if you just want to use it yourself—you'll want to test it to be sure it's safe to use. This means if you're making stoneware, you need to be sure your clay is vitrified, meaning it's safe to use in the microwave. If properly vitrified, stoneware can even be put in the freezer.

It's easy to test your stoneware clay body to make sure it's vitrified. Fire a bar of clay without glaze to your usual temperature. Weigh it in grams as soon as it comes out of the kiln. Soak it in water overnight, then boil the bar in a pot of water for several hours. Wipe off all surface water and weigh again. Subtract the dry weight from the wet weight, then divide this number by the original dry weight. Multiply by 100

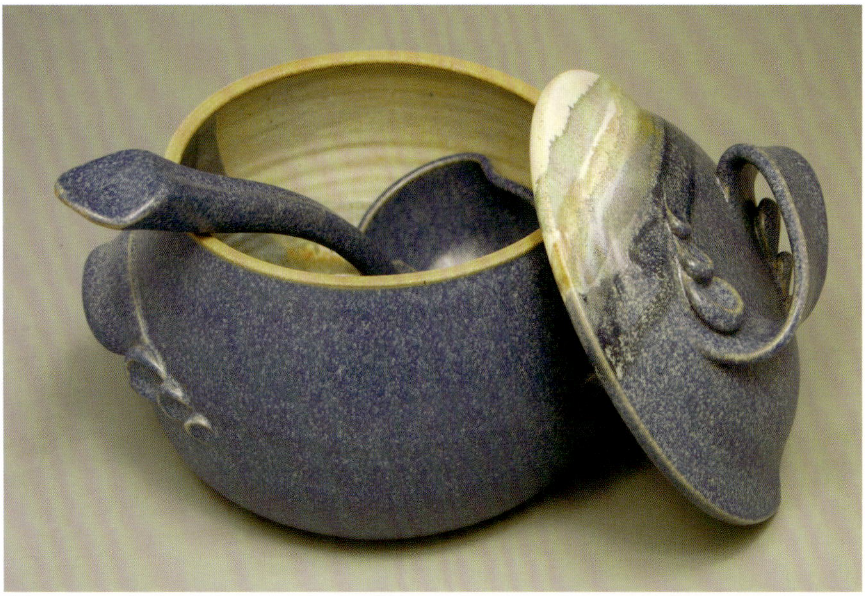

Soup tureen with ladle by Catherine Schroeder Abelson, 12 inches in diameter, stoneware, oxidation fired to cone 6. Abelson fires in oxidation, but her opaque, satiny, visually textured glazes resemble classic reduction-fired stoneware glazes. *Photo by Sumi von Dassow*

to get the percentage of absorbency. A properly vitrified stoneware clay will have an absorbency of around 3%. Porcelain should be less absorbent, around 1%. If your clay is more absorbent, it may not be safe to use in a microwave oven but there's no reason you can't bake in it: however, it may also be less durable if it isn't fired to its full maturity. You might want to consider changing your firing temperature or your clay body, if possible.

Stoneware that's properly vitrified should be safe to use in a microwave and here's a simple test. Soak the pot to be tested in water for a few hours to give it a chance to absorb water. Remove it from the water, dry it off, and place it in the microwave oven. Fill a microwave-safe mug with water and place it in the microwave along with the empty pot you're testing. Heat until the water is boiling. If the empty pot remains cool, it has not absorbed water and is safe to use in the microwave.

A rigorous test for stoneware is to soak your pot, dry it off, then place it in the freezer overnight. When you remove it from the freezer, pour boiling water into it. If it survives, you can be sure it's vitrified and it's safe to freeze food in it. You can also be sure that a mug stored in a cold pantry will survive when hot coffee is poured into it.

If you plan to make a great deal of stoneware pottery for sale, you might want to try testing your ware in the most adverse conditions your customers can possibly subject your pottery to. Dick Lehman came up with a series of tests after having several cracked baking dishes returned by customers. His first test is to put an empty baking dish into a 500°F oven for ten minutes then remove it and examine it for cracks. Tap it to see if it still "rings" (a dull thunk means it's cracked somewhere). Try filling it partway with water and putting it in the 500°F oven for ten minutes then examine and tap it. For a very severe test, fill it partway with water, freeze it, then place it in the hot oven. If your ware survives this test, probably anything a purchaser might do won't break your ware. Lehman tried one last test—pouring cold water into a dish hot from the oven. This treatment cracks almost every clay body, but if you find a clay that survives this, you know it will survive anything. You might also want to try these tests with different forms you make, to see which forms are more vulnerable to heat shock. Your ware doesn't need to survive the most rigorous level of testing to be useful; it just means you must warn users that it will break if they mistreat it. All of these tests defy the instructions that potters generally give their customers about how to safely use stoneware, but many customers may disregard these instructions.

Glazed earthenware is not microwave-safe, and no kind of earthenware can be put in the freezer, so don't use these tests on this kind of clay. In fact, there isn't any established test for earthenware at all. Because of its lower firing temperature, earthenware clay is porous and less dense than stoneware. Therefore, it will survive the thermal shock of heating, as long as it isn't placed directly on a hot electric burner or glass cooktop. Some cooks like to use unglazed earthenware in the microwave oven, soaking the pot in water first so the absorbed water will heat up and help to steam the food inside. The pot will heat up when it's soaked in water and used in the microwave oven, so it may be quite hot to the touch when cooking is done. This may also shorten the

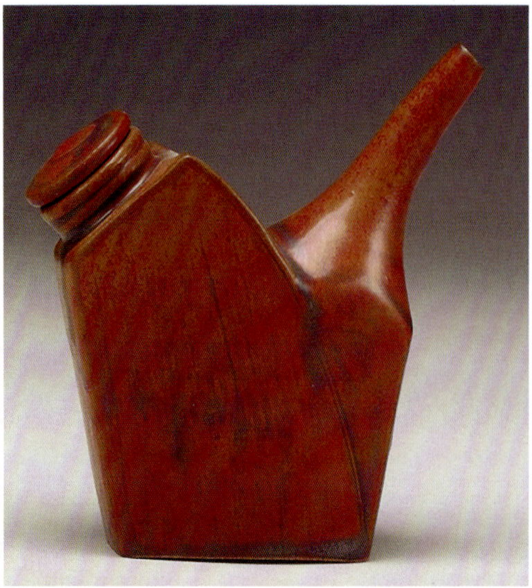

Reduction-fired stoneware offers a variety of rich glazes that are ideal for enhancing a finely crafted, almost sculptural form such as this Red Soy Bottle by Ellen Shankin. Stoneware, thrown and altered, cone 10 reduction. *Photo by Tim Barnwell*

life of a pot, but unglazed earthenware isn't expected to last forever anyway. Earthenware must be used with care and with the understanding that it's likely to break in use sooner or later. Nevertheless, people have been cooking in earthenware for millennia, and many traditional forms of earthenware pottery are made and used in great numbers. Many cooks are passionate about cooking in unglazed earthenware and prefer not to cook in metal pots. The fact that a pot will break eventually doesn't mean it shouldn't be used. It does mean that if you sell these pots for cooking in, you may end up with unhappy customers who don't fully understand that some kinds of pots last longer than others. For this reason many potters are reluctant to make earthenware for cooking in, especially for stovetop cooking.

Ware that is decorated with metallic lusters is not microwave-safe (the lusters will cause sparking), and shouldn't be washed in the dishwasher as the lusters will be damaged by dishwasher detergents.

Flameware can be tested in various ways. If it's truly flameware, you should be able to heat it empty, directly on a burner, then plunge it into ice water. It should also be tested in a lab with a dilatometer, which measures expansion. If you wish to market your ware as flameware you must perform repeated rigorous testing.

Choosing Glazes

Your choice of glazes is as important as your choice of clay. You must make sure your glazes are safe to use with food—in other words, that they won't leach toxins into the food. You want to be sure the glazes won't degrade when washed in the dishwasher. And you should make sure the glazes "fit" the clay body—that they don't develop a network of fine cracks, called crazing, or worse, that they don't "shiver" and pop off the surface. While crazing will render the surface less sanitary, shivering is an obvious safety hazard. Crazing happens when the glaze shrinks more than the clay body as it cools. Sometimes crazing may be acceptable, and glazes on earthenware bodies are likely to craze over time. Many beautiful classic pots exhibit crazing, and sometimes this is even a desired effect referred to as a "crackle glaze," but this flaw may weaken cookware and make it less suitable for everyday cooking. Shivering is the reverse phenomenon, the glaze shrinking less than the clay body as it cools. Shivering is never acceptable, but fortunately, shivering is far less common than crazing.

How Do I Make Sure My Glazes Fit My Clay?

If you use commercial clays and glazes, you shouldn't experience shivering. If you mix your own glazes, use tested recipes or consider using glaze calculation software to evaluate your chosen glaze recipes before using them. Avoid glazes that call for large

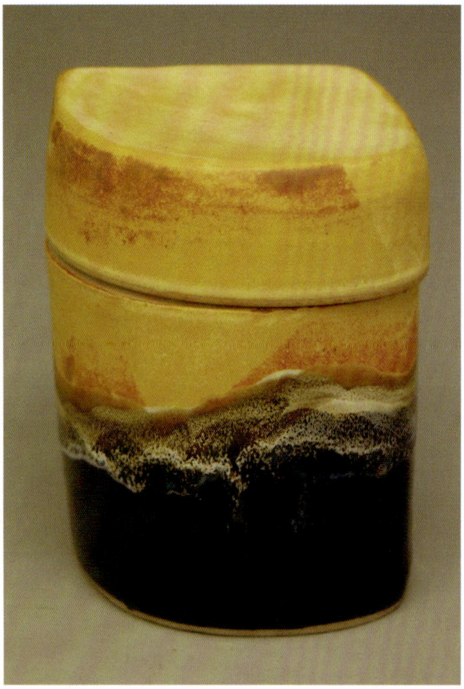

Canister by Sumi von Dassow, 8 inches in height, cone 7 reduction stoneware, thrown and altered. This canister is designed to fit into a corner under a cabinet. *Photo by Sumi von Dassow*

amounts of lithium. Lithium has a low coefficient of expansion and too much can cause a glaze to shrink far less than the clay as the pot cools. If you formulate your own glazes, you should use glaze calculation software to evaluate your recipes.

Crazing will often appear immediately, or within days after the pot is removed from a kiln. Sometimes a glaze that fits well may craze when applied too thickly. Sometimes a crazed glaze is obvious, though with light-colored glazes crazing may not be evident until the pot has been used for something like coffee, which will stain the crackles. To avoid crazing, it's desirable to have a glaze that shrinks slightly less than the clay; the glaze is considered to be "under compression," and glazes can resist a small amount of compression without shivering (popping off the pot). Shivering is more insidious—it may occur long after the pot has been fired. In severe cases, a glaze that will shiver may start out looking crazed, but in this case the shivering will probably happen pretty quickly.

To test your glaze for craze-resistance, make a thin bar of clay, glazed thickly on one side only. Fire it on its edge on a bed of alumina. Ideally it will bend slightly, with the glazed side convex (bent outwards). This indicates the glaze is shrinking slightly less than the clay, so on a normal pot the glaze will be under slight compression and will resist crazing. An extreme bend will indicate a glaze that is under too much compression and is likely to shiver. A bend in the opposite direction would indicate a glaze that will craze readily.

Another test for craze-resistance is called the Harkort test. To perform this test, heat a glazed piece to successively higher temperatures plunging it into cold water after each test. Examine the piece for crazing after each test; the higher the temperature you heat it to before the glaze crazes, the more craze-resistant the clay and glaze combination is.

How Can I Be Sure My Glazes Are "Food-Safe"?

A glaze that is safe for surfaces that come into contact with food must be stable, meaning it will not leach any of its components into food. This means you must be sure acidic foods won't attack the glaze and cause leaching. Many pottery buyers are aware of the dangers of lead glazes. If you're making earthenware and using commercial glazes, check to see if they contain lead. If they do, consider switching to lead-free glazes. Though commercial glazes containing lead are safe if fired exactly as the label instructs, every kiln is different and it can be difficult to be sure you're firing to the exact temperature indicated. If you're mixing your own earthenware glazes, you'll want to avoid lead for your own safety.

Stoneware glazes don't contain lead, since this material is only useful at low temperatures; however, many of the colorants used in glazes are toxic. While only lead and cadmium are regulated, many other glaze ingredients are toxic. You should use a stable glaze inside ware that is meant for cooking or serving food, or consider using a liner glaze. A liner glaze doesn't contain any metallic oxides other than iron oxide. Iron oxide is not toxic to most people—though some people do accumulate toxic levels of iron in their tissues, so don't assume your customers can't be poisoned by iron leaching. In any case, you don't want your customers getting iron supplements from your pottery. There are lots of attractive glazes colored only with small amounts of iron oxide, but if you want color from metallic oxides other than iron oxide—or if you use a glaze with large amounts of iron oxide—then you should test them for leaching. A simple test is to fire a sample piece, then submerge it halfway in vinegar for several days. After this period of time, examine the sample piece. If the submerged half has changed color, this glaze is not safe for use on surfaces that come into contact with food. Even if your glazes pass leach testing, avoid using glazes colored with large amounts of any metallic oxide on surfaces that will come into extended contact with food. To be sure your glazes are safe and stable, have them tested in a lab (see page 163). Small percentages of copper and cobalt oxide (one or two percent) can be safely used in a stable base glaze that is fired to maturity, though testing again is necessary.

How Can I Be Sure My Glazes Are Dishwasher-Safe?

If you want to be able to use your pots for a long time and wash them in the dishwasher, you should test your glazes for durability. Boil a glazed sample piece in water with pearl ash (potassium carbonate) for several hours. This simulates multiple cycles in a dishwasher. If you detect any visible change in the glaze surface after this treatment, the glaze is not durable enough to consider it "dishwasher-safe."

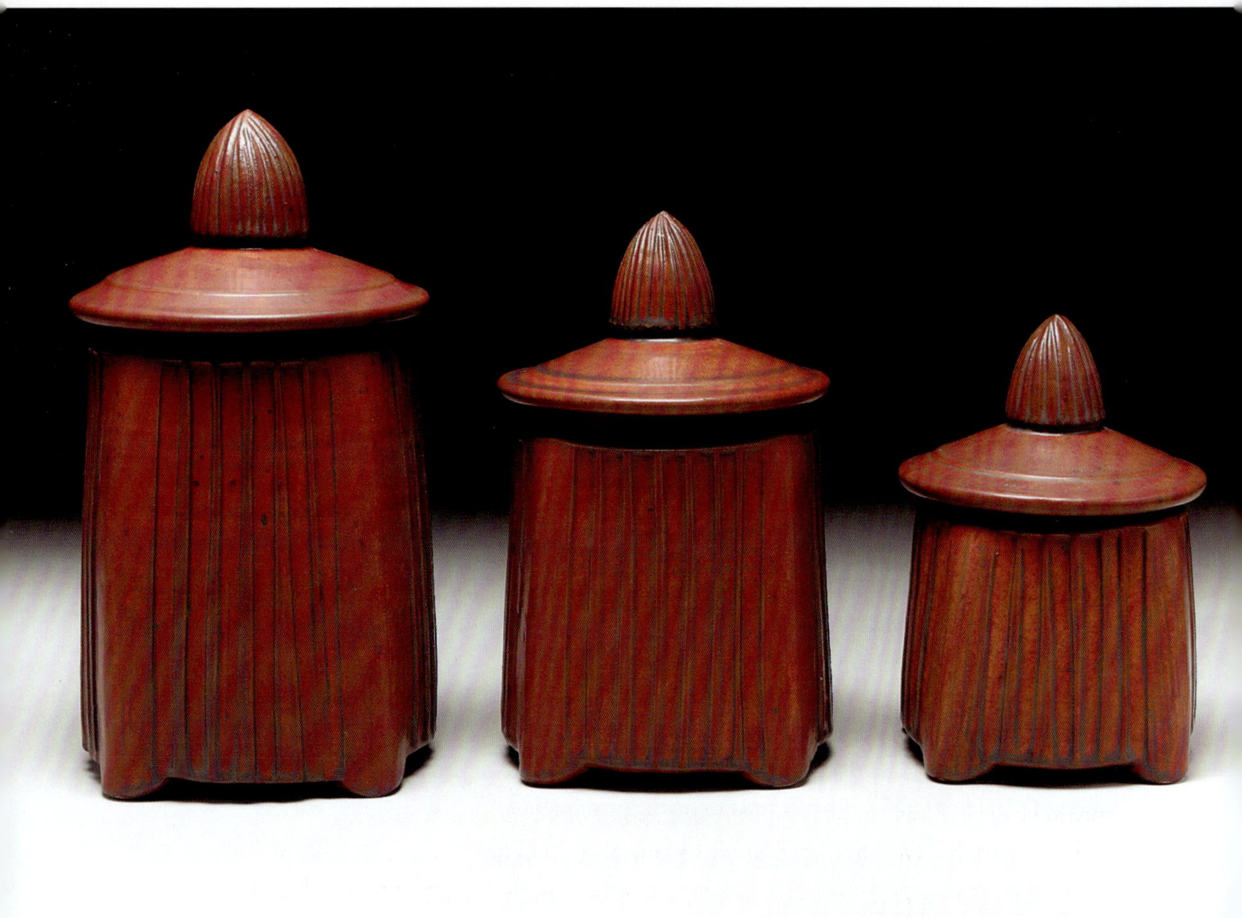

CHAPTER 3

Advice for the Cook

Chapter one describes the types of clay and what each type of clay is best suited for, so you can decide what kind of ware you want—or what you can do with the ware you have. But here are a few more questions for you to think about when selecting a piece of pottery.

How Do I Know What Kind of Pottery I Am Buying?

If you're buying it from the artist, ask! If it's flameware, it will certainly be sold with instructions for use. If you're buying it from a gallery, ask, but the owner or salesperson might not know. Look for a label or card with the ware that might tell you more about how to use the ware.

The colors of the glazes and the clay can give you a hint if it's stoneware or earthenware. Bright colored glazes, particularly vivid red, orange and yellow, are often hallmarks of earthenware. Earthenware glazes are typically opaque, uniform, and glossy. Stoneware glazes are often less vivid, but may seem richer in character and less uniform. Stoneware glazes are more likely to be translucent, to "break" over texture, and to have some variegation. If you look at the unglazed foot of a pot, earthenware clay is usually smooth and may be creamy white, brick red, or terra cotta orange. Some potters use terra sigillata on the unglazed parts of their pottery. In this case the foot will be very smooth, almost glossy or waxy to the touch, and usually brick red in color. Stoneware may be smooth or rough textured, and can range from white or tan to dark brown. A grayish-white clay is probably stoneware. Porcelain is very white, very smooth, and may be almost glassy or translucent. Unglazed cooking pots are almost sure to be earthenware and will probably come with instructions for use.

If you already have a piece of pottery, you can test it to see if it's vitrified. Draw a line on a piece of paper towel with a washable marker. Fill the pot with water and place it on the paper towel overnight. If the paper towel is damp, or the pen line is fuzzy, the pot is not vitrified and should be treated as earthenware. If the paper is dry and the pen line stays crisp, the pot is stoneware or flameware.

To test a piece of pottery for use in the microwave, fill a microwave-safe mug with water and place it in the microwave oven along with the empty pot you're testing. Heat

Canister set by Ellen Shankin, to 13 inches in height, thrown and altered stoneware clay with iron red glaze, and reduction fired to cone 10. *Photo by Tim Barnwell* until the water is boiling. If the empty pot remains cool, it has not absorbed water and is safe to use in the microwave. However, keep in mind that a brand-new pot may pass this test and then absorb water as it's used, at which point it would fail this test. Failing the "microwave-safe" test doesn't mean it can't be used, just that you shouldn't use it in the microwave oven—or if you do, you'll have to use a hot-pad to touch the handle.

How Do I Know if a Glaze Is "Food-Safe?"

It's hard to know for sure if a glaze is "food-safe," meaning it won't leach toxic minerals into your food, without testing it in a lab. Bright colors—including red, orange, yellow, green and blue—can be achieved with a variety of colorants that may or may not be toxic. The colorants that make blue and green are toxic, but glazes in these colors can be formulated safely. If a brightly-colored glaze is smooth and glossy, and especially if it's translucent rather than opaque, it's more likely to be safe. Stoneware glazes do not contain lead; earthenware glazes might be formulated with lead although most potters who mix their own glazes will avoid lead-based glazes, and most commercial glazes are lead-free. Again, if possible, ask the potter or gallery owner about the glazes.

If you're buying a pot that food, particularly acidic food, will be cooked in, avoid brightly-colored glazes on food-contact surfaces. White or earth-tone glazes are likely to contain no colorant or only iron oxide which is non-toxic for most people. Iron oxide

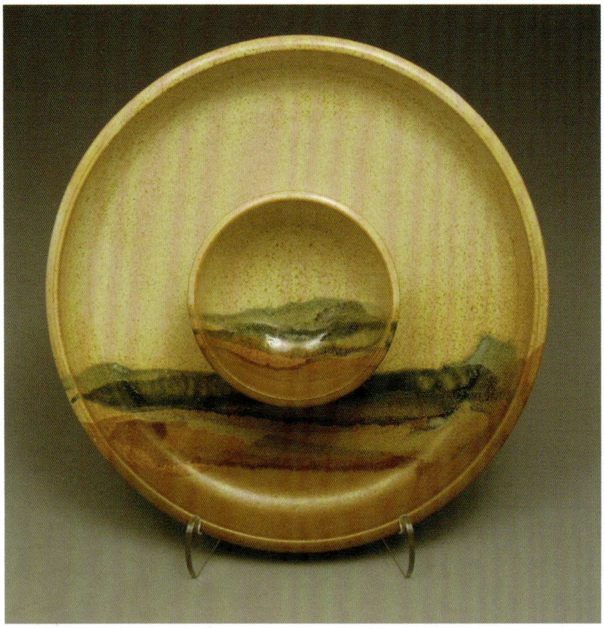

Chip and dip set by Catherine Schroeder Abelson, 15 inches in diameter, stoneware, oxidation fired to cone 6. This chip and dip set is glazed in oxidation with two glazes colored with iron oxide. The stripe of blueish glaze has a small amount of cobalt in it. *Photo by Sumi von Dassow*

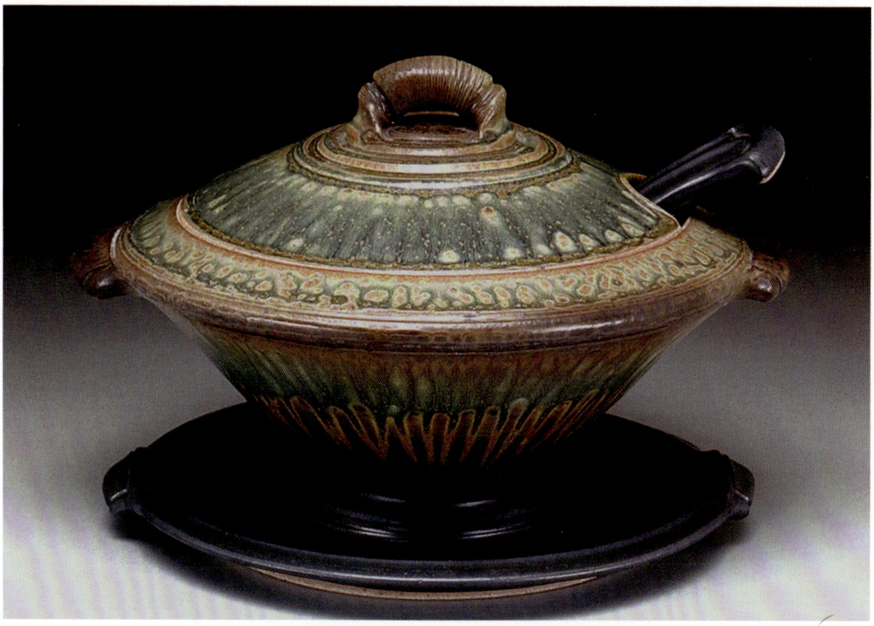

Soup tureen by Ellen Shankin, 12 inches in height, wheel-thrown stoneware clay, cone 10 reduction fired. The glazes on this tureen are a splendid example of the rich and earthy colors that can be achieved with reduction-fired stoneware. *Photo by Tim Barnwell*

can contribute to a great range of colors, including pale green, blue, or beige, bright yellow, red or orange, and black—so many colorful glazes, particularly on stoneware, are perfectly safe. Very dark or intense blue and green are achieved only with toxic colorants, so should be avoided inside cooking pots unless the potter can assure you the glazes have been tested for leaching.

Look for a smooth glossy cooking surface. Matte or semi-matte glazes in neutral colors can be perfectly safe but may be less easy to clean.

You might want to avoid glazes with a network of fine cracks, called *crazing*. Crazed glazes can certainly be stable and non-toxic, but they may be less sanitary. That said, an automatic dishwasher, and the heat of cooking, will kill germs, and there is no evidence that crazing harbors bacteria. But a crazed glaze can stain over time, and if the clay is not vitrified (that is, if the clay is still porous), crazing can allow moisture to seep through the ware.

Unglazed pottery in the typical terra cotta color should be perfectly safe, though if it has ever been washed with soap it may never lose the taste. If you're worried about cleaning unglazed ware, keep in mind that the heat of cooking kills germs, and earthenware has been safely used for cooking ware for millennia.

How Should I Use and Care for My Pottery?

Any bakeware, whether made by an individual potter or by a large factory, must be properly used and cared for if you want it to look good and function properly for a long time. Commercial ware such as Corning Ware, Römertopfs, or Le Creuset, all come with use and care instructions. If these instructions are not followed, you may not get the best results and the ware may even fail in use. Likewise, handmade ware should come with use and care instructions—but not all potters include printed instructions with their ware. There are some general rules that will apply to most handmade ware, although stoneware and porcelain, earthenware, and flameware have differing use and care requirements. If you have a handmade baking dish, you will first want to find out, or figure out based on the guidelines listed above, whether your dish is stoneware, flameware, or earthenware. While nothing made of clay will last forever, following a few basic rules of thumb should allow you to use a piece of pottery for many years.

Caring for Stoneware and Porcelain

- Always place stoneware or porcelain baking dishes in a cold oven instead of preheating the oven.
- Always fill your baking dish—don't use it to heat small portions of food. For best results when roasting meat, chicken, or fish, surround the meat with vegetables and liquid to protect the baking dish from uneven heating.
- Never pour cold liquid into a hot baking dish! This is a good way to crack ceramic or glass bakeware, and it's not good for cast iron or other metal either.

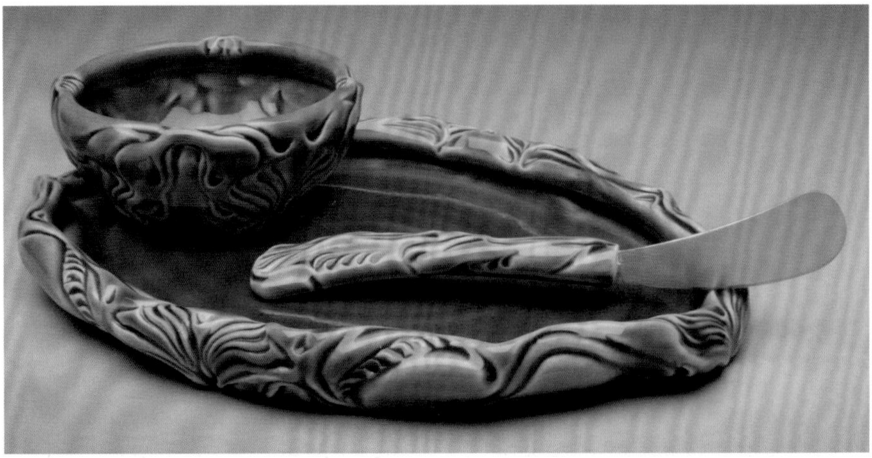

Three piece appetizer set by Lora Rust, to 11 inches in length, altered and handbuilt porcelain (stainless steel spreader blade), fired to cone 6 oxidation. Lora is careful to use glazes which are stable and nontoxic when fired. *Photo by Eddie Ing*

- Don't use stoneware or porcelain to freeze food. The food inside expands when frozen, which can crack pottery (or glassware).
- Stoneware and porcelain baking dishes are for oven use only—never place them on a burner. They shouldn't be used at excessively high oven temperatures, and they shouldn't be used to broil or grill unless they come with instructions indicating these uses are acceptable.
- Stoneware or porcelain dishes are generally safe to use in the microwave. The dish should be filled with food to avoid uneven distribution of heat. Use an appropriate power setting. Plates that are frequently used to heat a single serving of food may not last long as the center of the plate will repeatedly be subjected to rapid heating while the edges will stay cool.
- Stoneware and porcelain dishes can be washed in the dishwasher.

Caring for Earthenware

- Always place earthenware baking dishes in a cold oven. If cooking in a gas oven, the heat rise can be quite sudden so gradually turn up the heat.
- Unglazed earthenware may need to be soaked in water before it's used. If unglazed ware doesn't come with instructions, soak the pot by submerging it in water (or filling it with water) for 20 minutes before baking.
- Earthenware may be used to cook on the stovetop as well as in the oven, though it shouldn't be turned up too high. The pot may be placed directly on a gas burner but it should be placed on a diffuser when using an electric burner. Of course it shouldn't be heated empty and it should never be used on the highest burner setting.
- Never pour liquid into a hot baking dish! This is a good way to crack ceramic or glass bake-ware. (It's not good for cast iron or other metal cookware, either.)
- Don't use an earthenware dish to freeze food. Water may seep into the porous clay body and expand when it's frozen, cracking the ware.
- Glazed earthenware shouldn't be used in a microwave oven. Over time, water seeps into the pores of the clay, and when it's heated in the microwave, this water heats up and makes handles and rims hot. Eventually the glaze on earthenware that's heated in a microwave oven will develop a pattern of fine cracks, called crazing, from repeated expansion and contraction due to the heating of absorbed water.
- Unglazed earthenware can be soaked in water and used in the microwave oven. Micaceous clay pots can be used in the microwave oven without soaking. (Note that the bits of mica will not cause sparking—they aren't metal, they are silica).
- Earthenware shouldn't be cleaned in the dishwasher. The porous clay absorbs water and detergent. Earthenware should be cleaned by soaking in water and

scrubbing with a stiff brush (not steel wool). Glazed earthenware can be cleaned with dish soap.

- Micaceous clay pots and unglazed earthenware are cleaned by washing in very hot water and scrubbing with a plastic scrubber. Baking soda or salt can be used to scrub unglazed earthenware. After cleaning they can be rubbed with olive oil and placed on a very low burner or in a warm oven briefly to dry them. This makes it easier to clean them next time.
- Covered earthenware dishes, especially unglazed earthenware, shouldn't be stored with the lid on unless you're sure they're dry. Damp unglazed earthenware that isn't able to breathe may mold inside. If they do mold, they can be scrubbed clean and dried in the oven.

Do Earthenware Pots Harbor Bacteria?

Often a cook's—or potter's—main objection to the use of earthenware, especially unglazed earthenware, is the concern that a porous pot that can't be washed with soap or put in the dishwasher will harbor colonies of bacteria in the pores of the clay. There are several ways to respond to this concern. Of course, the first and most obvious answer to this objection is that if you're cooking in the pots, you're heating them up to a temperature that will kill any germs (if you're cooking meats to the recommended safe internal temperature, in addition to killing germs in the meat you will kill germs in the pot). This will be true whether you're cooking in the oven or on the stovetop. However, if you're merely gently warming food in earthenware, or serving in your ware but not cooking in it, you might not be killing all germs. There seems to be no documented evidence that people have ever gotten sick from their cookware and I haven't been able to find any studies about earthenware clay harboring bacteria.

It's also easy to say "people have been cooking in unglazed earthenware for thousands of years without dying from it" but that isn't really a satisfactory response. Over the millennia it's entirely possible many people have died of food-borne illness and only the strongest and healthiest survived. This "survival of the fittest" approach isn't reassuring! If you're young and healthy perhaps you're less concerned about germs, but if you're cooking for young children, the elderly, or people with compromised immune systems, you need to know you're not giving them food poisoning with your cooking. Also, in the last century due to the use of antibiotics, sanitizers, and intensive farming techniques, "superbugs" have evolved that are more virulent than anything that existed before. You want to be really sure you're not potentially harboring harmful strains of *e coli* in your pottery.

How Can I Protect the People I Am Cooking For?

- Don't put a damp pot away in the cupboard, and don't store porous pots with the lids on. Bacteria and mold thrive in a moist environment. If the pot is not moist, it may retain a few germs, but they won't be able to multiply. If you live in a humid climate, a pot that seems dry may actually be retaining enough moisture to mold.
- After scrubbing a pot and rinsing with very hot water, you can put it on a burner (on a diffuser if using an electric stove) on very low heat to dry it. If it's not stovetop ware, put it in the oven at 300°F for half an hour. You don't need to do this immediately; just wait until the next time you turn the oven on, or do it before each use.
- You can put your earthenware pots in the dishwasher during the heat dry portion of the cycle. This heats the ware enough to kill germs. You can do this either after using the pots, or before you plan to use them.
- Put your unglazed earthenware in the microwave oven after washing it. This heats the water retained in the clay, killing any germs. You shouldn't do this to glazed earthenware as this practice contributes to causing the glaze to craze, making it even less sanitary.
- Keep spray bottles of vinegar and hydrogen peroxide in the kitchen. (Keep the hydrogen peroxide in an opaque bottle so light doesn't cause it to degrade.) Before using, spray the entire pot with vinegar and then with hydrogen peroxide. This is an entirely non-toxic way to disinfect any surface, including cutting boards.
- Don't place raw meat in unglazed earthenware pots except during cooking. Raw meat is the source of the germs that cause most food-borne illnesses.
- Don't store food or liquid in porous earthenware, except for dry foods such as salt or sugar. Glazed earthenware may be effectively sealed with glaze and can be used for storing foods.

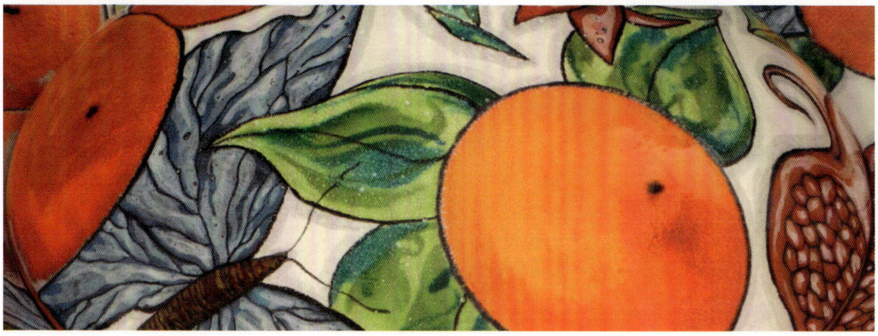

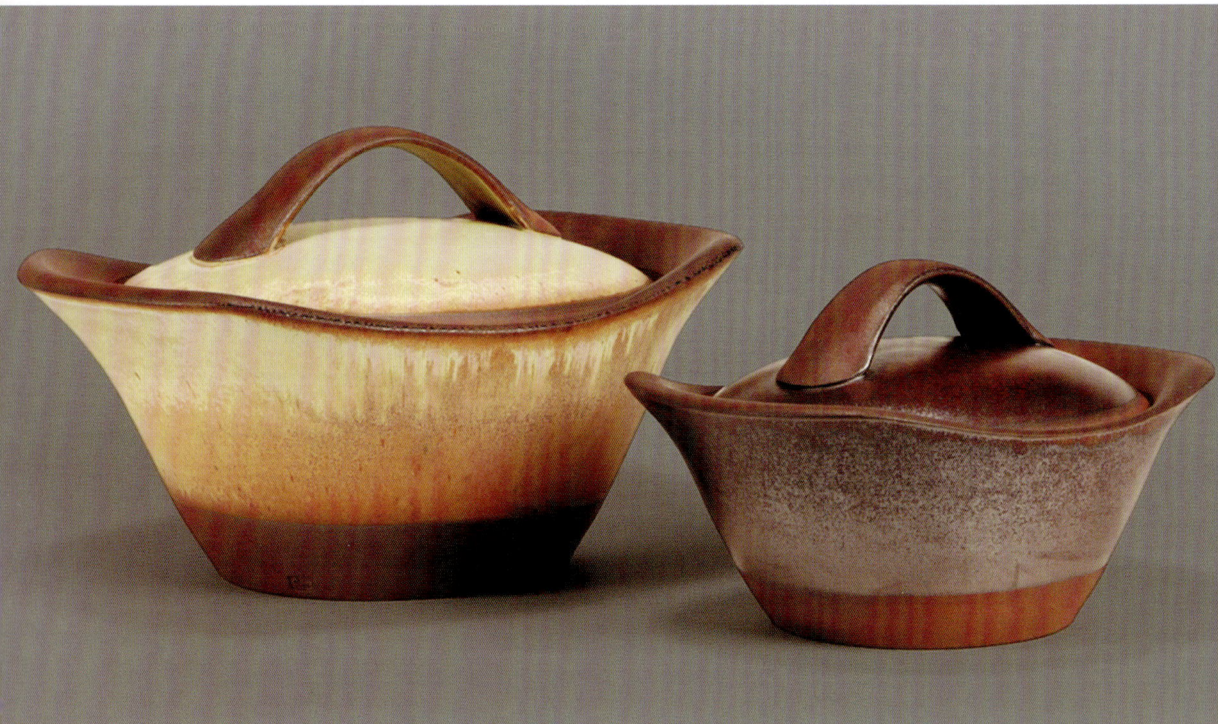

CHAPTER 4

Ovenware

When you think of ovenware you probably think of a casserole dish first. The lidded baking dish is a staple of both the kitchen and the potter's art, and can be used for casseroles, meats, roasted vegetables, and desserts. The lid can be used to cover the food while it's cooking, or to cover it after it comes out of the oven. It can be round, square, rectangular or oval, and it can be small enough to bake for one or two people, or large enough to serve a crowd.

Of course not all baking dishes have lids. Many wonderful foods are baked in uncovered baking dishes—think lasagna, brownies, pies, and breads. Just about any shape and size of dish can be useful, from a custard cup or ramekin holding a few ounces, to a 9×13-inch lasagna dish. Round baking dishes are used for pies, cakes, and many classic desserts such as crumbles, grunts and crisps. Square or rectangular baking dishes are especially useful for lasagna or some dessert recipes, such as baklava or brownies—though the only reason brownies need a square dish may be to facilitate cutting it into small equal pieces!

Breads and souffles want a deeper dish, to allow the contents to rise and to support them during baking. A loaf pan is usually rectangular, so the slices can all be the same size, while a souffle dish might be round or oval. A souffle dish can't be too wide because the delicate souffle needs to be able to cling to the sides as it bakes, so if it's large it needs to be oval.

What makes a casserole or baking dish useful and enjoyable to use? Is the glaze smooth and easy to clean? Is it deep enough to hold your favorite recipe? Does the lid fit well? Details like handles and knobs are important. Here are some questions to ask yourself when making a baking dish.

Is My Pot Useful?

- Does the lid have an unnecessarily high dome, which wastes oven space?
- Does the knob stick up so high the pot won't fit between the racks?
- Does the pot have a trimmed foot that may add excess height?
- Is the knob easy to grasp even with a pot holder?
- If it has side handles, can you get fingers under them with pot holders?

Robbie Lobell, two casserole dishes, two quart size and four quart size.
Soda-fired flameware. Photo by Michael Stadler

- If it doesn't have handles, can you grasp the pot's body with pot holders?
- Does it need a trimmed foot or should it be thrown flat on the bottom? There is some difference of opinion among potters in this regard. Common practice is to avoid a trimmed foot on bakeware. Most cooks prefer to use a pot with a flat bottom and no foot; in addition to adding unnecessary height, a trimmed foot may catch on an oven rack. Also, a trimmed foot catches water in the dishwasher, although this is easily avoided by cutting a notch into the foot. However, some potters put a foot ring on baking dishes to glaze across the entire bottom. This ensures that the bottom of the pot isn't stressed by having a glaze on one side only, since clay and glaze always expand and contract at slightly different rates with heating and cooling. In addition, if the clay is not fully vitrified—such as an earthenware clay—a trimmed foot ring allows for glazing as much of the surface as possible, thus helping to seal the clay from absorbing moisture. In general, however, a flat bottom with a slightly rounded corner helps protect the pot from heat shock and is an easy form to use.
- Should the pot have a gallery to hold the lid, or should the lid have a flange to hold it in place? Typically, the lid of a casserole dish sits on a gallery built into the rim of the pot. While this is functional, some potters think the pot should have a simple rim with a flange on the lid. To quote Vince Pitelka of the Appalachian Center for Craft at Tennessee Tech University, "With the normal 'cookie-jar' socket-style gallery on a casserole, where the gallery is on the pot rather than on the lid, anything that bubbles and spatters onto the underside of the lid flows down onto the gallery and makes a real mess, sometimes sticking the lid in place. Also, a casserole with this kind of gallery makes a less-attractive presentation when placed on the table

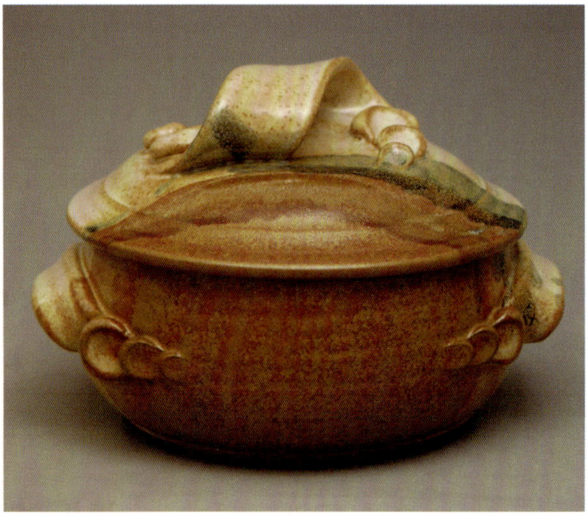

Stoneware casserole dish by Catherine Schroeder Abelson, 10 inches in height and oxidation fired to cone 6. This is classic stoneware—robust form and earthy colors. Photo by Sumi von Dassow with the lid. In contrast, with the gallery on the lid, anything that bubbles and spatters onto the underside of the lid simply drips back down into the casserole and does not contaminate the gallery. It's a fairly fine point, but worth considering." Also, a gallery built into the rim of the pot might make it more difficult to remove the first serving of a casserole. On the other hand, the traditional simple, slightly domed lid is easier to make and potentially easier to replace if broken. Some users believe that if there is a flange on the lid then it will end up getting into the food when it's placed on the pot. Some potters think that the profile of the dish when the lid is set on a gallery inside the rim of the pot is more clean and compact. Also, this kind of lid stores easily and compactly upside down inside the gallery. The decision about what kind of lid to make might depend on what is being cooked in the casserole, and whether it is being cooked with the lid on or the lid is going to be used to cover the dish after baking.

The Devil is in the Details

Making Lids

A casserole should have a slightly domed lid because a flat lid may slump in the firing, ending up concave; and an extremely domed lid has no function but wastes oven space. There are at least three ways to make the traditional slightly domed lid without a flange. It can be thrown upside down as a shallow bowl form, then turned right side-up when leather-hard, trimmed, and given a thrown knob or a pulled handle. It can also be thrown right side up, with or without a knob, then while still pliable, it can be turned upside down inside the gallery of the leather hard casserole dish and gently pressed until it develops a smooth curve. Alternatively, if thrown right side-up, it can be placed on a

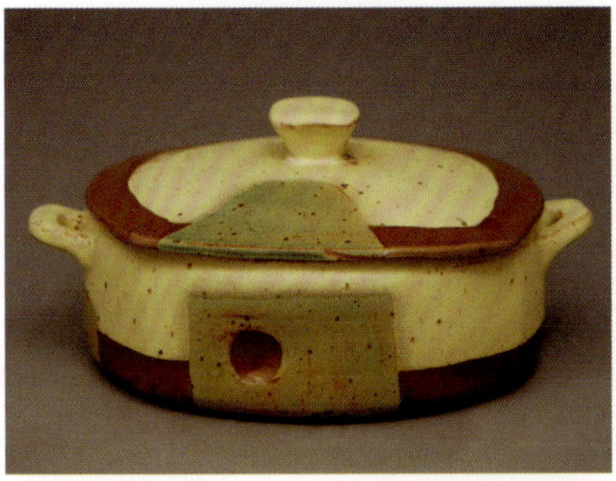

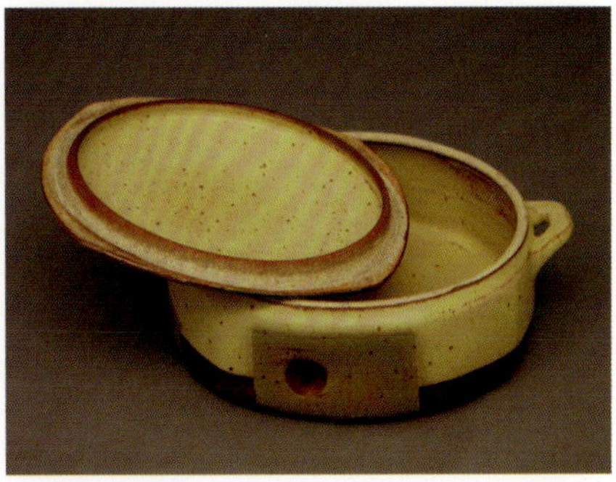

Casserole dish by Lynn Hull. 10 inches in length, reduction-fired stoneware. This casserole is slightly squared off so that the shape matches the rather contemporary decoration. The outer edge of the lid is thrown flat so that it can be cut slightly square, although the rim of the casserole and the flange on the lid remain round. The lid was fired in place. Photo by Sumi von Dassow small round hump mold on a bat, which is lifted and gently dropped to cause the rim to settle down around the hump. This method is very quick and easy, as long as you have several hump molds in different sizes to choose from. In either case, if the knob is not thrown on initially, a handle or knob can be added once the lid is formed. Either of these methods yields a lid that may be a bit less perfectly round and centered than one thrown upside down and trimmed, and the underside may need a bit of trimming to clean it up. Also with some clays the lid is more likely to slump and flatten out in the firing if it is thrown flat and reshaped. If you make a casserole dish without a gallery, you'll need to throw a lid with a flange. It will have to be thrown upside down like a shallow bowl with a double rim, one horizontal and one vertical. It will have to be trimmed and a handle or knob must be added after trimming.

Making Knobs

The knob is important—it must be big enough to grab with a pot holder, but no taller than necessary. If too tall, it will be vulnerable to accidents, and it may force the cook to move a rack to get the dish into the oven. It also shouldn't be too thick, or it might cause difficulty in the drying and firing processes. Two alternatives are to throw it as a small dish-shape on a stem, or a hollow round ball (with a hole somewhere to keep it from blowing up in firing). Of course, a handle can also be formed from a pulled or extruded strap.

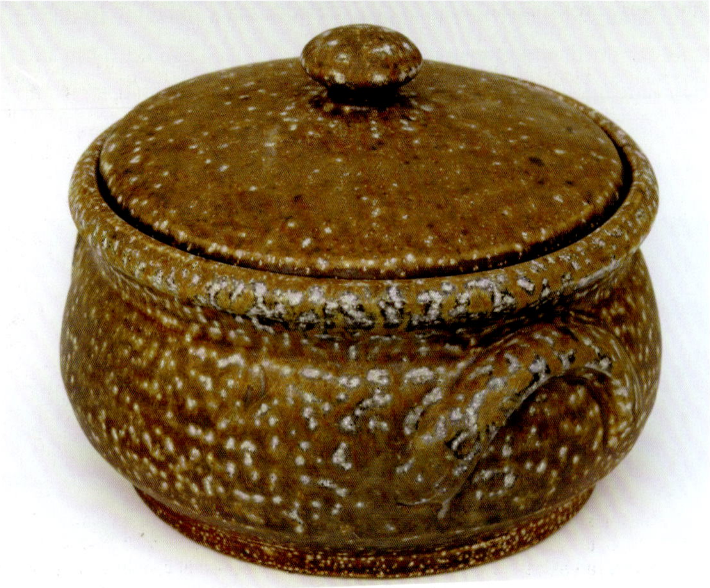

Casserole dish by Lynn Isaacson. 9 inches in diameter, salt-fired stoneware, unglazed exterior. Photo by Lynn Isaacson.

Making Handles

Side handles make a casserole or baking dish much easier to get out of the oven, as long as they are big enough to get your fingers under them with a pot holder. There are at least three basic ways to make side handles—you can throw a flange off the side of the pot and then cut away all but two sections; you can pull or extrude a strap and add two pieces to the dish when it's leather-hard; or you can attach two wide lugs to the sides of the dish and pull them into a wide strap. If this strap is then folded under itself it makes a very sturdy handle that is easy to grab. Which style you choose may depend on the size of the dish. If the dish is very shallow you'll want the handles at the rim, so you might simply throw the pot with a wide horizontal rim and cut off the excess. Attaching lugs and pulling the handles in place results in a rather bulky handle, so it is most appropriate for a deeper baking dish. For anything in between will you probably want to attach sections of a pulled or extruded strap.

What Will Your Baking Dish Be Used For?

It's important to keep the intended function in mind when making a baking dish. Of course you can make a dish and sell it and leave it up to the customer to figure out what to do with it, but if you know what your dish is suitable for, it will be easier to sell. By the same token, if you don't know what you're making your dish for, it's possible it won't suit any function very well.

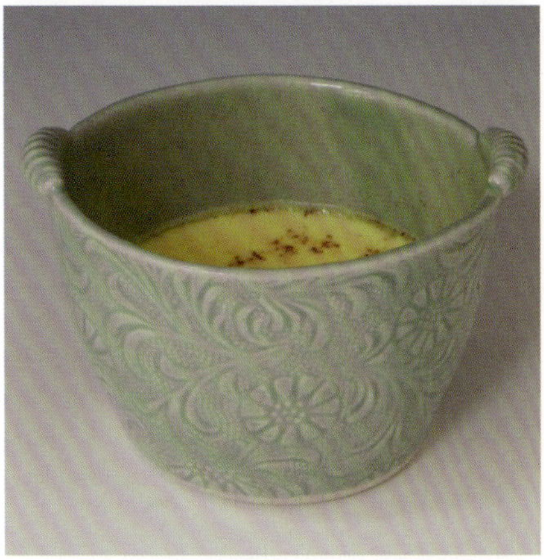

Ramekin by Alice DeLisle. Alice began making ramekins for her favorite custard recipe (see p. 74). Ovensafe, these ramekins are the perfect size for a single serving. Photo by Alice DeLisle

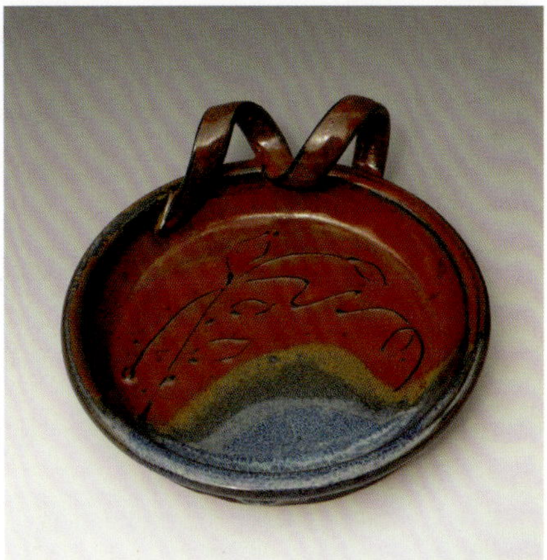

Brie baker by Dana Lehrer Danze, 6¼ inches in diameter, stoneware, oxidation fired to cone 6. Danze sells this very basic Brie baker with a knife and a recipe so customers don't have to ask what to use the dish for. Photo by Dana Lehrer Danze

Baking Dishes

Lasagna needs a relatively shallow (about 2 inches deep) rectangular pan without a lid. The sides should be vertical so a slice of lasagna can be removed with a spatula. If you really want a dish to be used for lasagna, then make it fit the dimensions of lasagna noodles. Plenty of other recipes can be made in relatively shallow round, square, or rectangular dishes. Handles placed on the short sides make these dishes much easier to remove from the oven. This sort of dish can also be used for brownies or cakes, for roasting vegetables, or for cheesy casseroles or desserts such as crisps and crumbles that are baked uncovered. Sarah Jaeger makes colorful porcelain baking dishes that are commodious with wide flat handles. They're altered from the round while quite soft to create a fluid, gestural effect that fits the character of their all-over decoration. She suggests using them to bake her favorite rhubarb crisp recipe. Pat Burns' soda-fired stoneware baker is equally functional, but quite different in character. It's a simple oval with minimal decoration and small handles, showing off the simple, honest soda-fired surface. She recommends a chile relleno recipe. Robbie Lobell makes rectangular soda-fired flameware baking dishes that can be used on a grill as well as in the oven. Her work is clean and spare, handles simply extensions of the walls, with earthy glazes and no surface decoration. They are handsome in their almost severe utilitarianism.

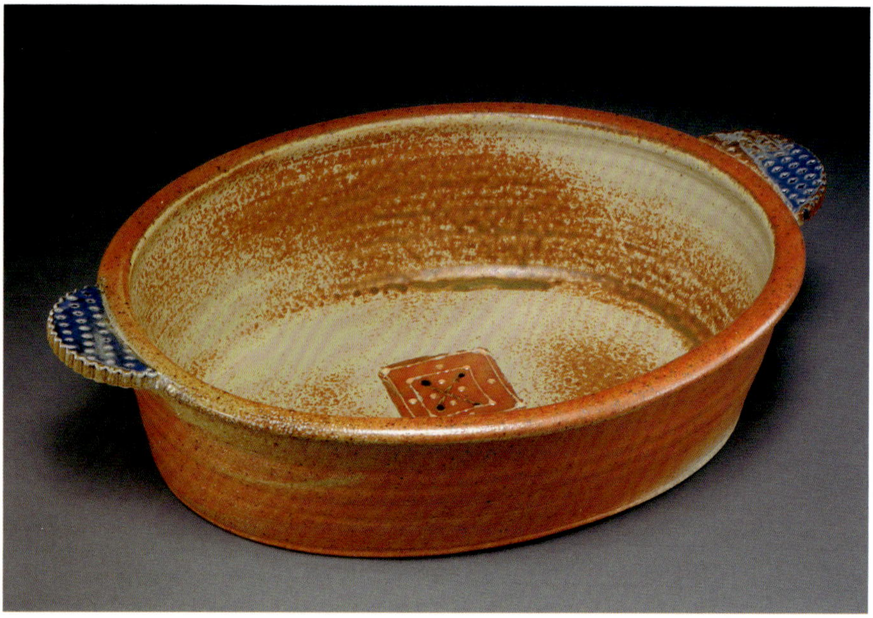

Oval baking dish by Pat Burns, 11 inches in length, soda-fired stoneware. Photo by Courtney Frisse

Casseroles

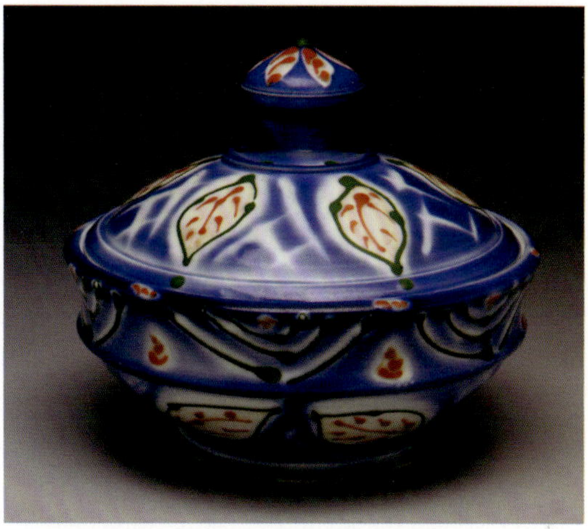

Casserole dish by Sarah Jaeger. 8½ inches in height, reduction fired to cone 10. Photo by Tom Ferris

A round casserole dish is usually used for recipes that don't need to be served in slices but may be scooped out with a spoon. While a round baking dish without a lid is useful for plenty of purposes, what we call a casserole dish has a lid. Many people never bake anything covered—or cover the dish only at the beginning or end of the baking period—but find the lid useful for keeping the food hot after baking or for storing leftovers. When the lid is used to cover the dish while it is baking, it has the function of keeping moisture in. Many meats benefit from cooking covered, with added liquid, to tenderize and moisten them. The covered casserole dish is the original crock pot, used for slowly cooking meals. It can be filled in the morning and left to simmer at low heat all day. A special category of covered casserole is the bean pot for making baked beans. The bean pot is like a smaller but taller version of a typical casserole dish. Catherine Abelson makes generously-sized stoneware casserole dishes, soup tureens, and bean pots, all with the flange on the lid, ideal for slow-cooking beans and stews. Sarah Jaeger's colorful porcelain casseroles are deep with a wide rim. With the flange on the rim of the pot rather than the lid, Jaeger recommends using them for baking in uncovered, and using the lid to cover the pot to keep the contents warm while serving. Robbie Lobell's round casseroles are deep, with the flange on the pot. Since they are flameware, they can be used with recipes that need to be started on the stovetop and then transferred to the oven.

While a round casserole is the easiest to make and useful for most purposes, it's fun to make square or oval casseroles, and such a shape might be more useful for a chicken or a roast. If you're making an oval casserole, it might behoove you to keep in mind the size of a typical chicken, because that is what people are going to want to use it for! In fact, while a chicken can be roasted many different ways, an oval covered casserole might be the ideal way to roast a tougher bird such as a guinea hen or a wild game bird, which will benefit from braising with added liquid.

Roasters

While a glazed stoneware or flameware covered roaster seals in the moisture from the food, roasters are often made from unglazed earthenware or micaceous clay. Roasters made from these porous clays are often soaked in water before use. This causes the food to cook slowly, but adds extra moisture to the food inside. Towards the end of the cooking period as the absorbed water dissipates, the porosity of the baking dish then allows the juices to evaporate and intensify in flavor, and foods such as potatoes and chicken skin become crisp instead of soggy. Bill Robbins makes a very basic earthenware roaster from a terra cotta-colored brick clay (see p. 14 and p. 69). It is completely unglazed, with a simple flat lid with a flange and an overhanging rim that allows it to be removed without the need for a handle. He includes use instructions and recipes with each roaster he sells, which instruct the user to soak the pot and lid in water before use, and to roast at a slightly higher temperature than typical. A chicken or roast takes longer to cook in this kind of roaster, but it comes out very moist. Many other forms can be made from unglazed earthenware and used in the same basic way, by soaking the pot first and baking at a relatively high temperature. Foods come out quite moist and evenly cooked in this kind of roaster, but they do take longer to cook. Finicky cooks who like to cook in unglazed earthenware will keep several of these pots—one for meat, one for fish, and one for vegetables, as the porous clay does tend to absorb odors that don't wash out. If you worry about these porous pots retaining bacteria in the pores, keep in mind they will be cooked to a temperature that will kill germs (see p. 28).

Actually, judging from the number of pots made just for roasting chickens, it would seem that roasting a chicken presents a special challenge that potters feel a great need to address. An old political campaign promised to provide Americans with "a chicken in

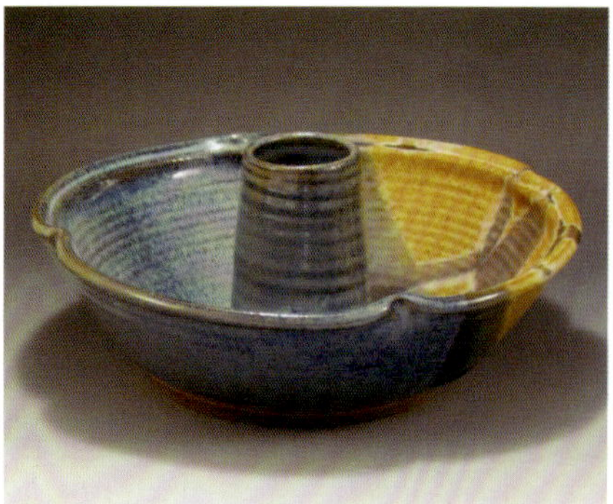

Chicken roaster by Tom Wirt, 10 inches in diameter, 4½ inches in height, Continental Clay Buff Stoneware, cone 10 reduction. by Tom Wirt.

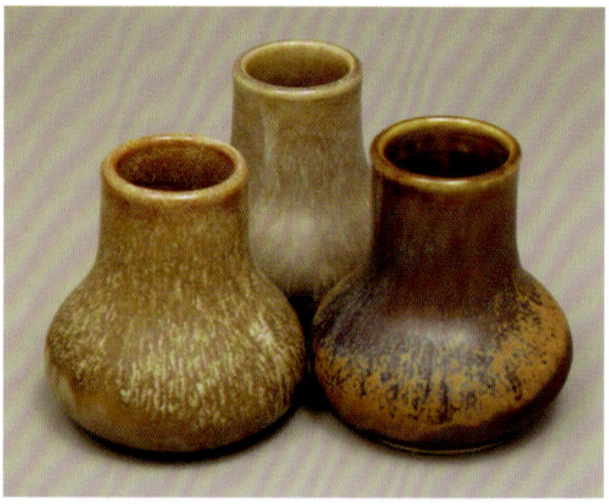

Three upright chicken roasters by Sumi von Dassow, 4 inches in height. These are designed to have a chicken set on them standing upright in a baking dish (see p. 70).

every pot," but potters seem determined to provide a pot for every chicken! You can use a stoneware or flameware casserole dish (round or oval, covered or uncovered); a covered earthenware casserole dish; or an earthenware "chicken brick" which is essentially a bottle form turned on its side and cut apart to create a pot with a lid. Traditionally, the chicken brick is made from unglazed earthenware, and it's soaked in water before each use; but of course, this is a fun way to make an interesting roaster out of any kind of clay. Another kind of chicken roaster that's fun and surprising is a simple cylinder with a bulbous bottom half. The chicken is placed over this form inside a baking dish in such a way that it stands upright instead of lying on its back. Some potters make a baking dish with a cylinder in the center for this purpose, although this solution is less versatile and may present something of a storage problem in a small kitchen. This form can stress some clay bodies; if you make it, you want to test your clay carefully and be sure it's very resistant to thermal shock.

Pie and Quiche Pans

The pie pan is a special sort of baking dish, always round. A round or square baking dish with vertical sides and no lid can be used for many purposes, but a pie crust will slide down vertical sides, and requires a shallow (one inch deep) sloping wall with a rim for the crust to rest on. Typical recipes are sized for a 9-inch pie pan, though 8- or 10-inch pans are also commonly made. In fact, if you include a recipe sized for a smaller or larger pie, you may be able to fill a niche making pie dishes in non-standard sizes.

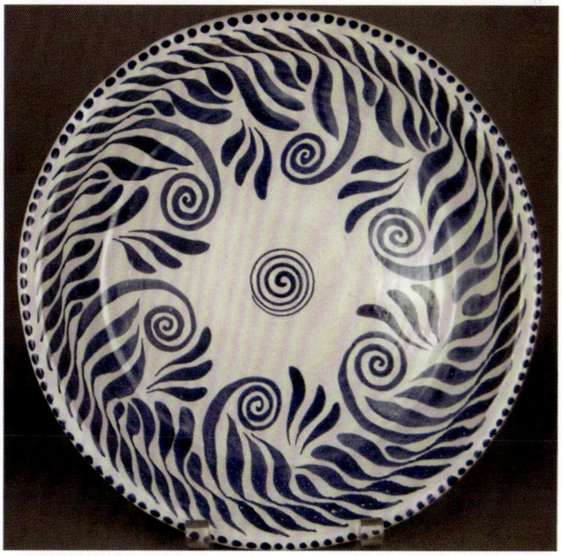

Pie plate by Eleonora Eden, 11¼ inches in diameter, slab-built and wheel-finished earthenware. Photo by Eleonora Eden.

A quiche, on the other hand, requires a shallow dish with vertical sides—fluting traditional but optional. Fay Krapf makes a traditional type of quiche dish with very slightly sloping sides and a small fluted rim, decorating it with a piece of lace impressed in the center. While this sort of texture might make the dish a bit more difficult to clean with many recipes, a quiche with a crust shouldn't present any such problem.

Loaf Pans

The last kind of baking dish that is commonly used is the loaf pan. A typical loaf of sandwich bread is baked in a 5x9-inch pan, about three inches deep. In addition to making conveniently-sized slices, these dimensions give the loaf support while it's rising. Of course, bread isn't the only thing that can be baked in a loaf pan—think meatloaf, for example. And bread doesn't need a loaf pan, either. Artisan-style breads baked in a round or oval shape are popular, and some potters make special lidded loaf pans for these crusty breads. Judith Motzkin, well-known for beautiful decorative saggar-fired vases, began

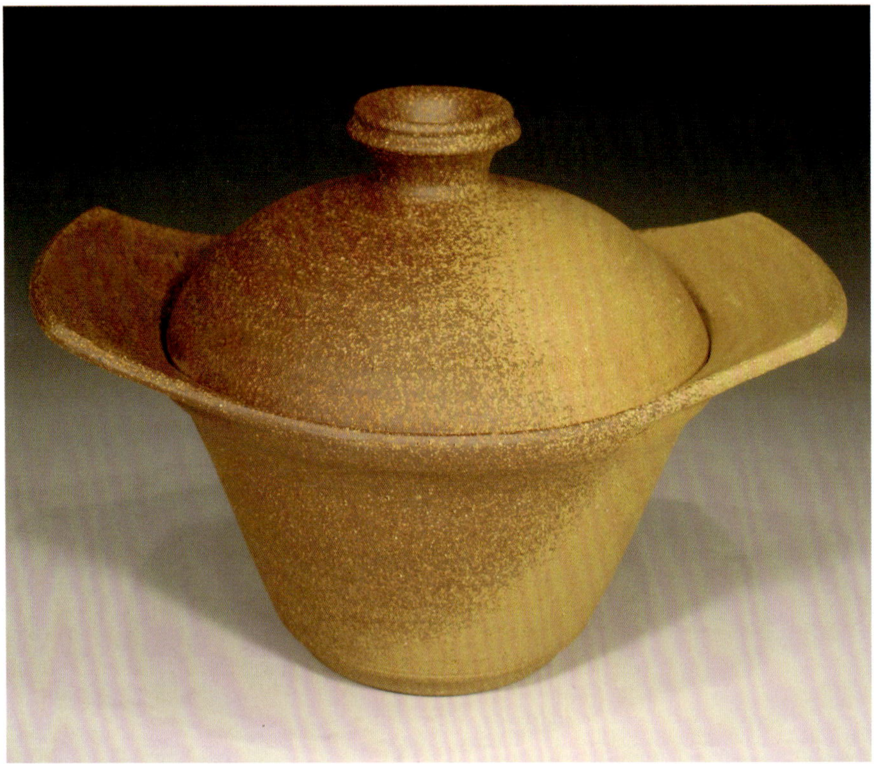

Bread pot by Judith Motzkin. Stoneware, 12 inches in width, fired to cone 9/10 in reduction, unglazed. Motzkin uses slip and/or sgraffito to paint a quote or recipe inside the lid. Photo by Judith Motzkin.

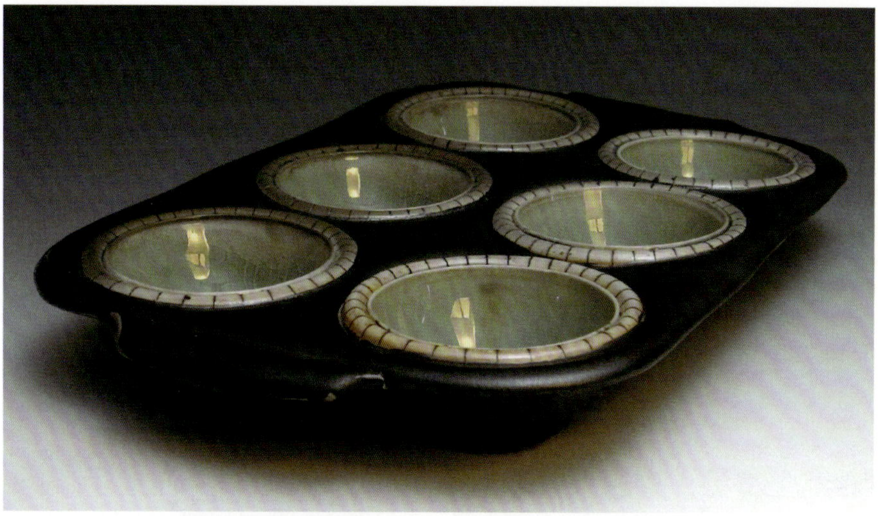

Muffin pan by Lorna Meaden, 8 inches in length, porcelain, wood/soda fired. Photo by Lorna Meaden

making round covered bread baking pots when she couldn't find what she wanted for a popular no-knead bread recipe. Now she makes hundreds of them, writing the recipe or a bread-related quote on the underside of the lid of each pot. She uses a variety of commercial stoneware clays, choosing them for their texture, color and low coefficient of expansion to avoid thermal shock in use.

One very specialized baking dish that is not commonly made outside of France is the cassole. The cassole is like a giant conical bowl, and it is use for baking cassoulet. Cassoulet is a very rich and complicated dish made of beans and a variety of meats, and it requires a conical stoneware baker in order to form the traditional crust.

Specialty Baking Pots

There are a number of smaller special purpose dishes for baking such as apple bakers for an individual apple. Ramekins are basically small flat-bottomed bowls for baking individual custards. Like Motzkin with her bread pots, Alice DeLisle began making ramekins for a favorite custard recipe. The garlic roaster is a round flat dish with a lip and a domed lid, sized for one or more heads of garlic. Baked Brie is a popular party dish that can be made in a covered dish similar to the garlic roaster, or in an uncovered roaster.

PROJECT 1: Making a Casserole

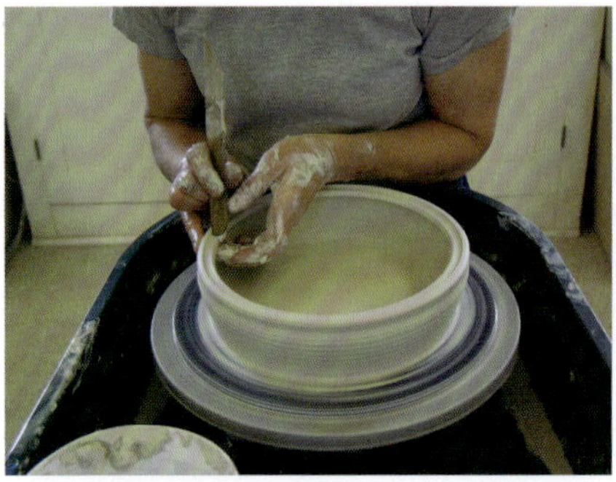

Throw 3 pounds of clay to form a 10-inch shallow bowl shape with a ¼ inch-thick bottom and a ½ inch-thick rim. Form the gallery by pushing down at the mid-point of the rim with a wood tool.

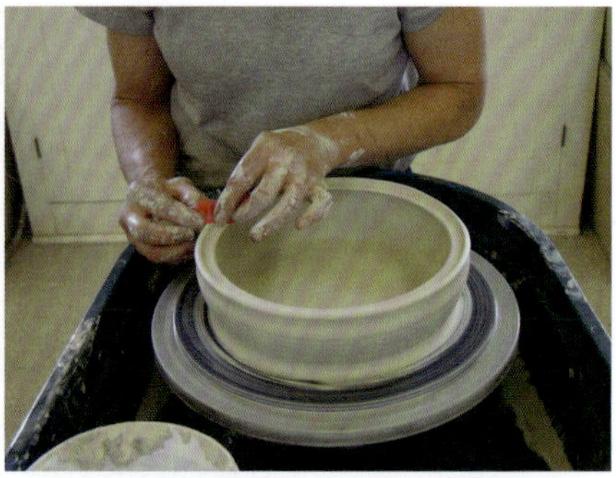

The wood tool has created a vertical and a horizontal rim. Smooth both with a chamois. Trim off excess clay from around the foot and run a cutting wire under the dish.

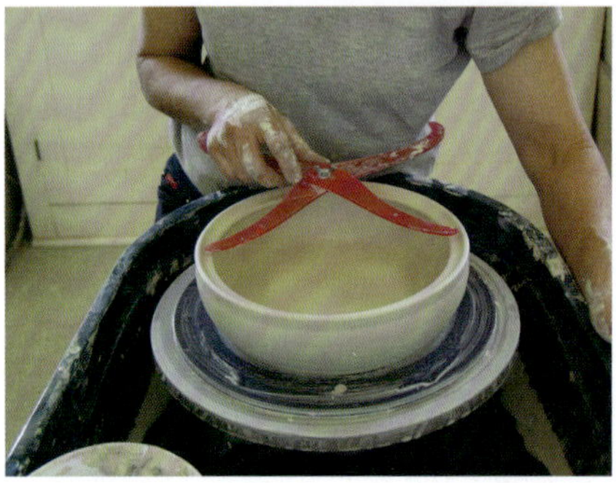

Using calipers, measure just inside the vertical rim. This tells you how wide the lid must be.

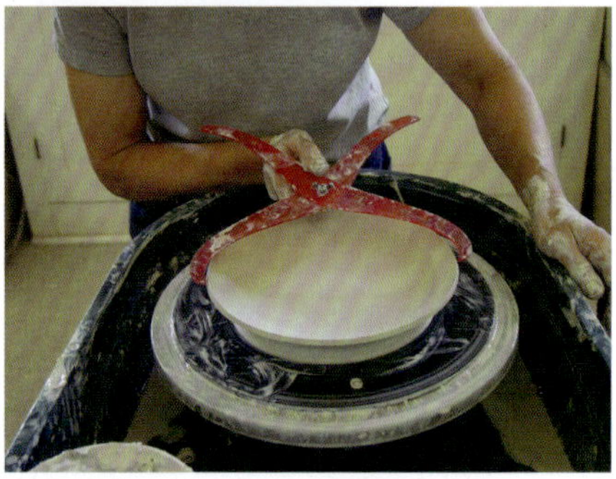

Throw a shallow curved lid upside down using about 2½ pounds of clay. Measure with calipers to make sure it will fit on the casserole dish.

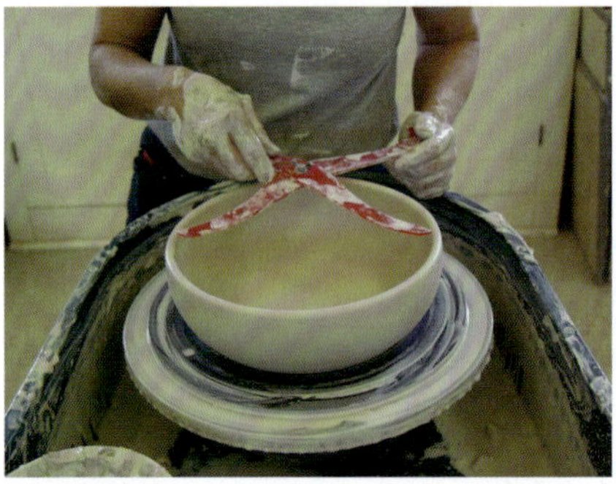

Alternatively, if you want to make the flange on the lid instead of on the dish, throw the casserole dish with a simple rim and measure with calipers just inside the rim.

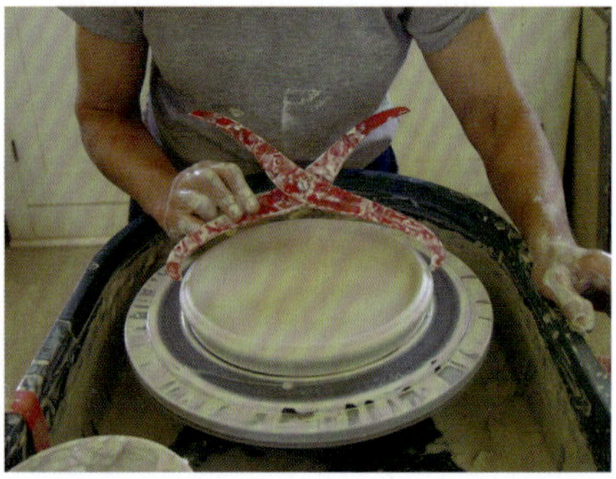

Throw a shallow bowl form to match your caliper measurement, leaving the rim quite thick.

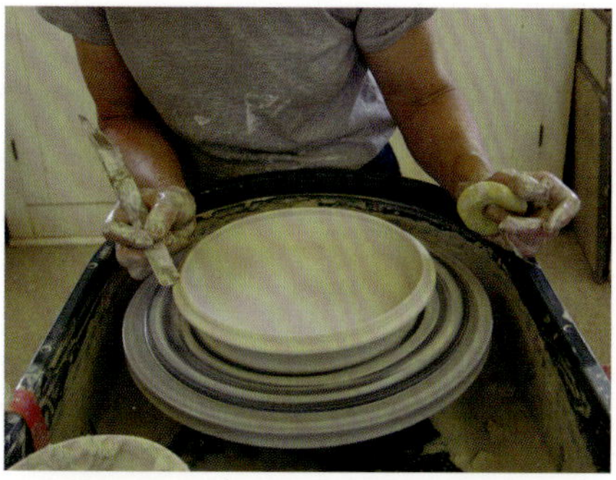

Using fingers or a wood tool, split the thick rim to form a horizontal rim with a vertical flange.

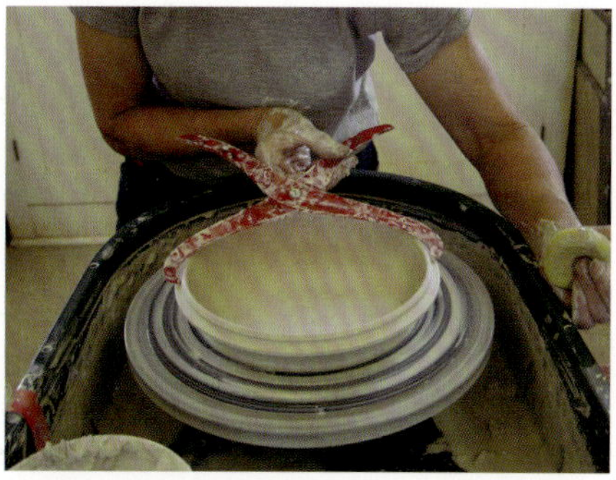

Using the calipers, measure to make sure the vertical flange will fit inside the rim of the casserole dish.

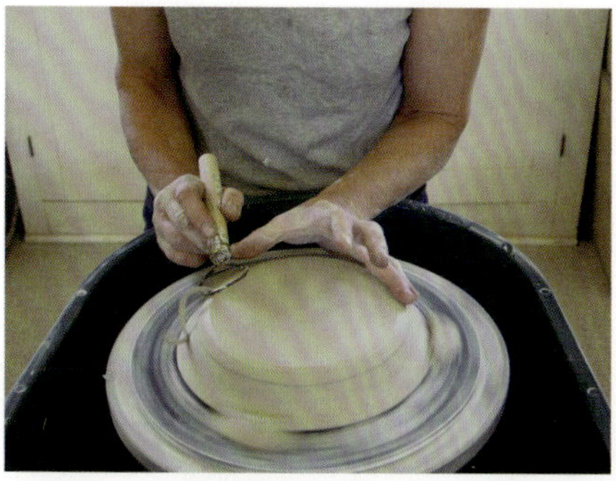

When the lid is leather-hard, center it right side up and trim excess clay from the top to leave a smooth curve.

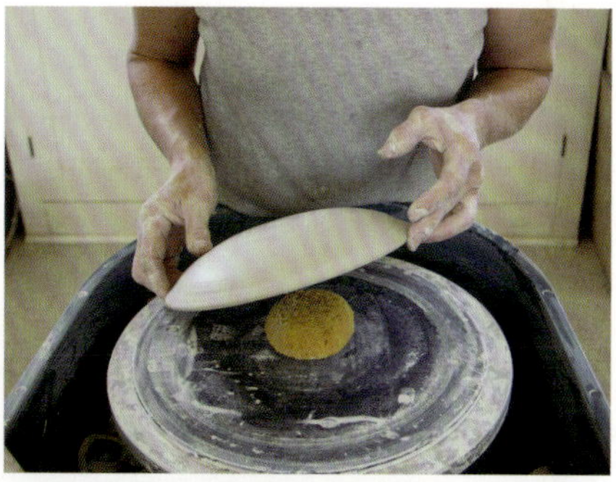

Check the thickness then put it back on the wheel with a clean, dry sponge under the center. The lid should just rest on the sponge to help keep it from collapsing when you throw the knob.

Making Magic Water

Instead of the traditional method of joining surfaces by "scoring and slipping," try magic water. Dip a toothbrush in magic water and scrub both surfaces to be joined. This method roughens the surface and creates slip in one step. Yes, it really does work better than plain water although plain water or throwing slip can be used if you don't have magic water around.

Magic Water

1 gallon water
3 tablespoons sodium silicate
1½ teaspoons soda ash

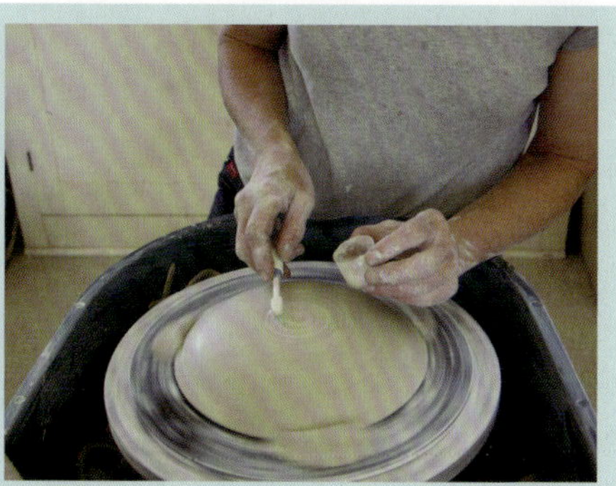

While the wheel turns, use magic water and a toothbrush to create a circle of slip in the center of the lid where you want to attach the knob.

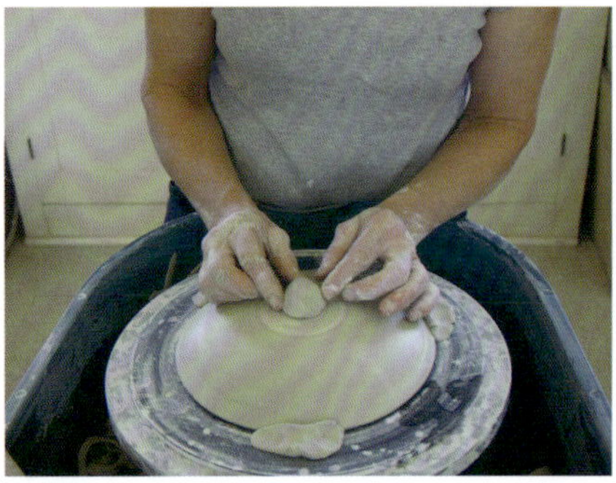

Place a small cone of clay in the center of the slipped area. Use a finger tip to gently adhere it to the lid all the way around.

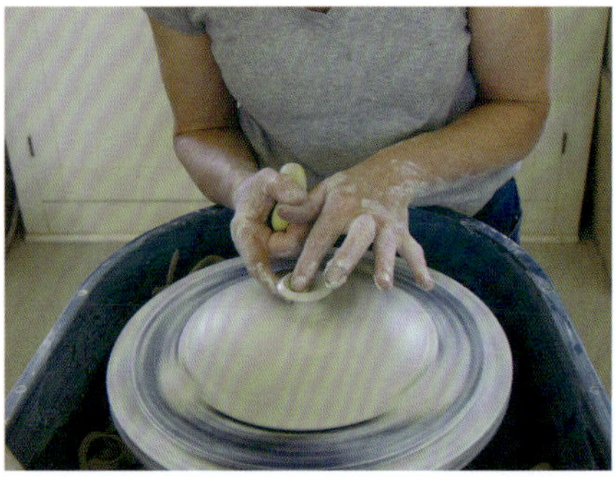

Using your fingertips and as little water and pressure as possible, throw the knob. Trim with a needle tool if necessary, smooth the edge with a chamois, and clean up with a sponge.

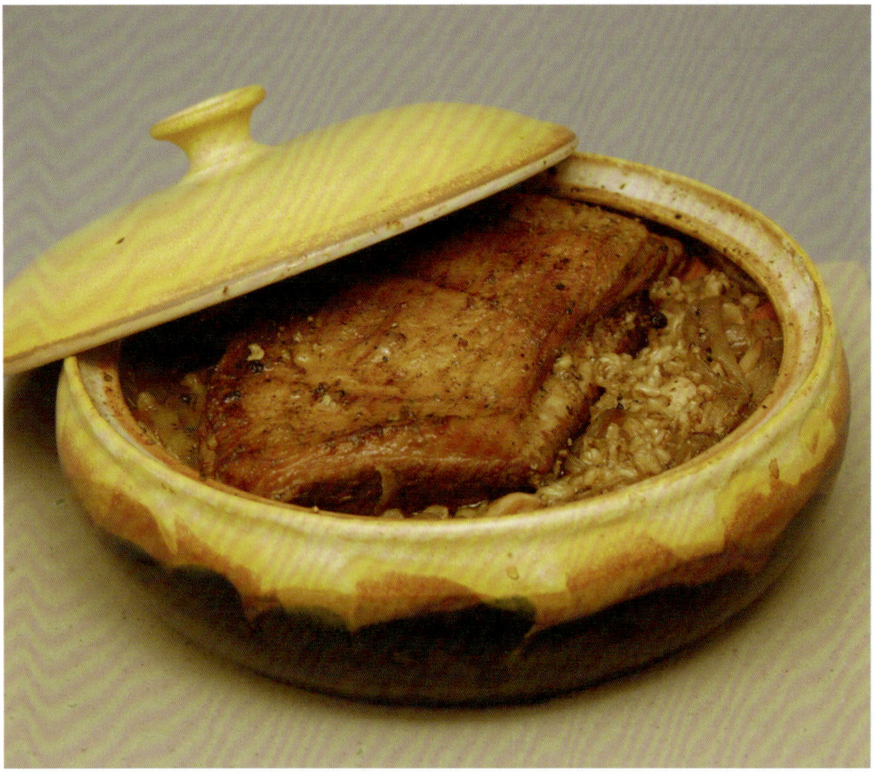

Casserole dish by Sumi von Dassow with cholent (recipe from Lili Krakowski, see p. 94).
Photo by Sumi von Dassow

PROJECT 2: Making an Oval Casserole

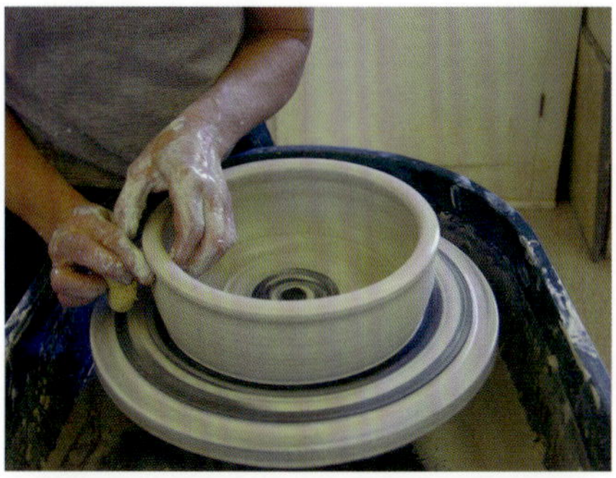

Using about 3 pounds of clay, throw a ring with no bottom. Pull up a wall, leaving the top ½ inch extra thick. Make a gallery as for a regular casserole dish (see Project 1).

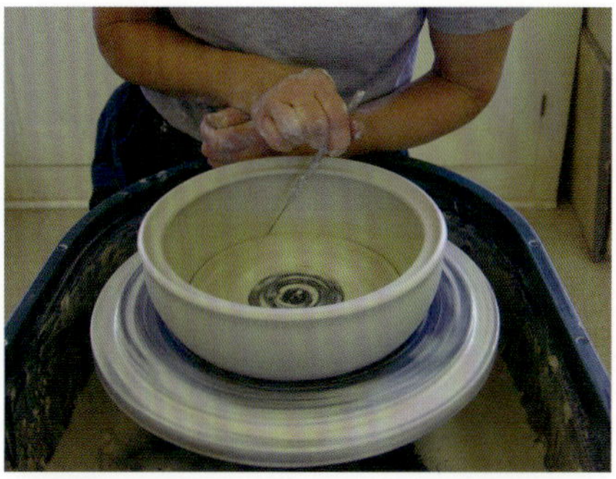

Using a needle tool, make a cut inside the ring, leaving some clay to join to the slab that will form the bottom of the casserole.

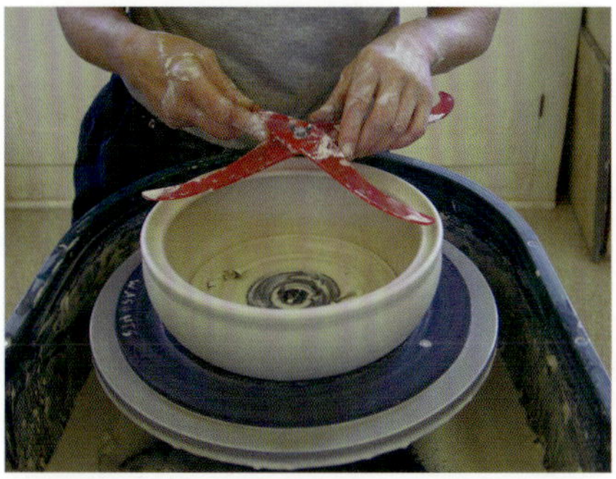

Measure roughly across the gallery. Remember this is going to be an oval so the exact measurement isn't critical.

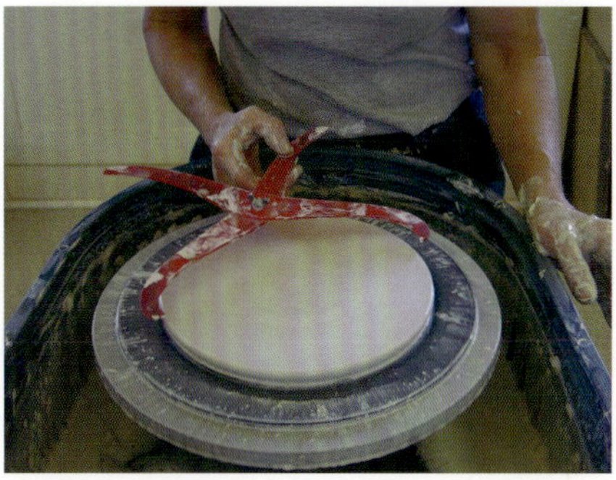

Throw two ⅜-inch-thick slabs to about the diameter of the gallery. Both will be stretched into ovals. One becomes the bottom, the other is used for the lid.

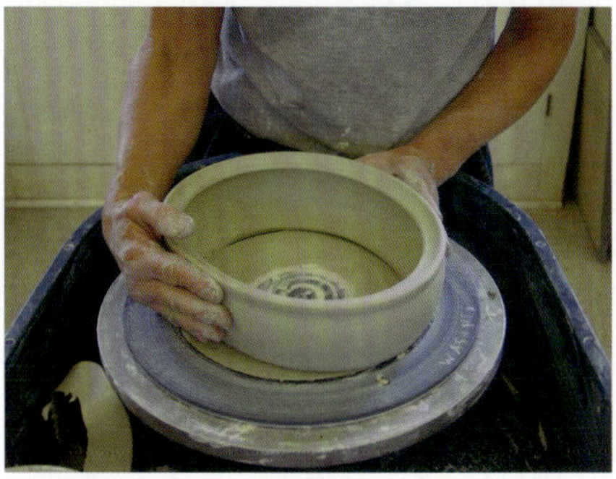

When the ring has stiffened up some, lift it off the bat and reshape it into an oval.

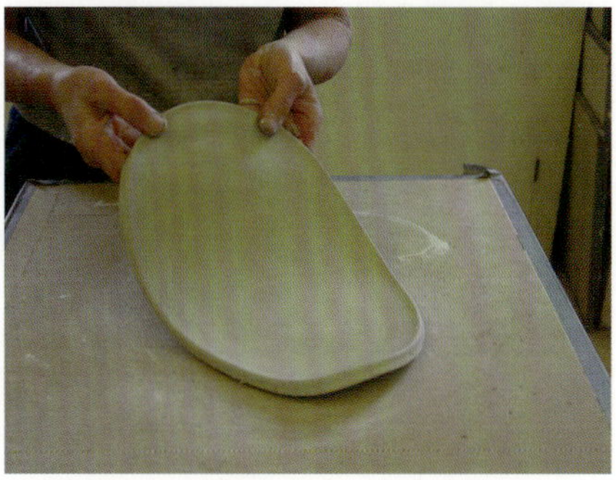

When the thrown slabs have dried a bit, toss both of them to stretch them into ovals.

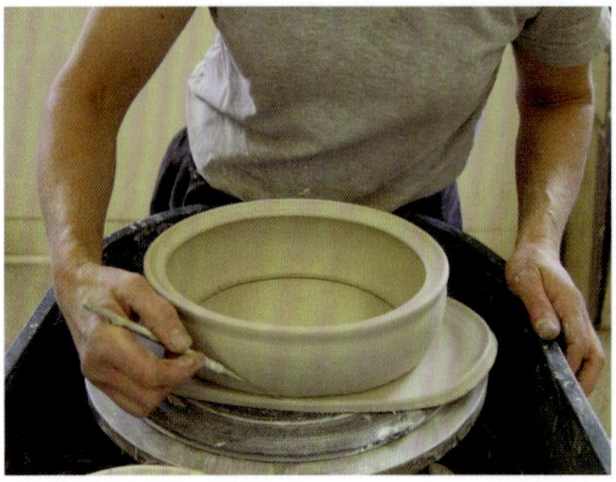

Place the oval wall section onto one of the oval slabs and trace around it.

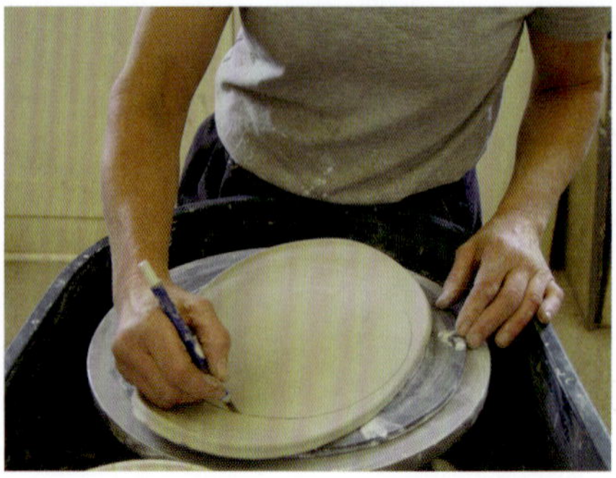

Set the wall section aside and cut on the line you drew.

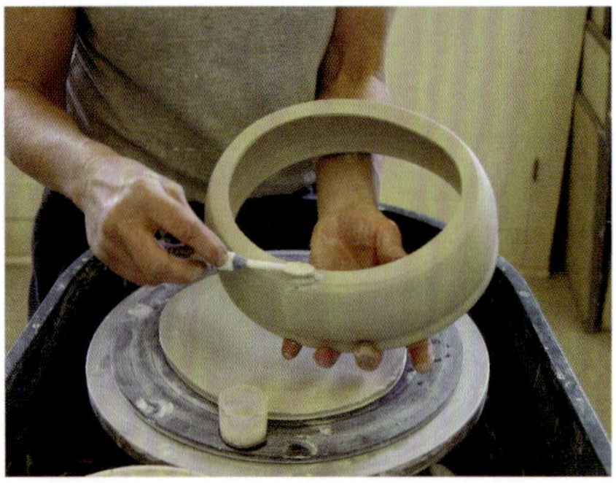

Using a toothbrush, apply magic water to both surfaces to be joined.

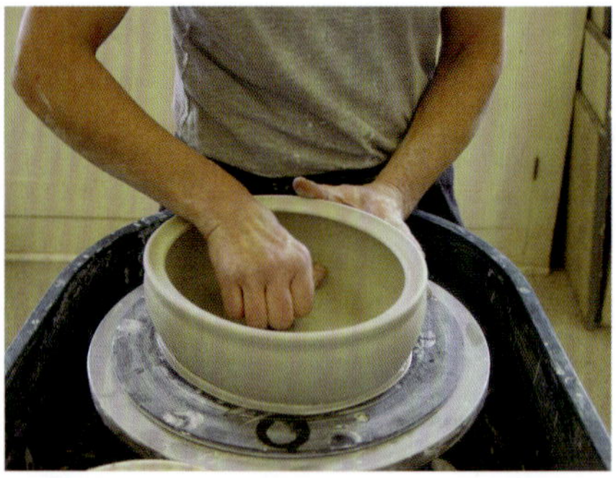

Set the wall on the slab and use your fingers and a rib to work the pieces together. If necessary, work a coil into the joint.

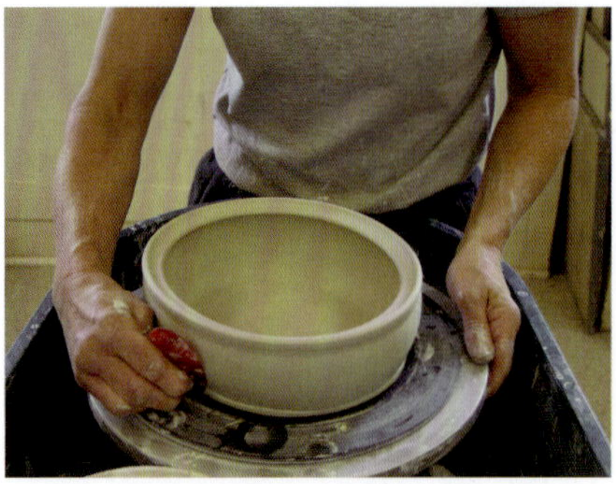

Using a soft rib, your fingers, and your wood tool, smooth over the join on the outside.

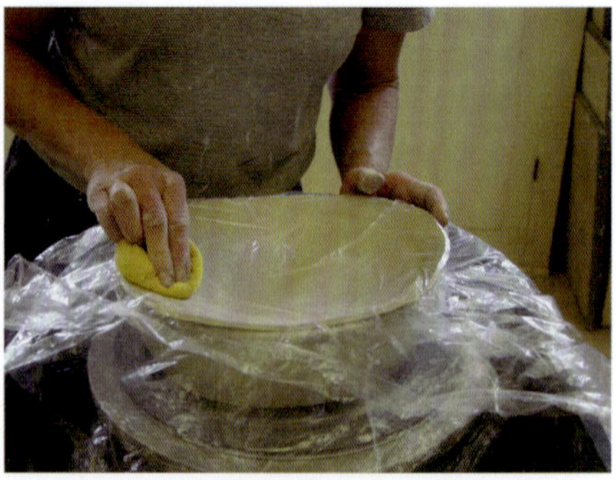

Place plastic over the rim and drape the second oval slab on top. Place another piece of plastic on top of the slab, then use a clean dry sponge to gently press the slab down to create a curve.

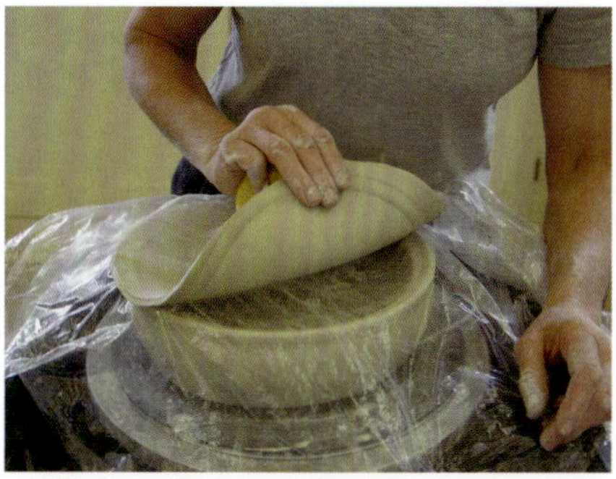

Press in all around the gallery to mark the slab. Don't lift the slab off while it is still this wet—this is just to show how the rim has marked the slab.

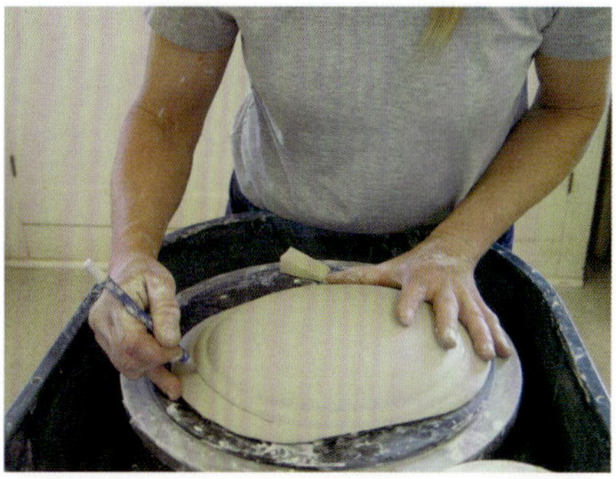

When the lid has set up enough, remove it and cut on the outer of the two marks.

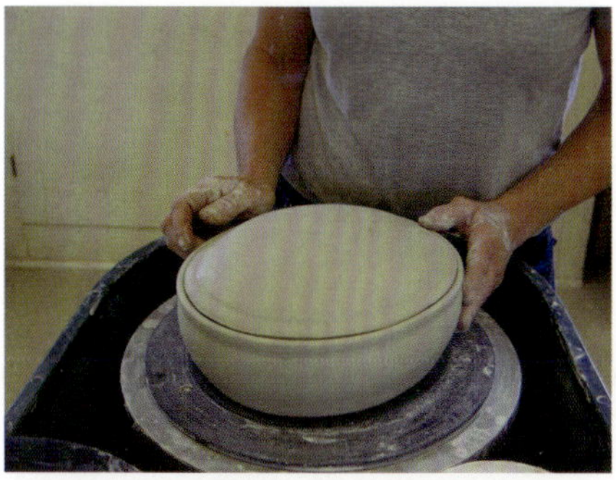

Set the lid into the gallery to check the fit.

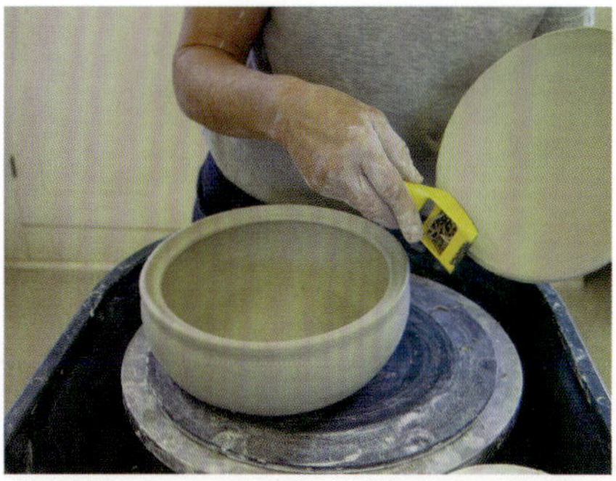

Use a Surform rasp to round the cut edge of the lid rim, and sponge it smooth.

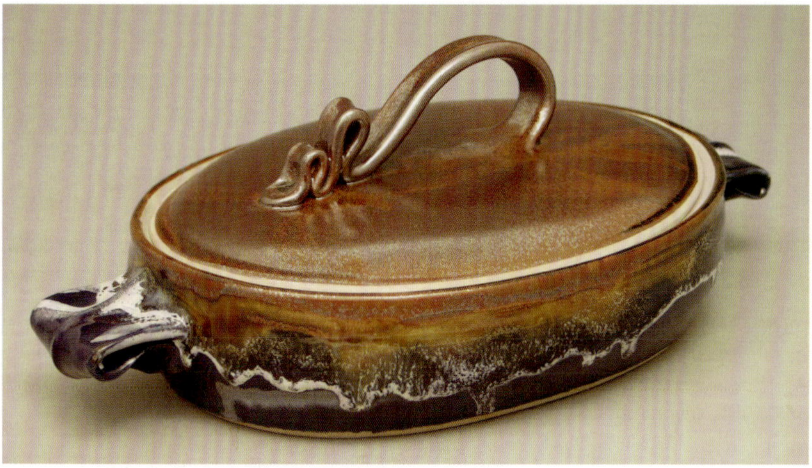

Oval casserole dish by Sumi von Dassow, 15 inches in length, reduction-fired stoneware.

PROJECT 3: Robbie Lobell Making a Square Baking Dish

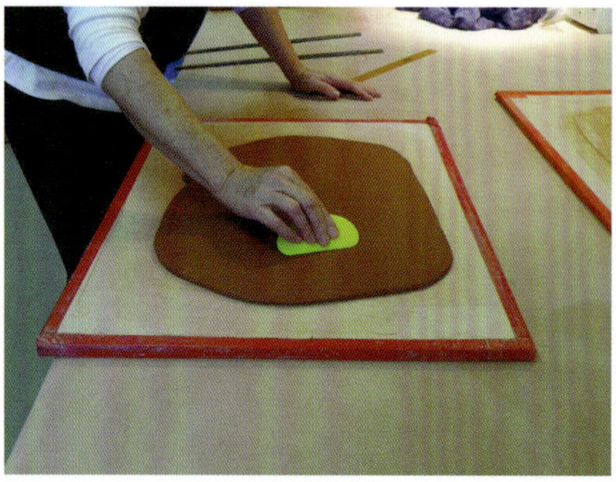

Robbie rolls a slab for the bottom of the baking dish and smooths it with a rib.

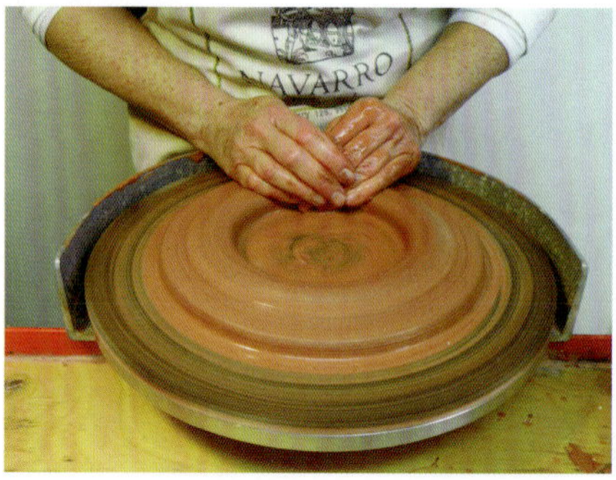

She then throws a ring without a bottom to form the walls of the baking dish.

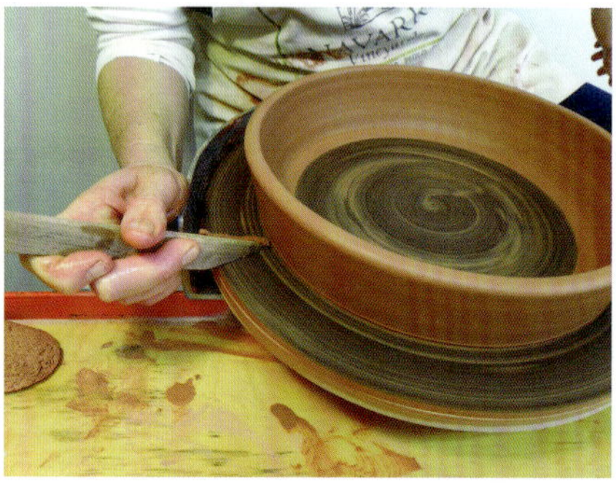

Trimming excess clay from the bottom of the finished ring.

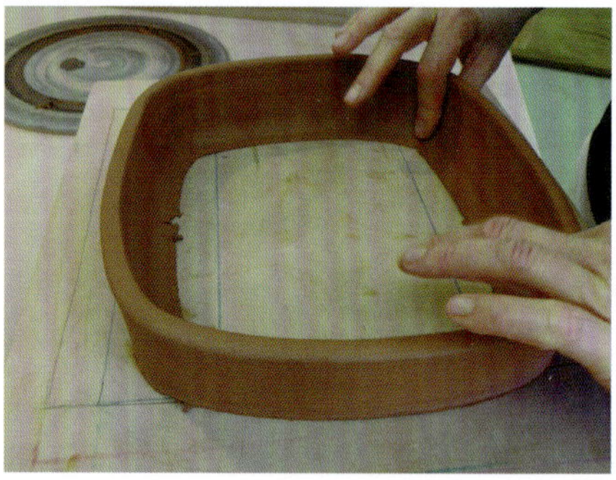

After the ring has set up a bit, it is reshaped into a square. Robbie leaves a little flange of clay inside the ring to aid in attaching it to the slab.

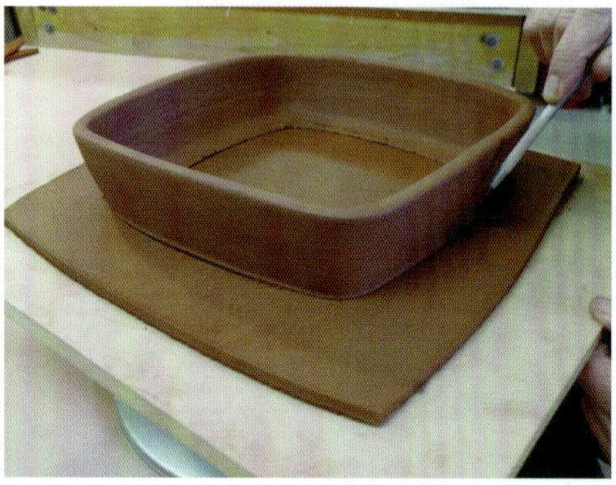

Robbie places the square on the slab and traces around it.

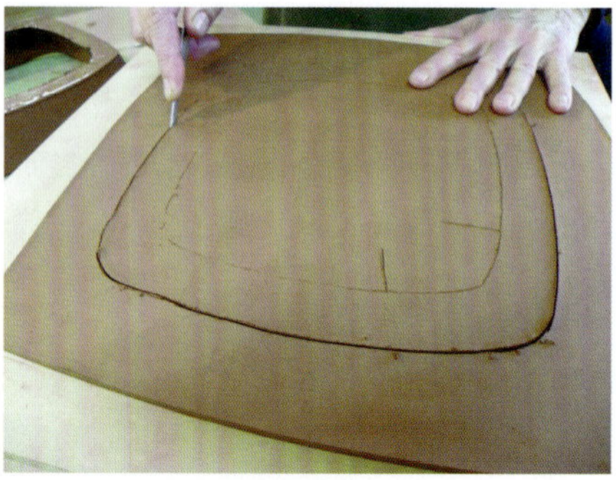

She then cuts the slab to size.

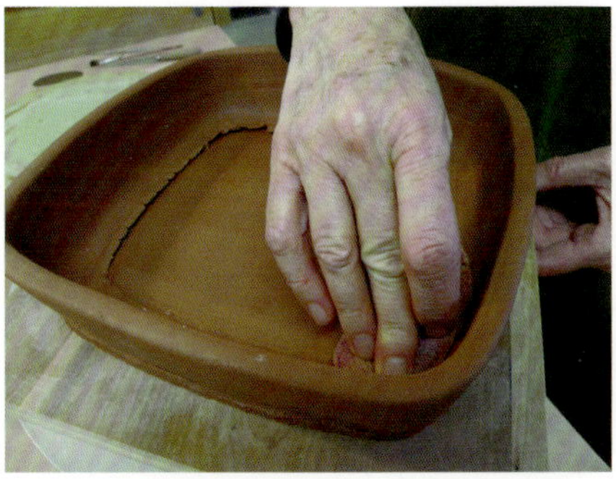

Using sponges and ribs Robbie smooths the join. There's no need to use an extra clay coil to join the pieces because of the flange inside the ring.

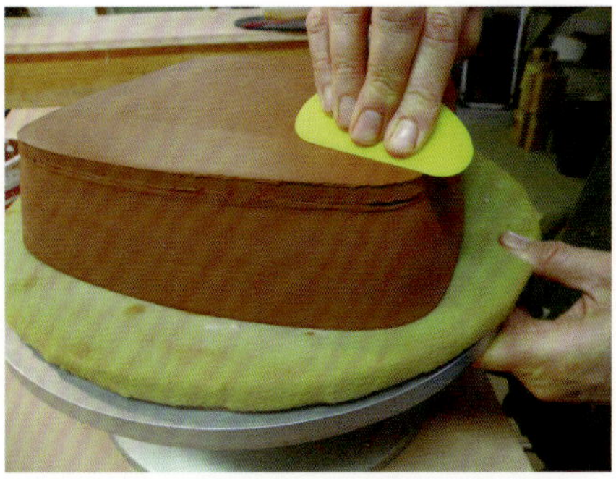

Robbie flips the dish over to smooth the bottom and compress it into the wall.

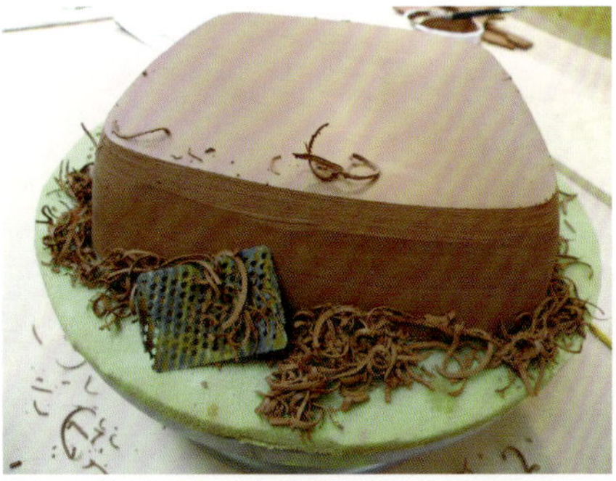

Using a Surform rasp to finish the bottom edge.

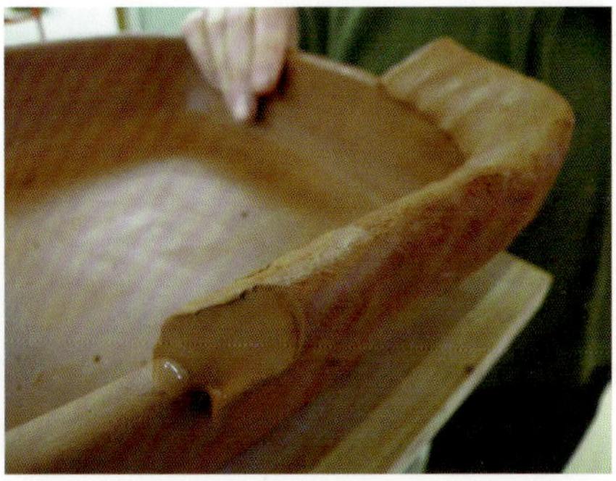

Robbie makes a unique style of handle by joining a thick coil of clay to two opposite corners and smoothing and stretching the clay into shape.

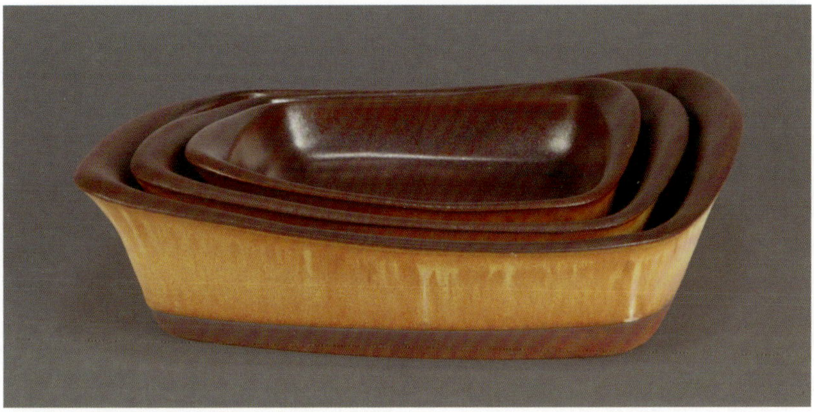

Three nested baking dishes by Robbie Lobell, to 13 inches in length, soda-fired flameware. Photo by Michael Stadler

PROJECT 4: James McLellan Making a Chicken Brick

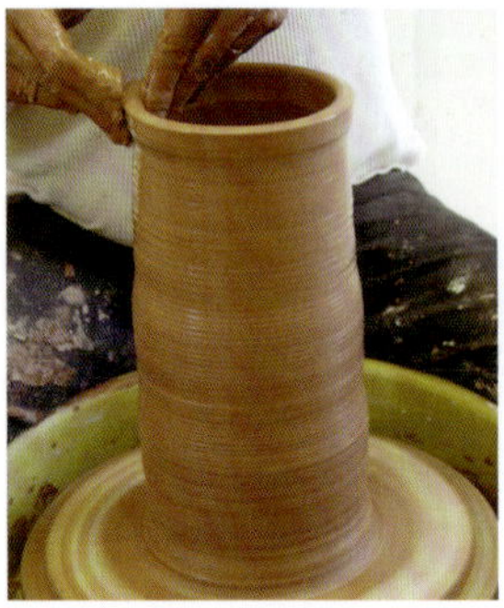

Starting with about 10 pounds of earthenware clay, James pulls up a tall narrow cylinder.

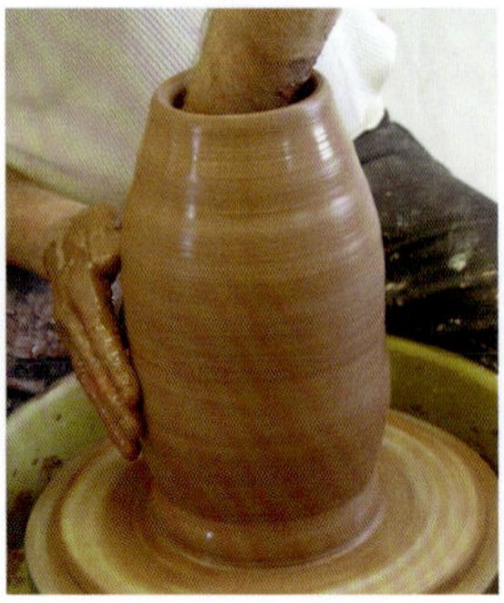

Once he has the height he wants, he bellies the clay out slightly then begins collaring the top of the form in.

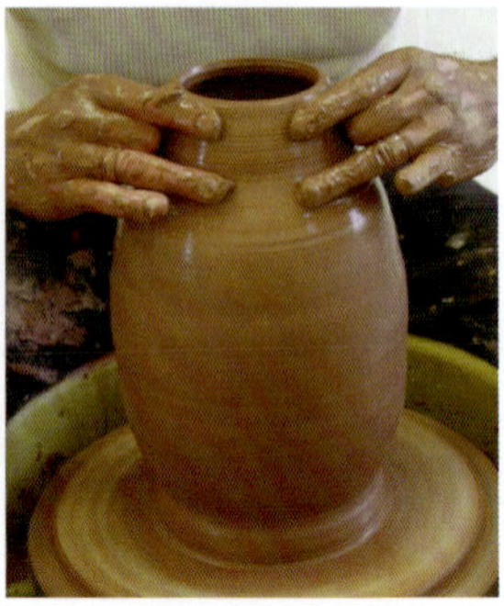

He alternates collaring with pulling up to keep the wall at a consistent thickness.

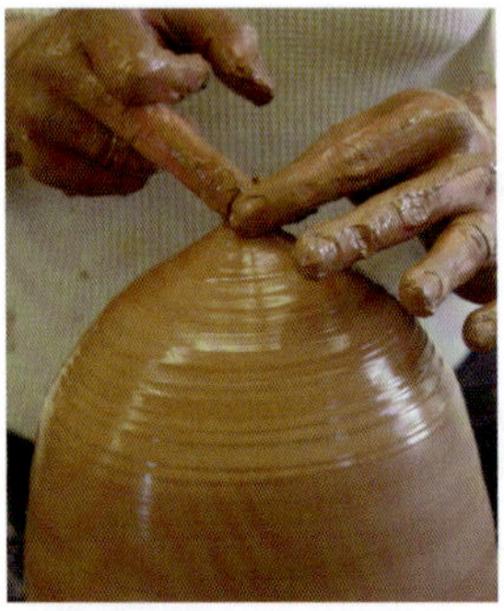

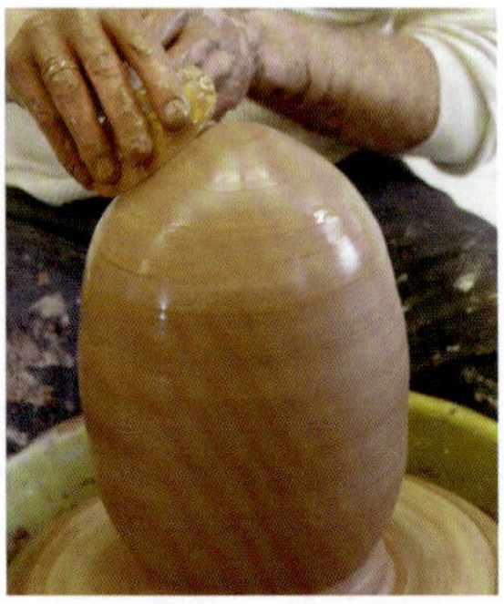

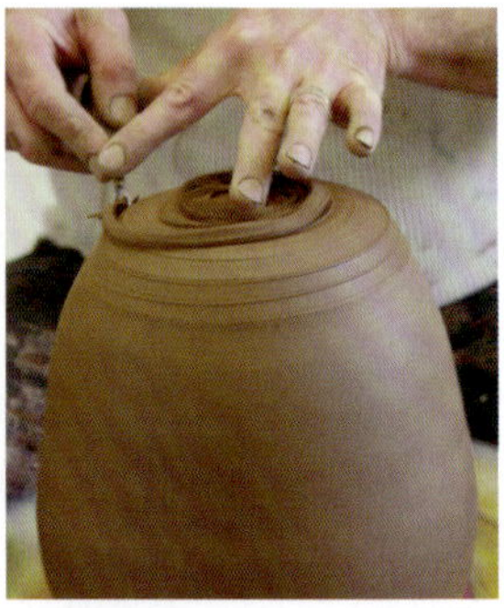

James closes the form completely and then ribs the entire form to smooth it and strengthen the area where he closed it. Alternatively, you can give this form a handle by throwing a vase with a long narrow neck. When turned on its side, the closed off neck becomes a handle. At soft leather-hard, James turns it in a chuck to trim excess clay.

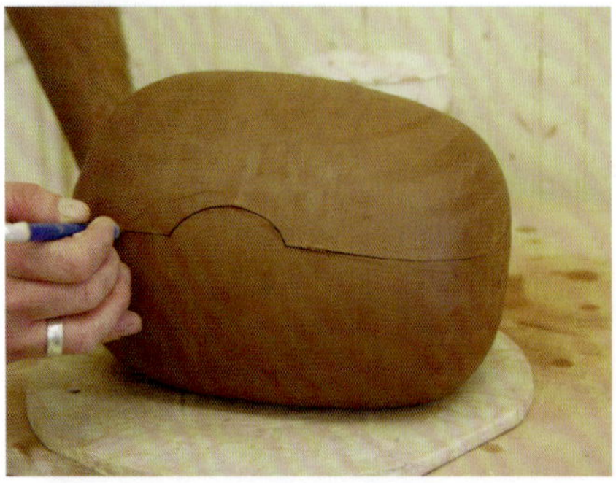

James marks and cuts the form with an X-Acto knife creating rounded keys on both sides so the lid will stay on and to seat the lid. When the form has set up a bit more he attaches handles.

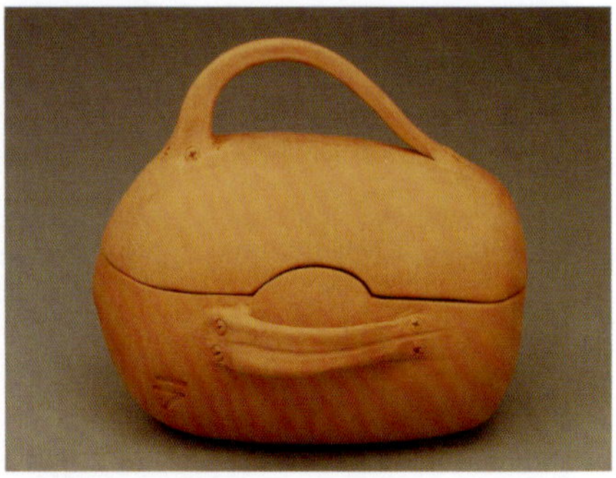

Finished unglazed earthenware clay (R2 from Laguna) fired to cone 05. Photo by Sumi von Dassow

PROJECT 5: Throwing a Chicken Brick in Two Sections

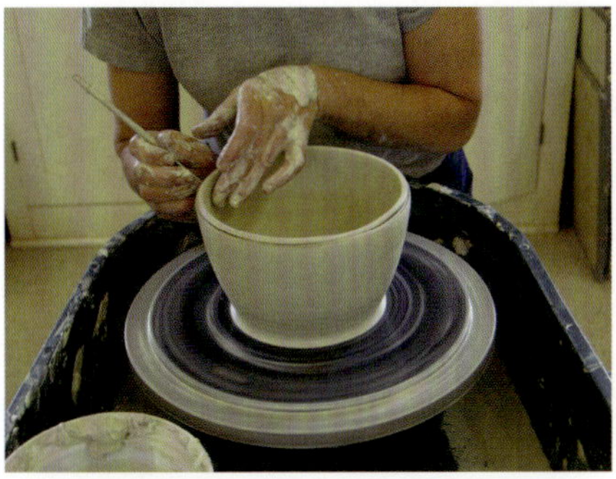

Center 5 pounds of clay and throw a bowl with a wide flat ¼-inch-thick bottom (no trimming required). Trim the rim at a downward angle with a needle tool. Do not wire under the form.

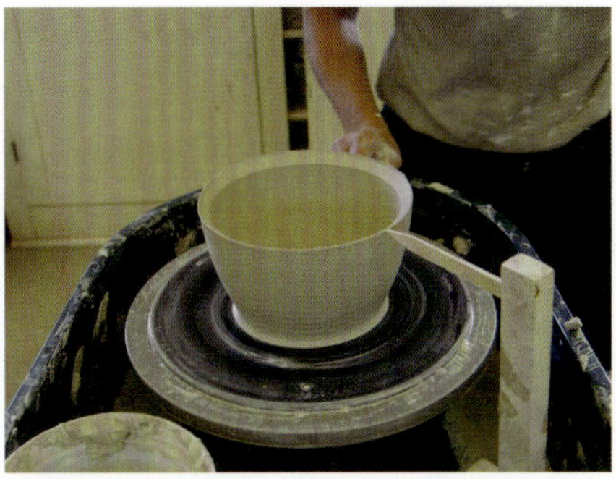

Throw an identical bowl using a pointer to measure height and width at the rim. Make a pointer from scrap wood or buy the Fulwood Measure (see p. 159).

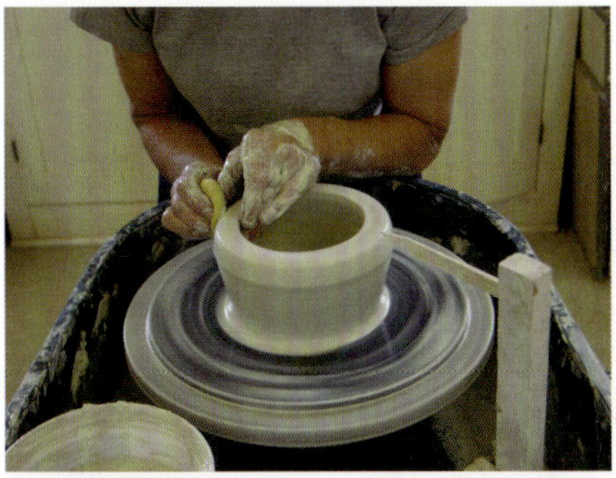

Without moving the pointer, center and throw a second bowl. Since the pointer is on the side away from your hands, it really doesn't interfere with throwing.

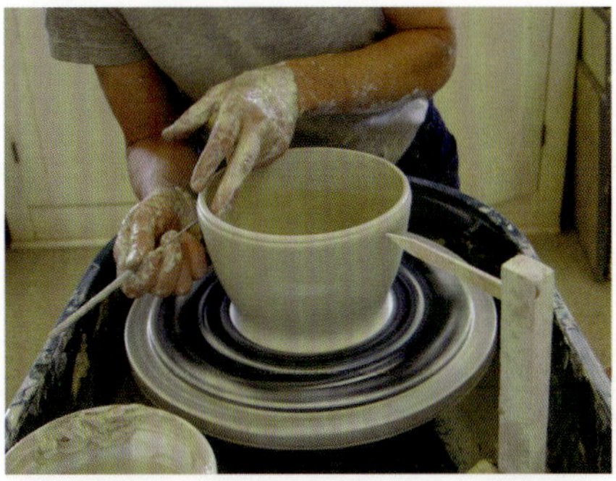

When the rim of the bowl touches the pointer, trim it at the opposite angle to the first one. Do not wire under the form. Wrap the rims of the two bowls and dry evenly in the open air.

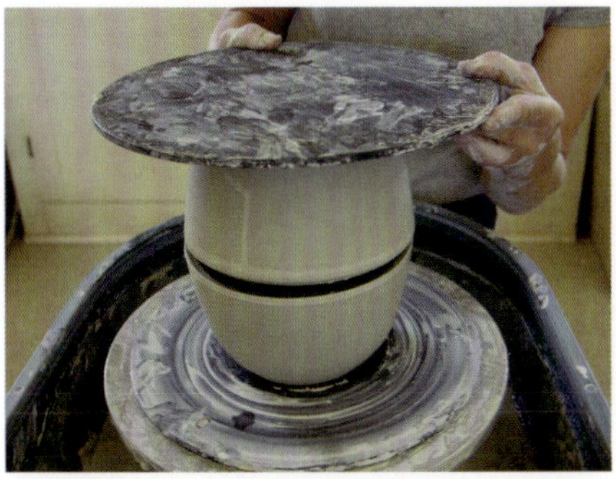

Scrub both rims with a toothbrush dipped in magic water. Place the first bowl back on the wheel, then pick up the second bowl by the bat and invert it on the first one.

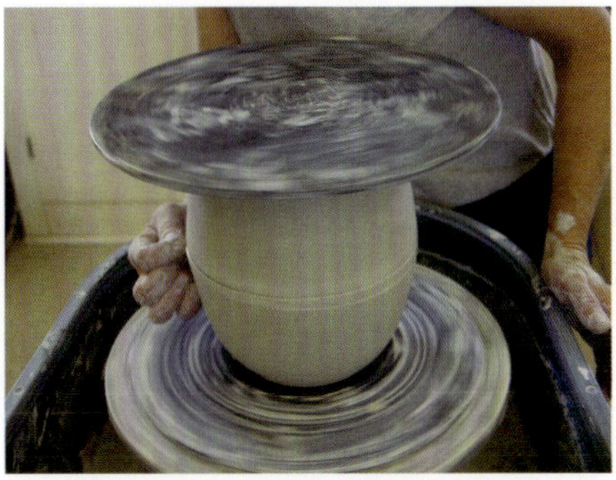

The angled edges should match up exactly. Use fingers and ribs to smooth over the join.

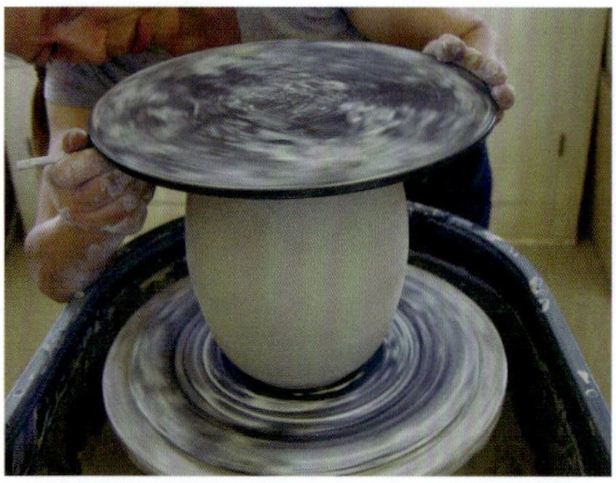

With the wheel turning, use a needle tool to cut a groove where the upper bowl joins the bat.

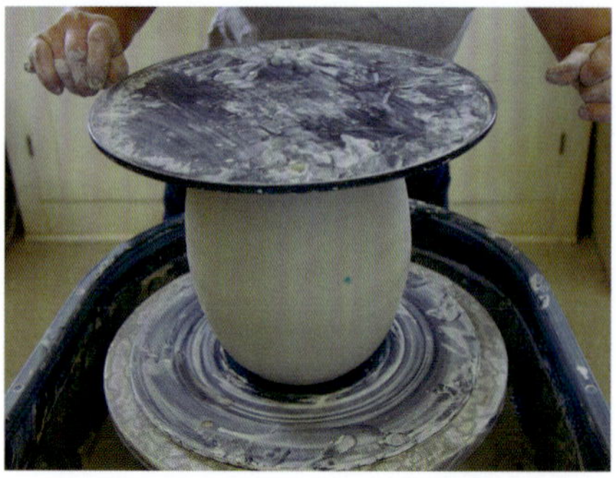

Work a wire into the groove you cut and, with the wheel turning slowly, pull the wire towards you to cut the bat loose. Use trimming tools and ribs to round and smooth the top.

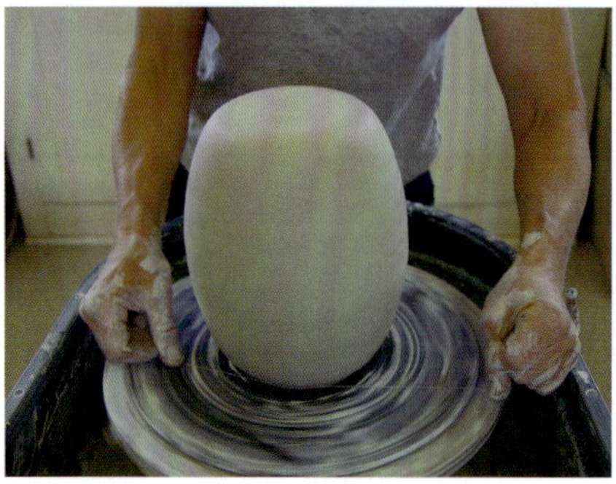

Wire under the roaster to remove it from the second bat.

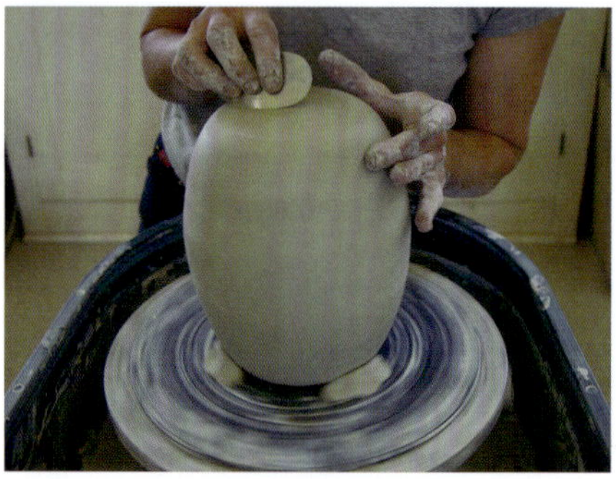

Flip the roaster over, secure it to the wheel-head with clay wads or a re-centering tool, and use trimming tools and ribs as necessary to round and smooth this end of the roaster.

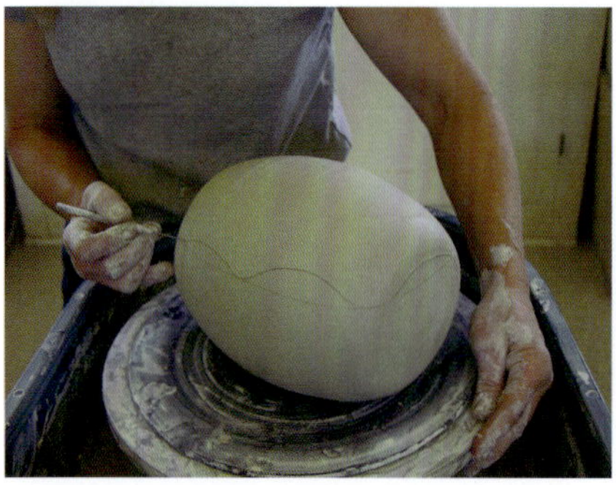

Now set the roaster on its side and draw a line around it a bit more than halfway up. Use this line as a registration mark to plan out a wavy cut.

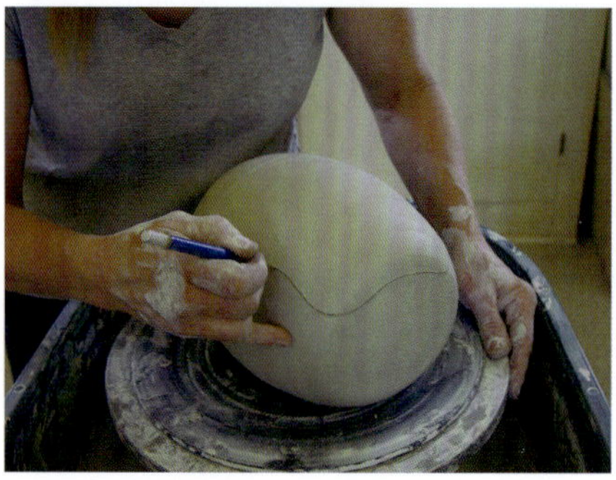

Using an X-Acto knife, cut the lid off.

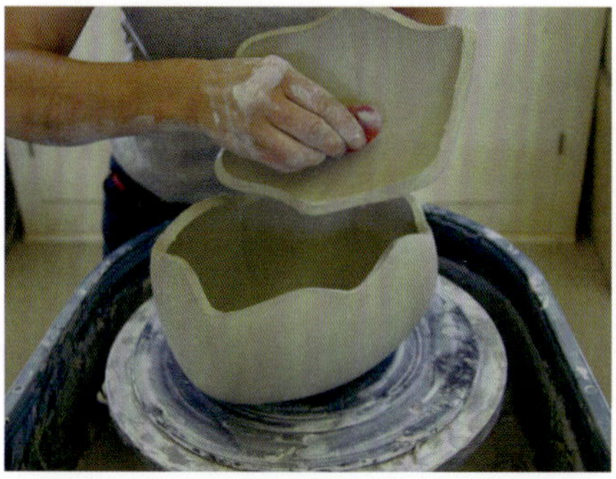

Lift the top off and smooth the inside of the join.

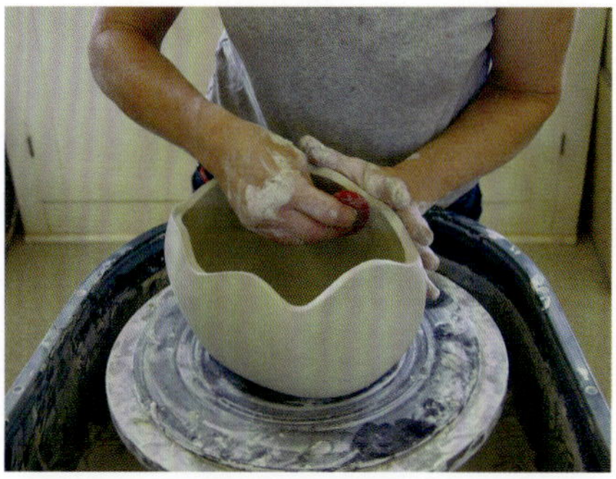

Smooth inside the join on the bottom section.

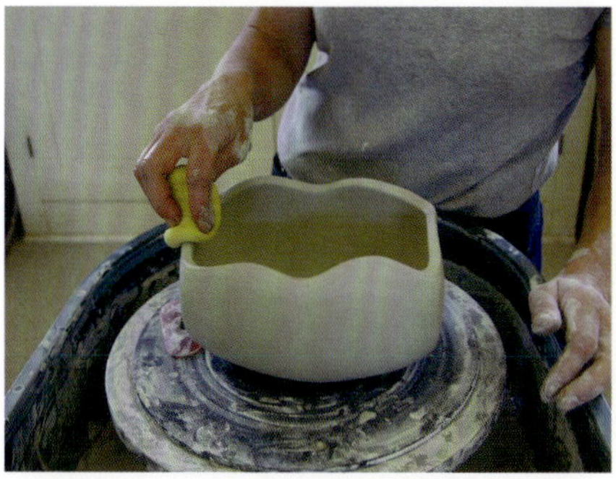

Smooth all cut edges with a sponge. Later you can use a Surform rasp if necessary.

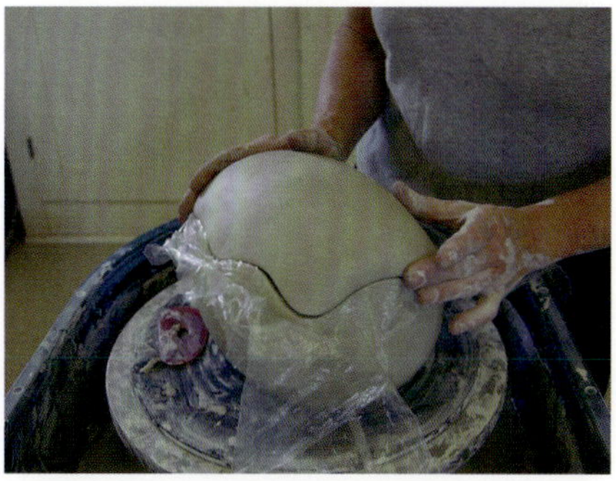

The pieces are still quite soft, so put plastic between them when you put them back together so they don't stick together. They need to dry a bit more before handles are added.

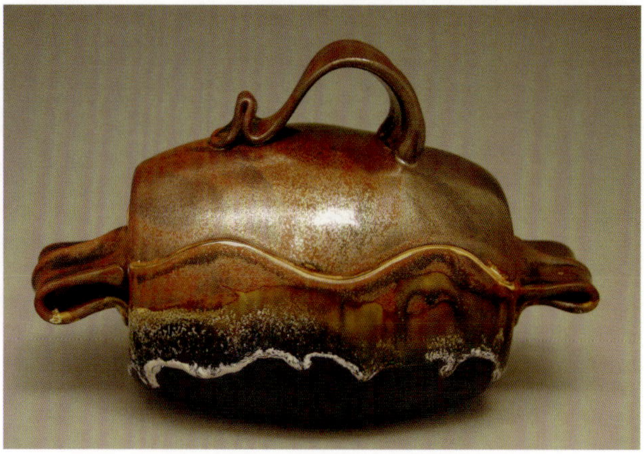

Chicken brick by Sumi von Dassow, 13 inches in length, stoneware, reduction-fired to cone 7. Thrown in two sections joined in the middle makes it more symmetrical and easier if you have trouble working with 10 pounds of clay. Photo by Sumi von Dassow

PROJECT 6: Making a Garlic Roaster

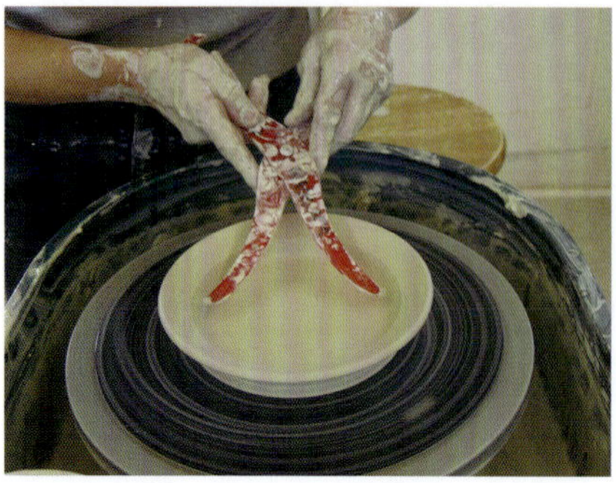

Throw a 3- to 4-inch saucer using a pound or less of clay. Measure across the bottom with calipers.

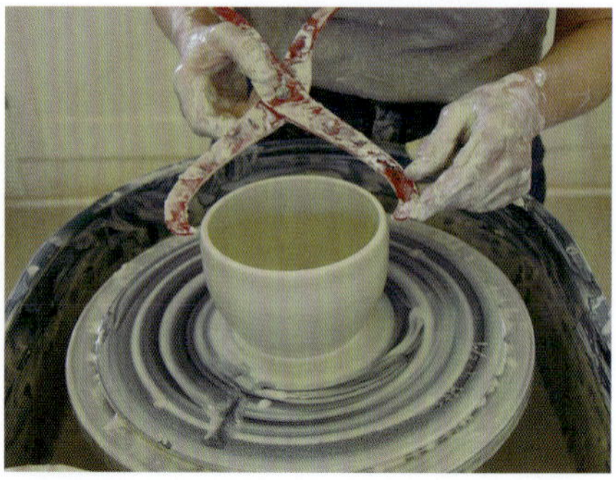

Throw the cover—a simple bowl form—and measure it. The outside of the cover needs to match the measurement across the bottom of the dish.

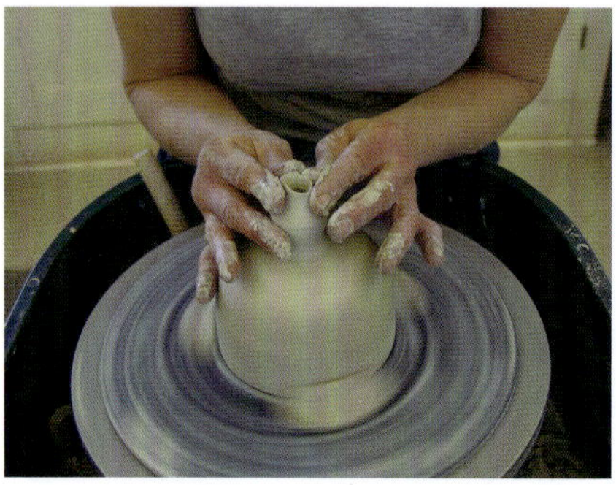

When it's leather-hard, turn the cover over and trim. Supporting it on a dry sponge inside, throw a knob. This is an onion-shaped knob, thrown hollow so it won't be too massive.

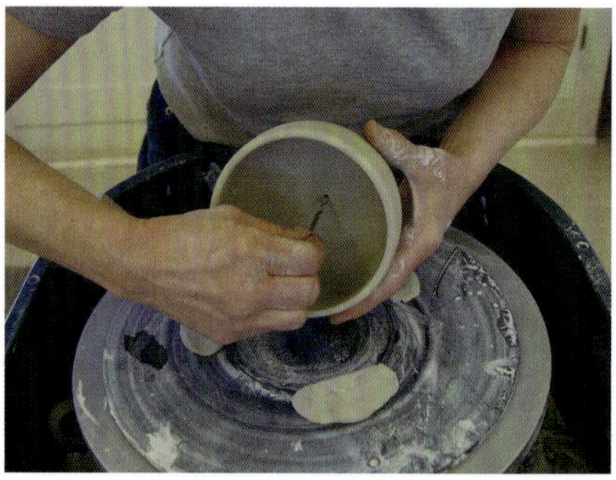

Drill a hole in the underside of the hollow knob so it won't crack while drying or trap moisture when being fired.

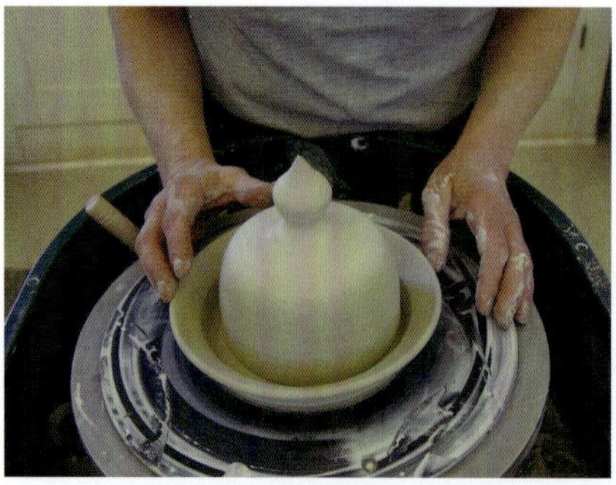

The finished garlic roaster. If you didn't make a rim on the dish, you might want to add handles. This same form can be made larger for a cheese bell.

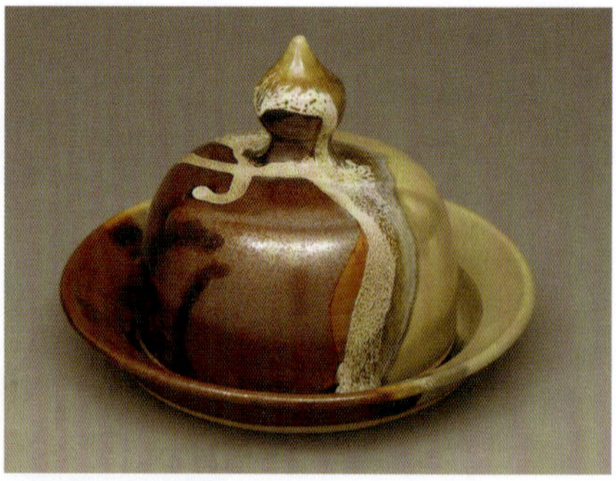

Garlic roaster by Sumi von Dassow, 6 inches in diameter, stoneware, reduction-fired to cone 7. Photo by Sumi von Dassow

Handle-making Workshop

There are many options for putting knobs and handles on baking dishes. You should choose a handle style that looks good, but also one that makes your baking dish easy to use.

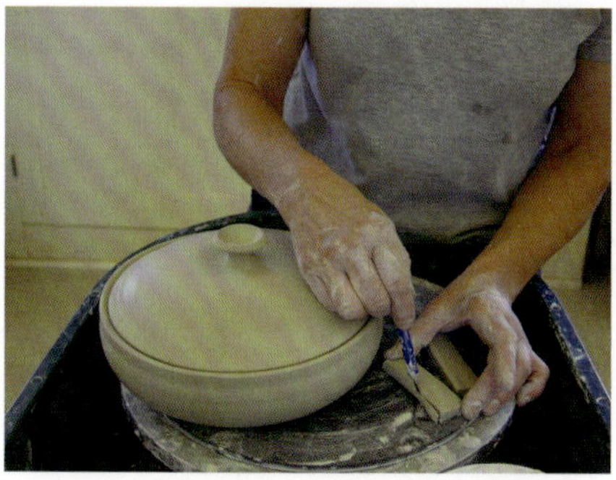

Pull a strap for handles. Cut two equal lengths and slice off one edge of each.

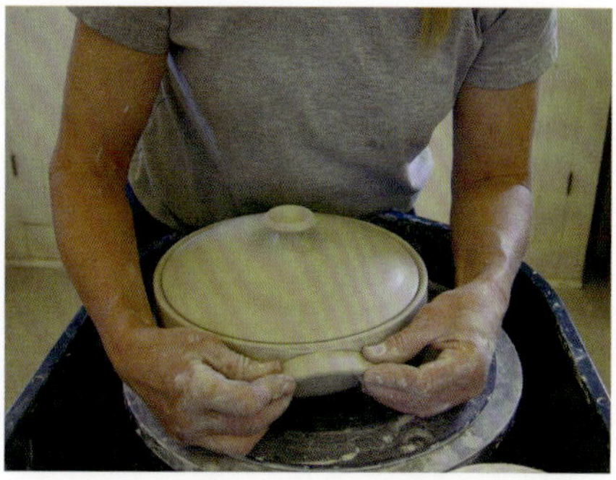

Scrub with a toothbrush dipped in magic water where you want the handle to attach, and press the cut edge of one length of handle on, giving it a slight downward curve.

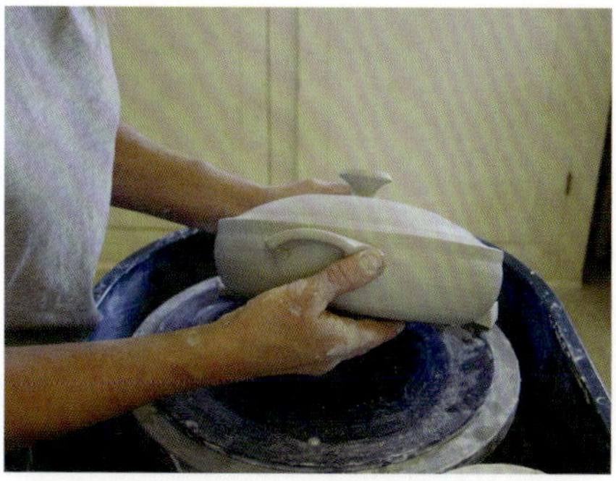

Use your fingers and a sponge to seal the join, then use the tips of your thumbs to push the corners of the handle down to seal it in place more securely.

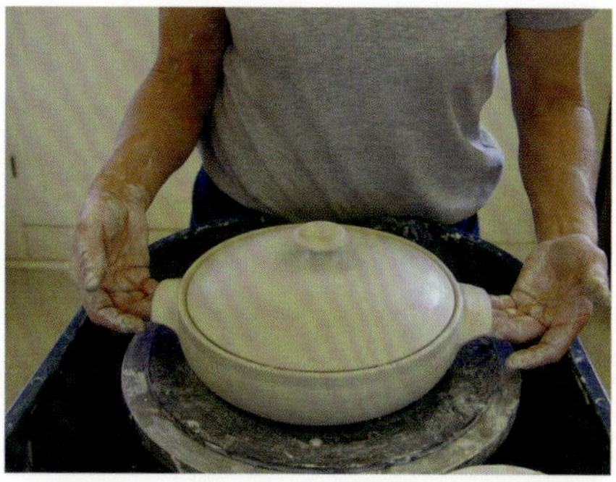

The finished casserole with both handles. This type of handle is securely attached, it's not too bulky, and it's easy to get your fingers under it when removing the dish from the oven.

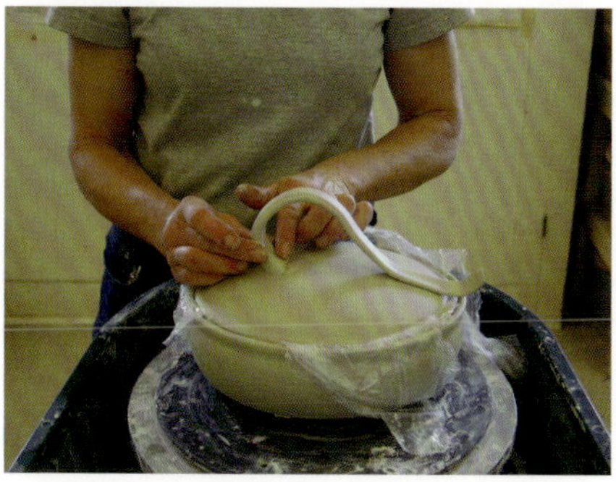

Pull a handle and attach it to the lid with a little magic water.

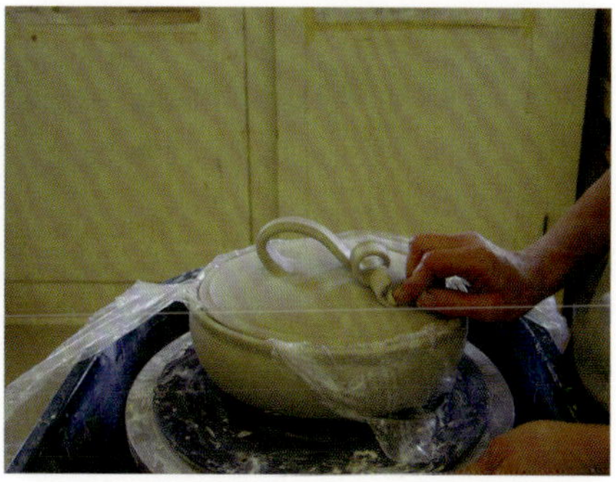

Make any flourishes you like in the handle.

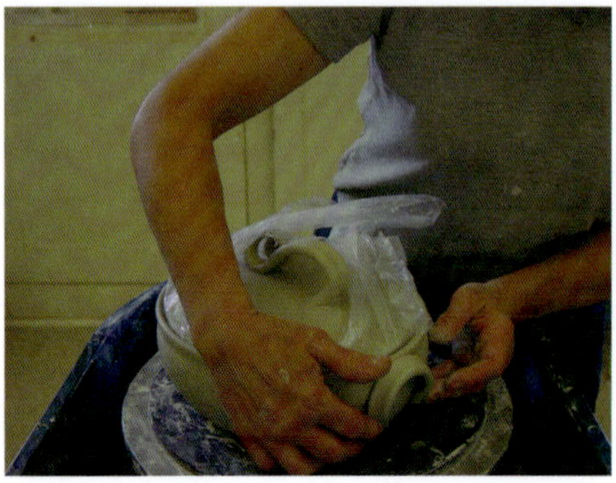

Pull another handle and cut two pieces for the sides of the dish. These handles are shaped into a C-shape and joined to the casserole dish at each end, using magic water.

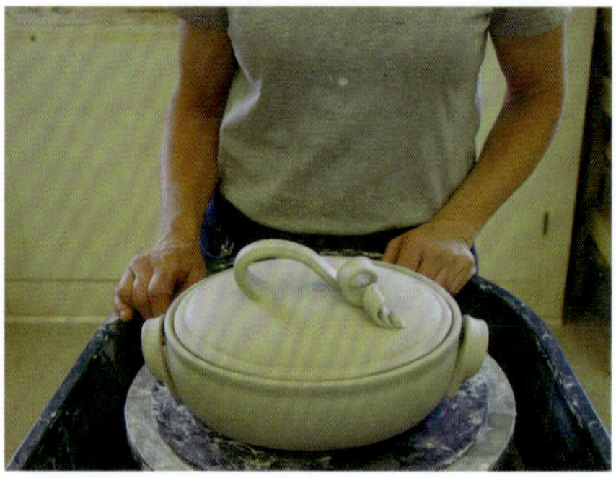

The finished oval casserole.

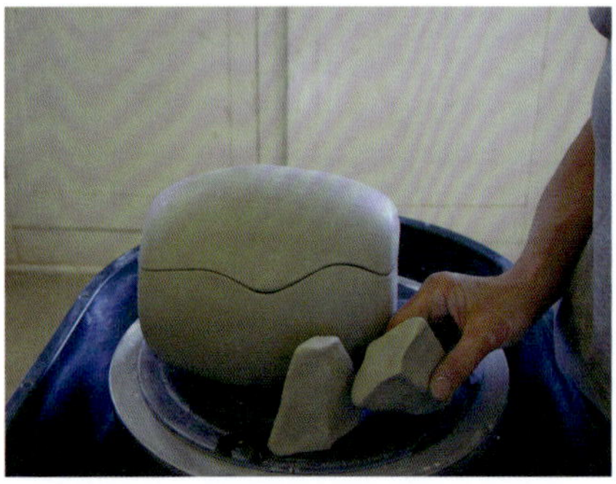

This form wants substantial handles. Start with two ½-pound chunks of clay and form them into flattened triangles with a diamond-shaped base.

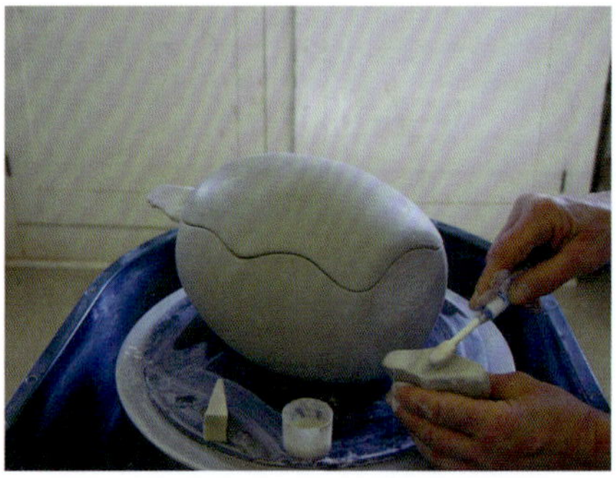

Using magic water and a toothbrush, stick both handle slugs on and seat them securely.

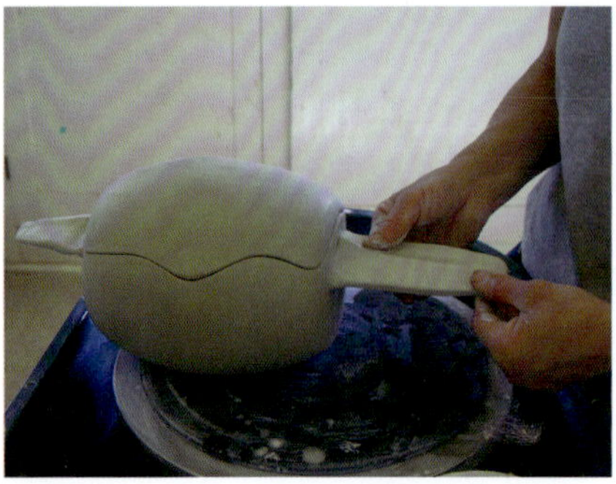

Pull the first handle, pulling straight toward yourself and alternating hands with each pull.

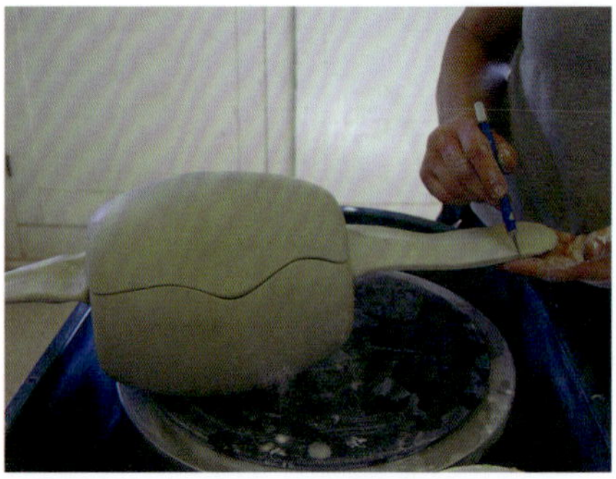

Cut the end of the handle when it is several inches long. Measure this one so you can make the other one the same length.

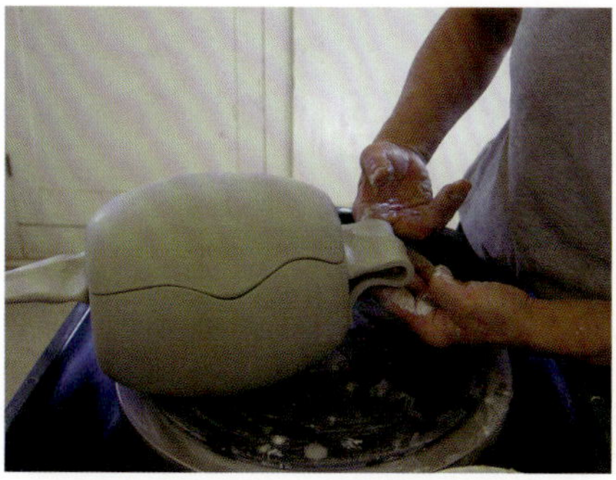

Fold the handle down around your finger.

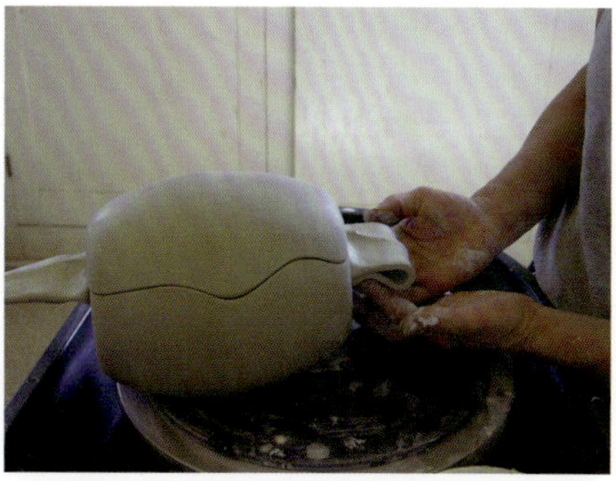

Secure the end of the handle with gentle pressure. Repeat the process for the second handle.

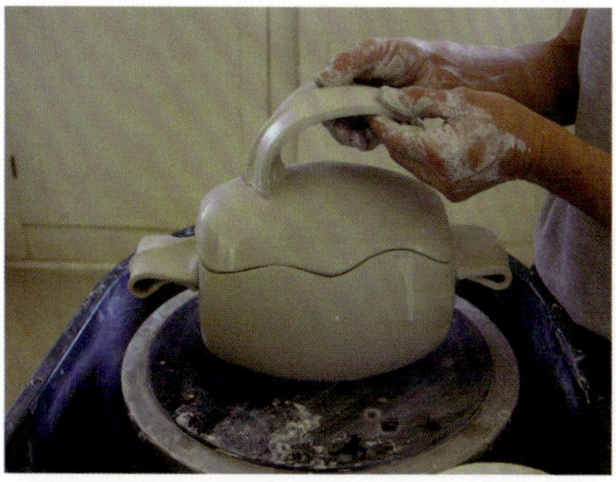

Attach a handle slug to the lid and pull a similar handle.

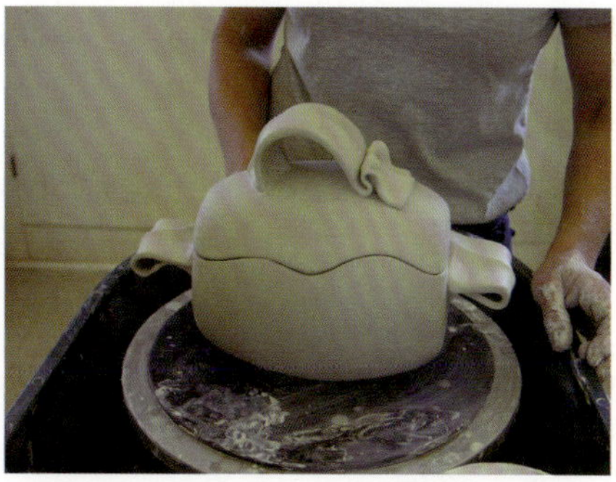

The finished chicken brick. These handles are very easy to grasp with pot holders.

Three rectangular baking dishes with different kinds of handles. The one in the middle is an example of yet another kind of handle. These handles are created by throwing the dish with a wide flat rim all around, then cutting off most of this rim, leaving just enough for two handles. This wastes a lot of clay but it makes a handle that is easy to grasp and is an integral part of the dish.

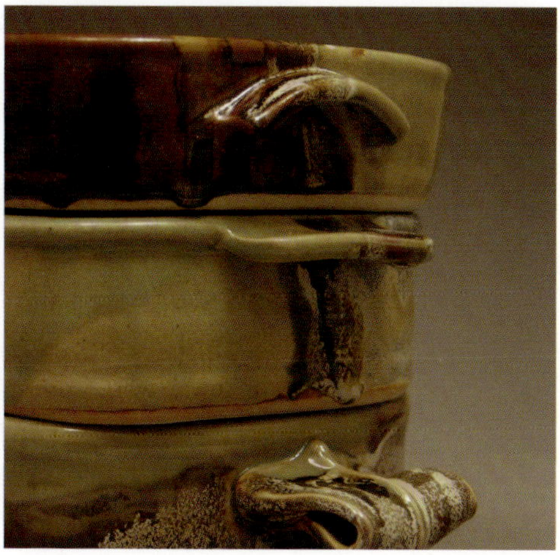

RECIPES FOR OVENWARE

Judy's Russian Rye

2 cups all-purpose flour (preferably King Arthur)
1 cup rye flour
¼ teaspoon instant yeast
1 teaspoon sea salt
Handful of caraway or nigella seeds
1½ cups water

Dry mix everything except water. Add water and stir until uniform and no dry flour remains. Cover bowl tightly with plastic wrap and let dough rest at room temperature for 14 to 18 hours or until top surface is dotted with bubbles. Turn dough out onto a lightly floured countertop. Dust top of dough lightly with flour, and fold the dough over itself once or twice. Cover loosely with plastic wrap and let rest 15 minutes.

Drape a cotton or linen towel over a large bowl, and dust liberally with flour. Dust top of dough lightly with flour, pat gently into a 6-inch circle, and fold edges into center of dough 4 to 6 times to form a ball. Place ball, seam side up, on center of towel, fold corners of towel loosely over dough, and cover loosely with plastic wrap. Let rise 1½ to 2 hours, or until doubled in size.

At least 30 minutes before baking, place bread pot or enameled cast-iron Dutch oven on lower middle rack and heat oven to 450°F. When hot, carefully remove pot from oven. Slide hand beneath towel and turn dough into center of pot (if using Dutch oven, shake pot from side to side to center it, if necessary). Cover with lid and transfer to oven. Bake, covered, for 30 minutes. Remove lid, and bake 15 to 30 minutes longer, or until loaf is golden brown. Transfer to wire rack and cool for at least 2 hours before serving. Experiment with different types of flour; use whole wheat instead of rye, or even soy or oat flour for part of the flour.

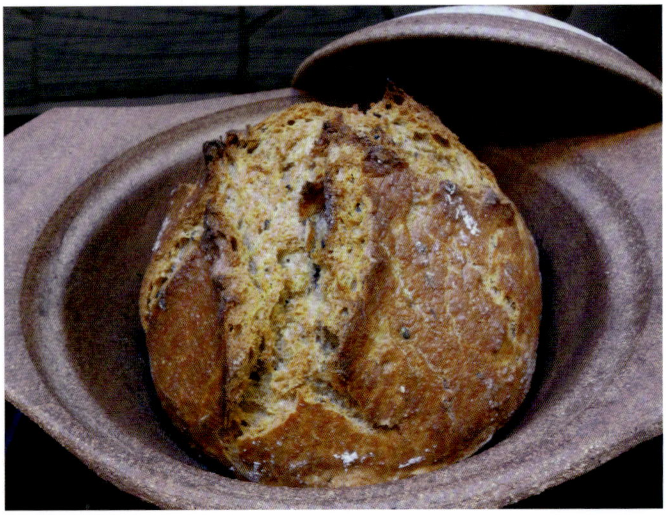

Bread pot with Judy's Rye, by Judith Motzkin. Photo by Judith Motzkin

Sumi's Sourdough Dark Rye Bread

1 ounce rye or wheat sourdough starter or ½ teaspoon active dry yeast
12 ounces cold black coffee (or water or cold tea) (1½ cups)
12 ounces non-chlorinated water (1½ cups)
12 ounces whole rye flour (3 cups)
12 ounces whole wheat flour (3 cups)
12¾ ounces all-purpose flour (3 cups)
4½ ounces molasses (⅜ cup)
1¼ ounce olive oil (3 tablespoons)
1 tablespoon caraway seeds
1 tablespoon salt
2 tablespoons anise seeds, ground
¼ cup cocoa powder

Dough Enhancer

1 cup wheat gluten
2 tablespoons lecithin granules
2 tablespoons pectin powder
2 tablespoons unflavored gelatin
1 teaspoon ascorbic or citric acid
1 teaspoon ginger
Mix all ingredients thoroughly; use 3 tablespoons per loaf.

If you have a kitchen scale, measuring by weight is quicker and more accurate. Mix sourdough starter or yeast with all the liquid and the rye and whole wheat flour in the bowl of a stand mixer. Cover and let sit for 8 to 12 hours (overnight). Then add all the rest of the ingredients. Dough should be elastic and slightly sticky. Knead by hand or in your mixer with the dough hook until the dough balls up on the hook; then remove the bowl, grease it, and cover it. After an hour, turn the dough out, press it out flat, and fold it over a couple of times without adding extra flour. Repeat this after another hour. After one more hour, divide dough in two, pat into loaf shape, and place into greased and floured 4x8-inch loaf pans. Allow to rise in a warm place until the top of the dough is an inch higher than the loaf pans. This may take up to 8 hours. Turn oven to 350°F and place loaves in; bake for 55 minutes or until loaves sound hollow when you knock on them. For a 100% whole grain variation, use 10¾ ounces (2⅝ cups) whole wheat or white whole wheat flour in place of the all-purpose flour, and add ⅜ cup (2 ounces) dough enhancer.

Granmur's Cranberry Bread

2 cups flour, sifted
1½ teaspoons baking powder
½ teaspoon baking soda
1 cup sugar
Juice and rind of one orange
2 tablespoons shortening or butter
1 egg
1 cup chopped nuts
1 cup raw halved cranberries

Mix orange juice and rind with butter or shortening and add enough boiling water to make ¾ cup liquid. Mix dry ingredients together, then add liquid mixture and beaten egg. Mix in remaining ingredients and pour into greased loaf pan. Bake at 350°F for an hour.

Maple Pumpkin Bread

1½ cups grade B maple syrup
1½ cups sugar
4 eggs
1 cup oil
3 cups mashed pumpkin or winter squash
¾ teaspoon salt
¾ teaspoon baking powder
1½ teaspoons cinnamon
4½ cups flour
1½ teaspoons baking soda
1½ teaspoons cloves
1½ teaspoons nutmeg

Grease and flour three standard bread loaf pans. Beat maple syrup, sugar, eggs and oil together; add pumpkin. Mix dry ingredients in separate bowl and add to wet ingredients. Pour into loaf pans. Bake at 300°F for 1 hour and 20 minutes. Test with cake tester. This bread freezes excellently.

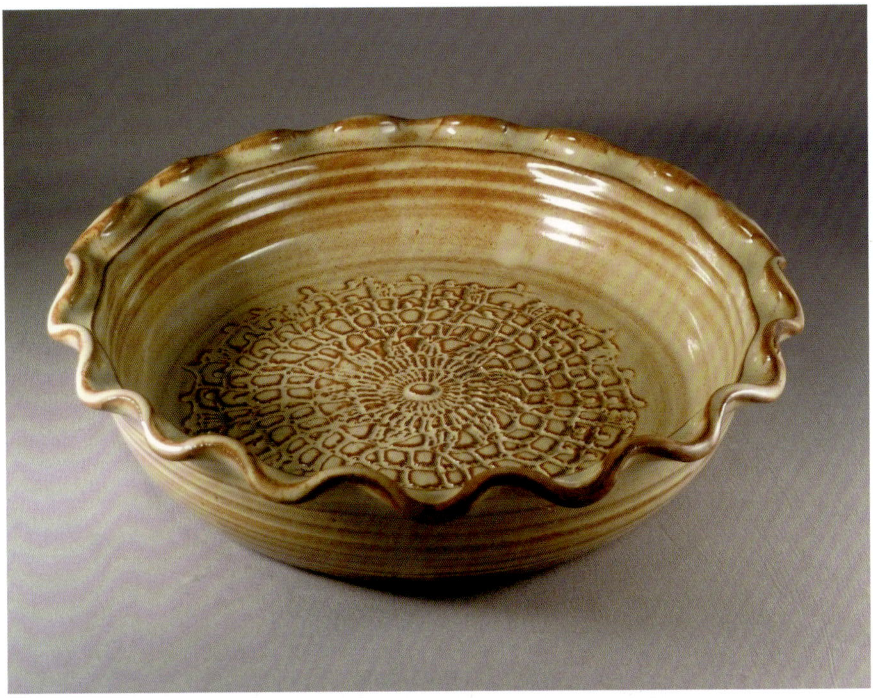

Quiche dish by Fay Krapf, 8 inches in diameter, oxidation fired to cone 6. Photo by Fay Krapf

Crustless Quiche

½ onion, chopped
2 cups vegetables—broccoli, spinach, zucchini, mushrooms, etc.
2 tablespoons oil or melted butter
1 cup milk
½ teaspoon salt
Pepper
1 cup grated cheddar cheese
4 eggs
½ cup flour or gluten free flour
1 teaspoon baking soda

Mix flour with baking soda; combine all the other ingredients, then add flour mixture. Pour into greased quiche dish or pie dish. Bake at 350°F for 45 minutes.

Onion Quiche

1 cup crushed saltine crackers or gluten-free rice crackers
4 tablespoons (½ stick) butter, melted
1½ cups chopped onions—can include green onions for color
2 tablespoons butter
3 eggs
1½ cups milk
½ teaspoon salt
¼ teaspoon pepper
1½ cups grated Swiss cheese

Combine cracker crumbs and melted butter. Place in bottom of quiche dish. Sauté onion for 10 minutes in butter. Cool, then place on top of cracker crumbs in the quiche dish. Beat eggs; add milk, salt, pepper, and Swiss cheese. Pour into quiche dish on top of crackers and onions. Bake until set, about 20–30 minutes. Do not over bake. May be stored in refrigerator. Warm in oven before serving. Can add other ingredients such as bacon, spinach, broccoli, etc.

Baked Brie

1 wheel of Brie (8 ounces)
1 tablespoon butter
¼ cup slivered almonds
1 tablespoon honey or apricot jam (optional)

Place Brie on baking dish. Spread softened butter on Brie. Sprinkle with almonds and drizzle with honey or jam. Cover and place in oven. Bake at 350°F for 5–10 minutes, until Brie just begins to soften. Serve with apple or pear slices or crusty bread.

Harvest Season Baked Tomatoes

4–5 pounds fresh tomatoes
1 teaspoon salt
3 tablespoons each chopped fresh basil and rosemary
Black pepper to taste
1 cup bread crumbs
⅓ cup ground flax seeds
1 cup grated Parmesan cheese
½ cup pine nuts
4 tablespoons butter, cut into small chunks
½ teaspoon salt
¼ teaspoon pepper
1 teaspoon Italian seasoning

Stem tomatoes and cut into 1-inch chunks. Place in a large colander, toss with salt, and drain at least 30 minutes. Grease a large baking dish with olive oil and put tomatoes in it. Add pepper and herbs and toss. Spread evenly. In large bowl mix bread crumbs and the rest of the ingredients, cutting butter into mixture with a fork or fingers until evenly distributed and crumbly. Sprinkle on top of tomato mixture and bake in 350°F oven until slightly browned and bubbly, about 45 minutes.

Roasted Butternut Squash Soup

1 butternut squash, peeled, seeded, and chopped
1 onion, diced small
1 teaspoon salt
1 tablespoon minced garlic (2 or 3 cloves)
Pepper to taste
1 bay leaf and two sprigs of fresh thyme if available
4 cups chicken or vegetable broth

Mix all ingredients, except for 2 cups of the broth, in bean pot or micaceous clay pot. Roast 30 minutes, then add warmed reserved broth. Stir and roast another 30 minutes. Remove bay leaf and thyme and purée in blender until smooth.

Oven Roasted Butternut Squash in Earthenware

1 butternut squash (2–3 pounds), peeled, seeded, and chopped
1 onion, diced small, optional
1 teaspoon salt
1 tablespoon minced garlic (2–3 cloves)
Pepper to taste
2 tablespoons coconut oil, butter or olive oil

Mix all ingredients in a 2 quart earthenware roaster or micaceous clay pot. Cover and place in cold oven set to 450°F and roast for 1 to 1½ hours until tender.

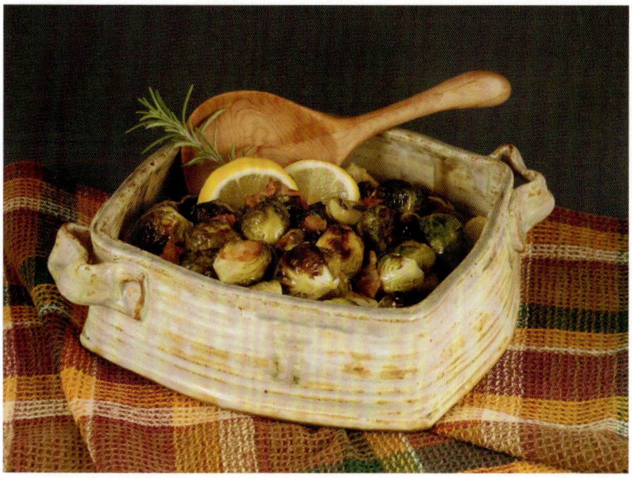

Baking dish with Oven Roasted Brussels Sprouts by Marcia Paul, 9 inches square, stoneware, wheel-thrown and altered, slips with ash glazes, reduction fired, cone 10. Photo by Robert Paul

Oven Roasted Brussels Sprouts

1 pound Brussels sprouts
2–3 tablespoons olive oil
Kosher salt
Lemon zest
1–2 slices bacon, chopped finely

Trim sprouts; slice in half and toss in a bowl with olive oil and salt to taste. Put in a baking dish and place in oven at 375°F for 20-45 minutes, stirring every ten minutes or so, until sprouts begin to brown. sauté bacon bits and toss with sprouts along with lemon zest.

Roasted Winter Vegetables

8 cups vegetables, peeled if necessary, and chopped into ½-inch chunks. Vegetables to use include potatoes, onions, carrots, parsnips, kohlrabi, beets, turnips, rutabaga, sweet potatoes and Jerusalem artichokes.
¼ cup olive oil or mixture of olive oil and coconut oil
1 teaspoon salt, or more to taste
½ teaspoon pepper
Several cloves garlic, peeled and minced
½ teaspoon each rosemary, thyme, and sage, or other herbs you prefer

Toss vegetables with oil and herbs and pour into a baking dish big enough to spread the vegetables out in a relatively shallow layer (or use two baking dishes). Place in oven and roast at 400°F for 1½ hours, or until vegetables are soft and beginning to brown around the edges. As they cook they will give off liquid; you want to roast them until most of the liquid evaporates. Stir once or twice while they are roasting.

Boston Baked Beans

1 pound (2 to 2¼ cups) dry white beans such as Navy beans or Great Northern beans
⅓ cup molasses
⅓ cup brown sugar
3–4 tablespoons Dijon mustard
⅛ teaspoon ground cloves
3 cups hot water
½ pound salt pork or bacon, cut into bite size pieces (omit for vegetarian version)
1 medium onion, chopped (1½ cups)

Soak beans overnight; drain and place in bean pot or covered casserole dish. Mix the next five ingredients. Put half of the salt pork or bacon in the bean pot and cover with half of the drained beans. Add all of the onions, then the rest of the beans and the rest of the pork or bacon. Pour the molasses mixture over the beans making sure to cover the beans. Cover and bake at 250°F for 8 hours or until tender. Add water as necessary. Add salt to taste when done.

Winter Veggie Cobbler

1 parsnip, peeled and cut into ¼-inch thick coins
½ rutabaga, peeled and cubed
1 potato, cut into bite-sized wedges
½ sweet potato, peeled and cut into bite-sized wedges
1 onion, chopped
1 turnip, peeled and cut into bite-sized wedges
1 cup chilled vegetable broth (best if homemade)
2 tablespoons cornstarch
1 teaspoon salt or miso paste
Freshly ground pepper to taste
1¼ cups all purpose unbleached flour
2 tablespoons baking powder
¼ teaspoon salt
6 tablespoons cold butter, diced
¾ cup cream or ¼ cup heavy cream and ½ cup milk

Place all the veggies in the casserole. Mix the cornstarch with the stock and pour over veggies. Add pepper and salt or miso and mix well. Combine dry ingredients in a food processor. Add butter and pulse until it resembles coarse meal. Transfer into bowl and pour in cream, barely mixing. Lightly knead dough on floured table. Place blobs of dough over the top of the casserole. Bake for 50 minutes at 350°F or until dough is nicely browned and veggies are tender.

"Cheesy" Vegan Potato Casserole

4 large potatoes, thinly sliced
½ cup (1 stick) margarine
½ cup flour
3½ cups boiling water
1½ teaspoon garlic powder
1 to 4 tablespoon extra virgin olive oil (cold pressed is best)
1 to 1½ cup crimini mushrooms, sliced
Salt to taste
¼ cup vegetable oil
1 cup nutritional yeast flakes or 2 cups cheese for non-vegans
4 ounce can diced green chilies (optional)
Paprika (optional)

Oil a large casserole dish and fill it with the sliced potatoes. Set aside. Heat olive oil in small saucepan and sauté mushrooms until edges are golden brown, then set aside. In a medium saucepan, melt margarine over low heat. Add flour and whisk continuously to form a roux. Add boiling water, garlic powder, and salt, whisking continuously for 1 to 2 minutes until the sauce is thick and bubbly. Add oil and nutritional yeast (or substitute 1 cup of cheese) and whip until smooth, then stir in mushrooms and optional green chilies if desired. Pour sauce over potatoes and combine thoroughly. Sprinkle with paprika if desired. Bake covered at 450°F for 30 minutes, then bake uncovered for 30 minutes more, or until potatoes are tender and the top is browned. Remove from oven. If you used cheese, add remaining cheese to top. Let stand for 10 minutes before serving.

Grilled Tomatoes

Lucia Zucconi, chef at La Meridiana International School of Ceramics, for Robbie Lobell

4 tomatoes
1 tablespoon bread crumbs
1 tablespoon parsley, minced
10 black olives, pitted
1 tablespoon capers (preserved in salt)
1 garlic clove
Sugar, just a pinch
Olive oil
Salt and pepper

Wash the tomatoes and halve them with a horizontal cut. Gently push out the seeds. Mix the bread crumbs with minced olives, capers, garlic, parsley, salt, pepper and pinch of sugar. Put a spoonful of the mixture in each tomato half. Drizzle some olive oil over the stuffed tomatoes. Arrange tomatoes on a baking dish and bake in the pre-heated oven for 20 minutes. (Using a pre-heated oven requires a flameware dish.)

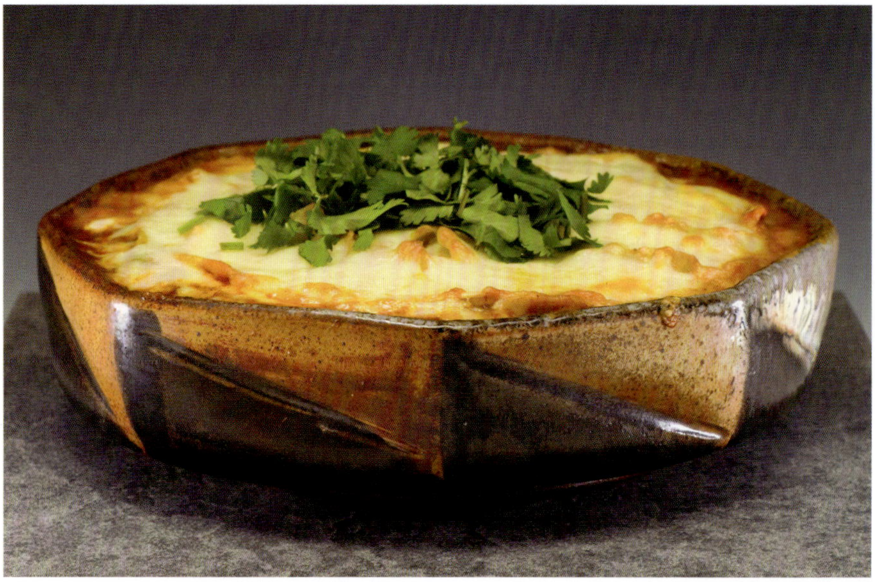

Baking dish with Chicken Enchilada Bake by Marcia Paul, 9 inches in diameter, stoneware, wheel-thrown and altered, slips with ash glazes, soda-fired to cone 10. Photo by Marcia Paul

Chicken Enchilada Bake

1 medium onion, chopped
1–2 jalapeño peppers seeded and chopped
2–3 cloves garlic peeled and minced
Crushed cumin seed
½ of a cooked chicken, shredded
½ cup chicken broth
1 cup enchilada sauce or more
½ cup mole sauce (optional)
¼ cup tequila (optional)
Tortillas (flour or corn)
Cheeses (white cheddar and/or jack), grated

In a sauté pan, heat olive oil and add chopped onion, jalapeño and garlic. Sauté about five minutes. Add cumin, toss, and sauté another two minutes. Add chicken and toss. Add liquids, mix, and allow to simmer, uncovered, gently for 10-15 minutes to cook down. Place 1 or 2 spoonfuls of sauce in baking dish and spread evenly. Place a tortilla on top of sauce, top with chicken mixture, add grated cheeses, spread evenly. Repeat layers but don't put cheese on the top layer yet. Bake covered at 350°F for 20 minutes. Uncover, add cheese to the top layer, and return to oven for another 10–15 minutes until cheese melts and begins to brown. Garnish with cilantro or finely chopped lettuce and serve with refried beans or rice.

Chile Relleños

1 tablespoon flour
½ teaspoon garlic salt
1 teaspoon baking powder
¾ cup milk
6 eggs
12 ounces shredded pepper jack cheese
28 ounces poblano chilies, roasted, seeded and stemmed, or canned chilies

Grease a 7x11-inch baking pan or an 11-inch oval baking dish. Mix together flour, garlic salt and baking powder in a small bowl and then, in a medium bowl whisk dry ingredients into milk until lumps are gone. Break eggs into milk and whisk well to combine. Set aside ½ cup shredded cheese. Layer half of remaining cheese on bottom of pan. Cover with a layer of peppers. Repeat layering of cheese and peppers. Pour egg/milk mixture over all and use a fork to ensure that it penetrates all layers. Sprinkle reserved cheese over top. Bake 30 minutes, or until puffed and golden brown.

Spinach Lasagna

1 16-ounce package lasagna noodles
2 16-ounce packages frozen spinach or 32 ounces fresh spinach, chard, sorrel, or beet greens
8 ounces goat cheese or cream cheese
8 ounces crumbled feta cheese
16 ounces grated mozzarella or mix of mozzarella, cheddar, and Parmesan
1 28-ounce jar pasta sauce (you won't use it all) or home-made pasta sauce
Sweet basil, oregano, minced garlic or garlic powder, onion powder

Cook twleve lasagna noodles until *al dente*. Drain and rinse with cold water (or use 12 no-boil noodles). If using fresh spinach or other greens, cook until soft and drain thoroughly. Mix spinach/greens with feta cheese and cream cheese and/or goat cheese. Add herbs to taste. Spread some pasta sauce on the bottom of a 9x12 lasagna pan and lay three noodles over the sauce. Spread on more sauce, then top it with one third of the spinach mixture. Top with grated cheese. Add two more layers of noodles, sauce, spinach mixture and cheese. The top layer will be three noodles, sauce and cheese. Bake at 350°F for 45 minutes to an hour. If using no-boil noodles they will soften up better if made at least several hours before baking.

Sausage, Peppers and Potatoes, Roasted

2⅓ pounds baking potatoes, cubed (can substitute sweet potatoes)
2 pounds sweet Italian sausage, cut into 2 inch pieces
4 large green peppers, seeded and cut into eight pieces each
2 large onions, sliced
1 tablespoon olive oil
Salt and pepper
Mix all ingredients in a large baking dish. Bake at 350°F until potatoes are done, stirring occasionally, about 50 minutes.

Baked Ziti

½ package (8 ounces) uncooked ziti pasta
28 ounce jar of your favorite prepared tomato sauce
1¾ cups (15 ounces) ricotta cheese
2 cups shredded mozzarella
½ cup grated Parmesan cheese or other cheese mixture (asiago, etc.)
1 teaspoon dried oregano
1 teaspoon dried basil leaves
Salt and pepper to taste

Cook the pasta and drain, reserving about ¼ cup of the cooking water. Combine ricotta, 1 cup mozzarella, oregano, basil, salt, pepper, and most of the Parmesan. Add the reserved cooking water to the cheese mixture so that it will spread easily (optional). Add sauce to the pasta and stir. Pour ½ the pasta/sauce combination into 9x11-inch baking dish. Cover evenly with ricotta mixture. Pour balance of pasta/sauce on top. Sprinkle with remaining mozzarella and Parmesan cheese. Cover and bake at 350°F for 45–60 minutes until bubbling throughout. Uncover for last 15 minutes to brown cheese on top.

Roasted Garlic

1 head garlic
1 tablespoon olive oil

Cut off the top of the head of garlic to expose the end of each clove. Place in garlic roaster and pour olive oil on top. Place roaster in cold oven and set it to 350°F. Roast for 45 minutes or until garlic is soft. Squeeze cloves out of skins and use in recipes or spread on bread.

Braised Lamb Shanks

2 leeks
1 tablespoon olive oil
2 teaspoons minced garlic
3 lamb shanks
Handful dried sour cherries or prunes
⅔ cup port
¼ cup Cointreau or other liqueur
½ teaspoon each salt and pepper

Split, wash, and chop leeks and cook slowly in olive oil in a frying pan. Rinse lamb shanks and pat dry. Add lamb, 1 cup water, port, liqueur, salt, pepper. Cover and bring to a simmer. Transfer to a casserole dish and place in cold oven. Set oven to 325°F and bake for two hours. Add dried fruit after one hour. Check occasionally and add a bit of water as needed to make a nice brown sauce. Uncover and bake until meat is browned for 10 or 20 minutes longer. Also suitable for a flameware casserole dish.

Exotic Pot Roast in Earthenware

4 pound rump roast or top round
½ cup chopped onion
1 clove garlic, minced
1 teaspoon salt
¼ teaspoon cinnamon
½ teaspoon oregano
2 8-ounce cans tomato paste
2 teaspoons chili powder
¼ teaspoon nutmeg
½ cup dry red wine
1 ounce unsweetened chocolate, melted
1 teaspoon grated orange peel
1 pound carrots, peeled and cut lengthwise
1 pound onions, peeled and quartered
¼ cup slivered almonds, optional

Soak the earthenware roaster in water for 15 minutes. Brown the meat in hot oil. Add the garlic and chopped onion and sauté briefly. Place the meat and the sautéed onions in the pre-soaked roaster. Sprinkle with salt. Combine the next 8 ingredients and pour over the meat. Add the onions and carrots. Place in cold oven and set to 400°F. Bake for 1½ hours or until meat is tender. Garnish with slivered almonds if desired.

Simple Chicken Roasted in Earthenware

Soak earthenware roaster in water for 15 minutes. Cut up a 3–4 pound chicken, arrange pieces in the roaster and sprinkle salt, pepper, and 1 teaspoon poultry seasoning over the top. Arrange 6 small potatoes around the chicken. Place cover on and set in cold oven. Set at 450°F and cook 1–1½ hours. Add seasonings and additional vegetables for infinite variations.

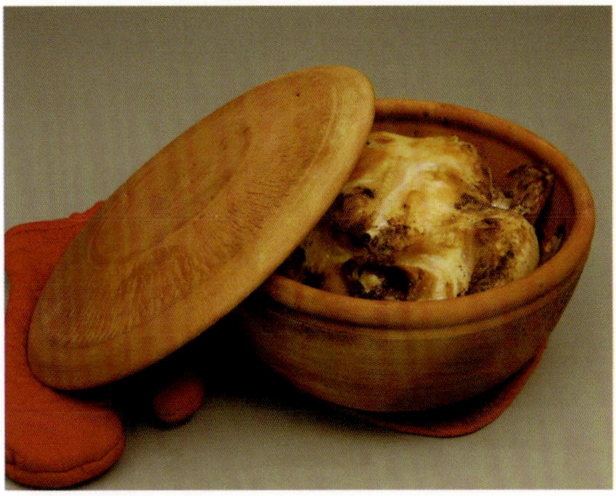

Chicken roasted in Bill Robbins Clay Cooker. The cooker is big enough for lots of vegetables to be roasted under the chicken. Photo by Sumi von Dassow

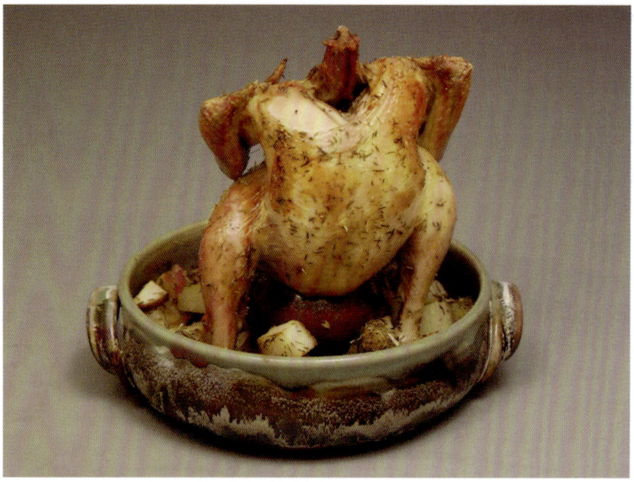

Chicken standing up on a chicken roaster, just out of the oven. Photo by Sumi von Dassow

Upright Roasted Chicken and Vegetables

Fill chicken roaster with beer, wine or your favorite marinade, add some cloves of garlic or some chopped onion, rub the chicken with garlic salt, and place it upright on the baker in the center of an 8-inch square or round baking dish. Chop an onion, a carrot, a few mushrooms, a potato, or other vegetables and arrange around the chicken. Pour more beer or liquid of your choice over the vegetables. Roast at 350°F for 1½ hours or until done. Serve the pan-roasted vegetables with the chicken and enjoy the extra-crispy chicken skin! Make broth by boiling the bones with the pan juices; add rice or noodles and the leftover meat and vegetables to make a delicious soup.

Guinea Fowl in Earthenware Roaster

1 guinea fowl, 3–4 pounds
2 or 3 potatoes, cut into chunks
¼ cup white wine
1 cooking-type apple, cut into small chunks
2 tablespoons slivered almonds
Salt and pepper
3 tablespoons butter, softened
1 teaspoon dried thyme or 1 tablespoon fresh

Soak roaster in water for 10 minutes. Mix apple, almonds, salt, pepper and 1 teaspoon thyme and stuff into the cavity of the guinea fowl. Mix butter and thyme and push under the breast skin of the bird. Place potato chunks in the bottom of the roaster, sprinkle with salt and pepper, and put the guinea fowl on top. Pour wine around the bird. Cover the roaster and put in a cold oven. Set oven to 450°F and roast 60–75 minutes. Uncover roaster and roast another 15 minutes until skin is browned. Scoop stuffing out, mix with potatoes and serve atop portions of meat.

Salmon in Earthenware Roaster

1 onion sliced thinly
2 pounds mixed small potatoes and parsnips, sliced in thin rounds
1 teaspoon rosemary
Salt and pepper to taste
3 tablespoons butter, diced
1 cup chicken or vegetable broth
1 pound skinless salmon fillet, cut into four pieces

Soak roaster in water for 10 minutes. Place a layer of potatoes and parsnips in the bottom of the roaster and sprinkle with salt, pepper, and rosemary. Add a layer of onions, then more potatoes and parsnips, sprinkling each layer with salt, pepper and rosemary. Repeat layers, ending with potatoes and parsnips. Dot with butter on top and pour broth over. Cover roaster and place in cold oven set to 450°F and roast 60–75 minutes until vegetables are tender. Sprinkle salmon fillets with salt and pepper and place on top of vegetables. Cover roaster and roast for 15 more minutes. Uncover and roast for another 5–10 minutes until salmon is cooked through.

Meatloaf

2 pounds ground beef
½ cup oats, bread crumbs, or rice cracker crumbs
1 small yellow onion, chopped
1 cup grated carrots
1 egg, lightly beaten
1 can tomato sauce, divided
2 teaspoons yellow or Dijon mustard
1 tablespoon Worcestershire sauce
Salt and pepper to taste
2 teaspoons brown sugar
Lightly grease a 9-inch loaf pan.

In a large bowl, combine beef, cracker crumbs, chopped onion, carrots, egg, 1/4 cup tomato sauce, mustard, Worcestershire, salt and pepper. Transfer mixture to prepared pan. In a small bowl, combine remaining tomato sauce with sugar. Pour sauce over the meatloaf. Bake at 400°F until cooked through and deep golden brown, about 1 hour. Set aside to let cool for 10 minutes before slicing and serving.

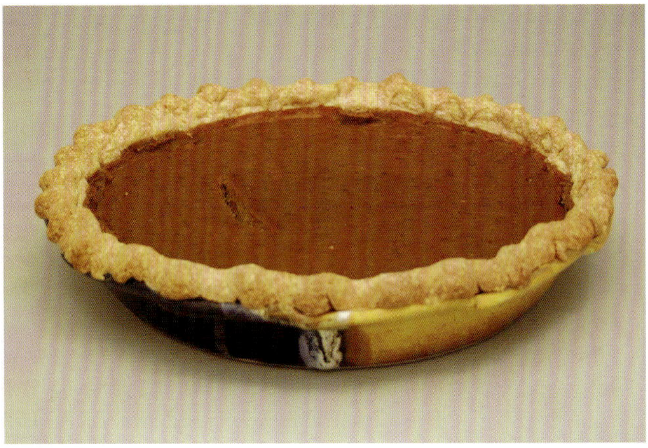

10-inch pie plate with pumpkin pie by Sumi von Dassow

Pumpkin Pie

1 9-inch pie crust, unbaked
3 cups roasted pumpkin or a winter squash
1 cup cream
½ to ¾ cup honey, to taste
2 tablespoons molasses
4 eggs
2 teaspoons ground ginger
2 teaspoons ground cinnamon
¼ teaspoon ground cloves
¼ teaspoon salt

Place crust in pie pan and crimp edges. Put the rest of the ingredients in a blender and blend until fully liquefied. Taste and add more honey if necessary. Pour into crust and place in oven. Bake at 350°F until crust is brown and filling is puffed up and barely jiggles when tapped. Remove from oven and cool at least 30 minutes before cutting.

100% Whole Wheat Pie Crust

2 cups whole wheat flour
1 cup very cold butter, cut into chunks
1 tablespoon sugar, optional
⅔ cup cold water or buttermilk

Place first three ingredients into bowl of food processor and process until butter is cut into little crumbs. Pour in water or buttermilk and process again until a ball of dough forms. Depending on the flour, you might have to add a tiny bit more water to get it to ball up. Transfer to a covered bowl and leave at room temperature overnight or 8 hours. Roll out on a lightly floured pastry cloth. The dough will be elastic and much easier to roll after the resting period. Makes two crusts.

Lemon Meringue Pie

1 cup white sugar
2 tablespoons all-purpose flour
2 tablespoons cornstarch
¼ teaspoon salt
1½ cups water
Zest and juice of 2 lemons
2 tablespoons butter
4 eggs, separated
6 tablespoons sugar
1 9-inch pie crust, baked

In a saucepan, mix 1 cup sugar, flour, cornstarch, and salt. Add water, lemon juice and lemon zest. Cook over medium-high heat, stirring frequently, until mixture begins to boil. Put egg yolks in a small bowl and gradually stir in ½ cup of hot lemon mixture. Pour egg yolk mixture back into lemon mixture. Bring to a boil again and cook stirring constantly until thick, about one minute. Remove from heat and stir in butter. Pour filling into baked pastry shell. To make the meringue, beat egg whites in a large bowl until foamy. Add 6 tablespoons sugar gradually, and continue to beat until stiff peaks form. Spread meringue over filling, sealing the edge at the crust. Bake at 350°F for 10 minutes, or until meringue is golden.

Flaky Pie Crust

3 cups all-purpose flour
2 tablespoons sugar (omit for savory pie)
½ teaspoon salt
½ stick butter and equivalent amount of lard (frozen preferably or at least very cold)
½ egg yolk
½ teaspoon vanilla
¼ cup lemon juice
½ cup ice water with some more ready at hand

Measure dry (first three) ingredients into large mixing bowl and whisk together. Whip wet (last four) ingredients together separately. Take either butter or lard out of the refrigerator. Dip the block and your hands in the flour. Using a grater with regular size holes, grate some of butter or lard into the flour and mix immediately. Repeat until the block is all grated into the flour. Repeat with the next stick. Pour wet mixture in and mix in with rubber spatula and fingers. Add water if necessary to make the whole thing stick together. Ample for two large crusts. Double recipe and freeze half to avoid using half an egg yolk.

Egg Custard

3 cups milk
½ cup Splenda (or sugar)
4–6 large eggs
2 teaspoons vanilla extract or other flavoring
Ground nutmeg or cinnamon for garnish
2 tablespoons unsalted butter, for greasing ramekins

Place milk into a medium saucepan and bring it almost to a boil over medium heat, stirring frequently. Remove milk from heat when it begins to froth and simmer. Cover the pan and place it in the refrigerator or freezer to cool to room temperature, about 1 hour in refrigerator.

Bring a kettle of water to a boil. Preheat oven to 325°F. Grease six 6-ounce ramekins with butter and dust them with sugar (dusting optional).

Whisk eggs briskly in a medium bowl until uniformly lemon-yellow in color. Stir in sugar or Splenda and vanilla and beat until dissolved. Stir in milk. Strain mix through a fine-mesh strainer and pour into ramekins. Garnish with nutmeg or cinnamon. Put a layer of newspaper in the bottom of large metal baking pan. Place ramekins in the baking pan and carefully pour hot water into the pan to reach halfway up their sides. Bake for 30–40 minutes until custards appear firm on edges and loose in center, and a knife or toothpick inserted in the center comes away clean. Remove pan from oven and immediately remove the ramekins from the pan. Serve immediately, or refrigerate until cool.

Gluten-free Flourless Brownies

1 can (15 ounce) no-salt black beans, drained and rinsed (or 2 cups cooked black beans)
3 eggs
½ cup butter
¼ cup cocoa powder or ½ cup carob powder
⅛ teaspoon salt
2 teaspoons vanilla extract
⅔ cup sugar (or ¼ cup honey)
½ cup arrowroot, rice, potato flour, or gluten-free flour mix
½ cup chocolate chips
½ cup chopped walnuts

Melt butter and pour into 8-inch square baking dish. Place black beans, eggs, cocoa powder, salt, vanilla, sugar, and flour in food processor. Swirl melted butter around baking dish to grease the dish, then pour the remainder into the food processor. Process mixture until smooth. Stir in chips and nuts by hand. Pour into baking dish and bake at 350°F for 30 to 40 minutes, until set.

Blackberry Crisp

2 cups (1 pint) fresh or frozen blackberries
2 tablespoons sugar
1 teaspoon tapioca
1 teaspoon grated lemon zest
½ cup quick-cooking oats
¼ cup whole wheat pastry flour
¼ cup packed brown sugar
¼ teaspoon ground cinnamon
¼ cup cold butter

Place blackberries in a buttered baking dish. In a small bowl, combine the sugar and tapioca and pour over berries and mix in gently. Let sit while you make the topping. Combine the oats, flour, brown sugar and cinnamon; cut in butter until crumbly. Do not over mix. Use a pastry blender or pulse in a food processor. Sprinkle over berries.

Gluten-free Apple Crisp

4–5 cups apples, peeled (or not) and chopped
Juice and zest of one lemon
1 tablespoon arrowroot flour
2 tablespoons sugar (or 1 tablespoon honey)
½ teaspoon cinnamon
¾ cup almonds
¾ cup arrowroot, rice or potato flour, or gluten-free flour mix
6 tablespoons butter, chopped
¼ cup sugar
¼ teaspoon salt
1 teaspoon vanilla extract

Mix apples with lemon juice and zest, 1 tablespoon arrowroot flour, 2 tablespoons sugar, and cinnamon and place in baking dish. Grind almonds in food processor and add flour mix. Add butter and process just until crumbly. Add sugar, salt and vanilla and process briefly. Pour over apples and bake at 350°F for an hour.

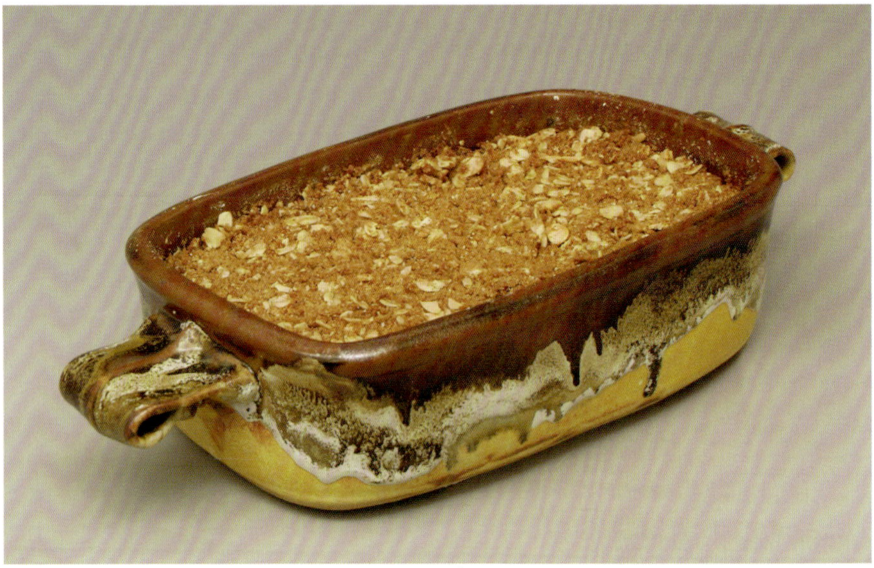

8x12 baking dish with rhubarb crisp by Sumi von Dassow. All the glazes on this dish are colored with iron oxide, except for the white, which has no colorants at all. It is safest to use a white glaze or a glaze colored with iron oxide inside baking dishes, especially for acidic foods such as rhubarb. Reduction-fired stoneware. Photo by Sumi von Dassow

Rhubarb Crisp

8–10 cups diced rhubarb or combine with strawberries, apple, etc.
1 cup sugar (or less, to taste)
Grated zest of one orange
2 tablespoons cornstarch
⅓ cup cognac
¾ cup unsalted butter
2 cups flour
1 cup rolled oats
¾ cup brown sugar
1 tablespoon cinnamon
⅓ cup nuts (slivered almonds)
Pinch of salt
1 egg

Mix the fruit, orange zest and sugar. Dissolve the cornstarch in cognac and add to the fruit. In a separate bowl, combine the flour, cinnamon, sugar and a pinch of salt. Cut the butter into the flour until it is evenly distributed (pea size). Add the rolled oats and almonds. Break the egg into a small bowl, beat it lightly, then add it to the dry mixture to bind it loosely. Place the fruit in an appropriate size baking dish, then spread the topping over the fruit. Bake at 350°F for approximately 50 minutes.

Apple Cake

3 tablespoons butter
1 cup sugar
1 egg
½ teaspoon each cinnamon, nutmeg, and salt
1 teaspoon baking soda
1 cup sifted flour
3 cups diced apples
¼ cup chopped nuts
1 teaspoon vanilla extract

Cream butter and sugar. Add egg and mix well. Sift dry ingredients together and add to butter mixture. Stir in remaining ingredients. Pour into greased 8-inch square pan. Bake at 350°F for 40 to 50 minutes.

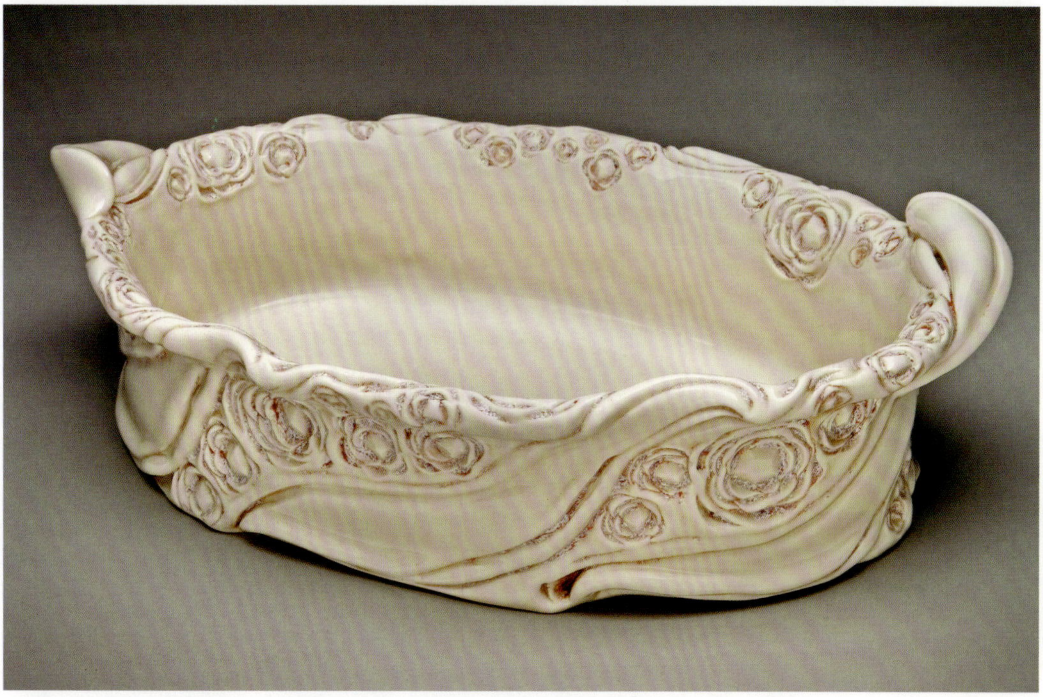

Oval baker by Lora Rust, 11 inches in length, altered and handbuilt porcelain, fired to cone 6 oxidation, with clear glaze over rutile wash. The decoration on Rust's work is neither impressed nor carved, but formed in the wet clay with handmade wooden tools. Photo by Walker Montgomery

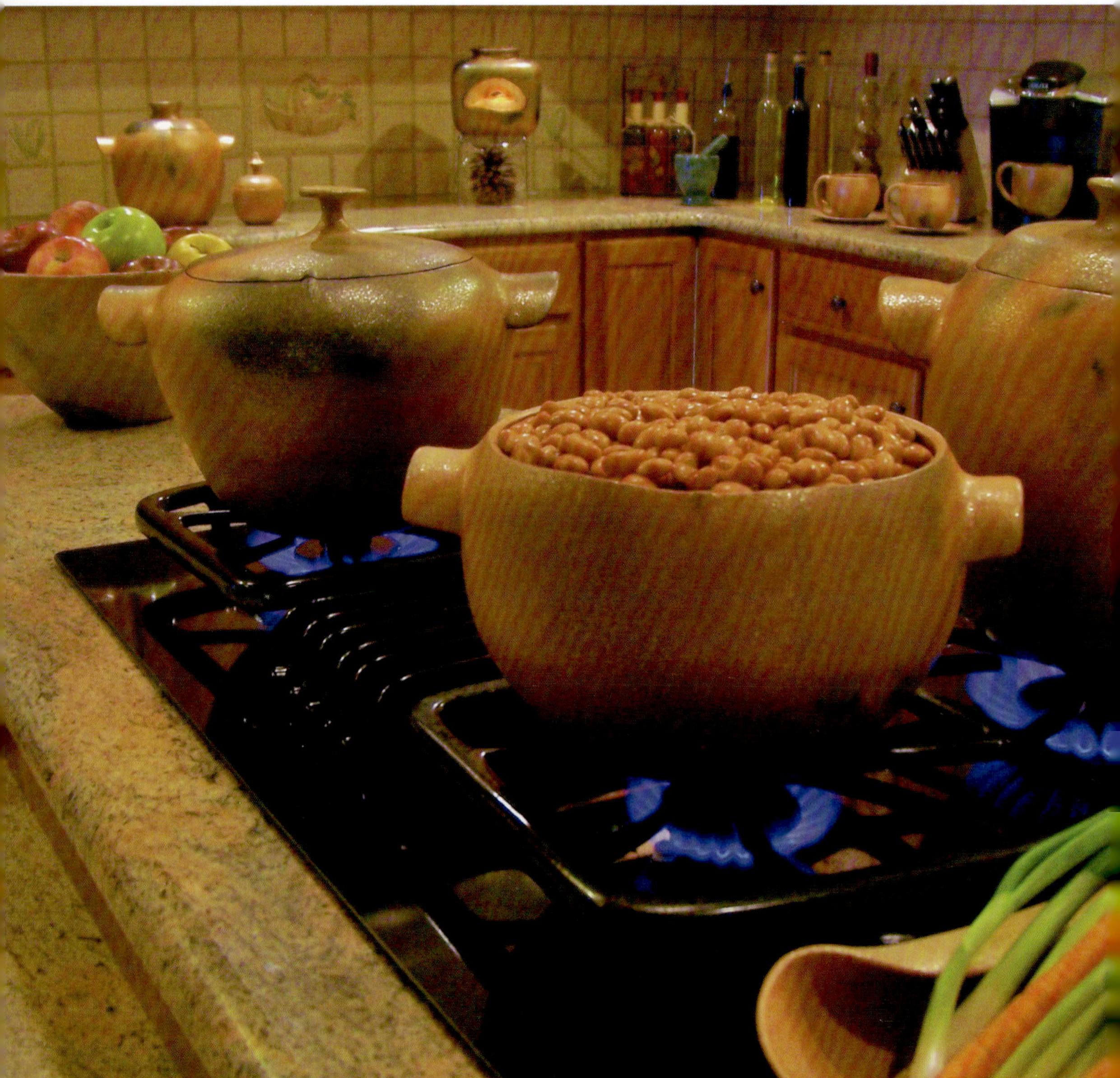

CHAPTER 5

Stovetop Ware

Stovetop ware is ware that may be used on a burner on the stovetop. While ovenware typically can't be used directly on a hot burner, any pot that can safely be used on a burner can also go in the oven. In this respect, cooking in clay on the stovetop resembles cooking in cast iron, and makes this kind of ware very convenient to have around—if all your burners are occupied you can just pop your pot in the oven. In fact, if it can be used on a burner, it can usually be used on a campfire or grill, too. This kind of pottery is ideal for use with recipes that need to be started on a burner then moved to the oven. Some kinds of ware should be used with a diffuser if cooking on an electric burner or glass cooktop to protect the ware from direct contact with the heat source. Also, when a pot is removed from the hot burner it should be placed onto a potholder or wooden cutting board rather than a cold counter.

Why cook on the stovetop in a clay pot? While you have to be very careful to avoid cracking your ware when using clay pots on the stovetop, some cooks believe that food cooked in clay tastes better than food cooked in metal. If you're a potter, it's a fun challenge to make your own cookware, but if you're squeamish about being able to adequately clean porous earthenware pots, don't be—it's easy to clean and disinfect any kind of pottery (see p. 26).

Handmade stovetop pottery is not easy to find in the United States. Most potters work in stoneware, and stoneware can't be used on the stovetop. Thus, at your typical craft fair or gallery you probably won't find ware for the stovetop. There are many traditional earthenware forms such as the Spanish cazuela, the Moroccan tagine, the Japanese donabe pot, or the Chinese sand pot, that are made for using on the stovetop, but few (if any) American potters make them to sell. This is both because Americans aren't accustomed to using pottery on the stovetop, and because potters perceive stovetop ware as being more dangerous and likely to break in use. These pots are still handmade by anonymous crafts people around the world where they are traditional, and they can be purchased online or from large retailers. People who cook in them love them, and some potters make them for their own use. These unglazed earthenware forms are traditionally quickly made, fired once to a low temperature, and used until they break—almost like disposable ware.

Greg "Kele" Hardy, bean pots in the kitchen. Greg "Kele" Hardy makes his bean pots by coil-building a round, closed form and cutting the lid like a jack-o'-lantern. This way there are no flanges to clean on the lid or pot, just a wavy or notched cut to keep the lid from slipping off. Photo by Greg Hardy

Micaceous Clay Cookware

One type of traditional earthenware pottery for the stovetop is micaceous clay cookware made from clay that has a large proportion of mica mixed into the body, making the clay extremely resistant to heat shock. Mica has a chemical composition similar to clay, with a similarly low coefficient of expansion, but, unlike clay or silica, it doesn't change its crystalline structure when heated. A low coefficient of expansion is vital for stovetop ware because it means the clay is resistant to cracking due to being heated unevenly. Mica also doesn't absorb water, and can withstand very high temperatures without breaking down. Micaceous clay pottery, traditionally made by Southwestern Native American potters, is burnished and fired in a bonfire. Many enthusiasts say food cooked in micaceous clay has a special flavor. Some assert that because the clay is alkaline, it neutralizes the acids in foods, making food taste sweeter. These pots are treasured and kept for years—they are not considered disposable!

Micaceous clay and powdered mica can be purchased from suppliers in New Mexico. Depending on the source of the clay, how much mica is in it, and how the pot is finished, micaceous clay pots may not be porous, or not very porous, and become "sealed" with use. Traditional potters burnish the clay, coating it first with several coats of slip containing extra mica—the more the better—making the clay much less

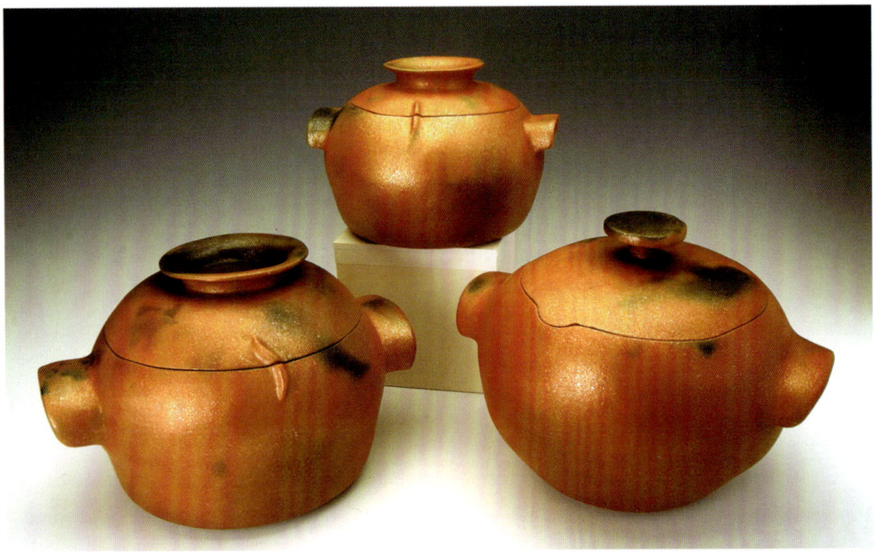

Bean pots by Greg "Kele" Hardy. 3 to 4 quart cooking capacity. Each about 8 inches in height (including the lid) and 10 in. wide (with the handles). Micaceous clay, coil-built and smoke-fired. Photo by Greg Hardy.

porous. Many potters temper a new micaceous pot with oil to make it easier to clean. One interesting feature of micaceous clay cookware is that the outside of the ware stays relatively cool so you can lift the lid or pick up a pot of hot chili by the handles without pot holders. Micaceous clay is equally suitable for campfires or cooking on a grill. When earthenware pots, including micaceous cookware, are used on an electric burner or glass stovetop, a diffuser must be placed under the pot to protect it. A diffuser is not necessary on a gas burner.

Flameware

Flameware is a modern kind of clay body formulated to not expand or contract when heated and cooled, and thus isn't subject to thermal shock. Few potters have the resources to formulate, fire, and test this kind of ware, so it's relatively uncommon and understandably expensive. A few clay manufacturers now make flameware bodies, although, if you use one, you must formulate a glaze that fits the clay. Standard stoneware glazes craze because flameware does not expand and contract like stoneware, so a glaze that fits stoneware won't fit flameware. Search the Internet to locate suppliers who carry flameware clay. A few potters make flameware from clay they formulated and either mix it themselves or have it mixed.

Tom Wirt formulates and mixes his own clay for his flameware tagines, a Moroccan-

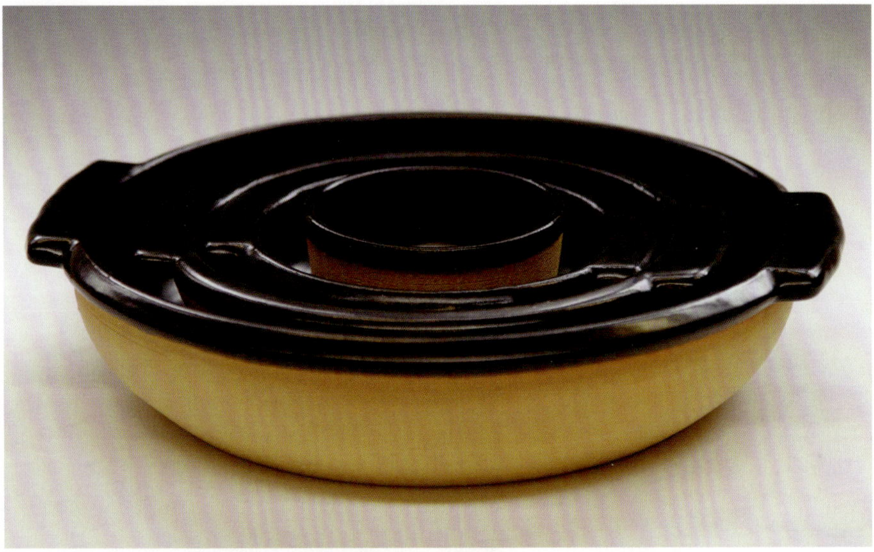

Travis McFlynn's flameware pots and pans look and function very much like classic saucepans and skillets. These nested flameware dishes measure 12, 8, 6, and 3 inches in width and were fired to cone 7 oxidation. Photo by Travis McFlynn style covered dish. The base is made from flameware while the lid is stoneware. Bay area potter Travis McFlynn uses Leslie's Ceramic Supply's clay to make a line of cookware for restaurant chefs. For a dedicated cook, such as a professional chef, handmade flameware is very exciting to use. It's inert and won't flavor or contaminate food; it's beautiful and unique, so it can go directly from the stovetop to the table; and the clay conducts heat evenly into the food and keeps the food warm longer than a metal pot. Compared to cooking in earthenware it can be used much more like metal cooking pots, so it doesn't require learning new recipes or cooking techniques. The only rule is that the shape of the foot of the pot must be the same as the shape of the heat source; that is, you can only use a pot with a round base on a round burner, though a square pot can be used on a grill or under the broiler.

Flameware potter Robbie Lobell makes elegant lidded pots that are like a deep casserole dish, suitable for simmering soup on the stove, cooking beans or rice, or for use in the oven. Her pots have handles that are extend from the slightly flared rim, and lids that sit on a gallery inside the rim of the pot.

For some recipes, such as paella, you might want a shallow, open form, similar to a frying pan. Robbie Lobell makes very shallow flameware pots which she calls paella pots with handles that are simple wing-like extensions of the rim. Her pots can be used on the stovetop or on the grill.

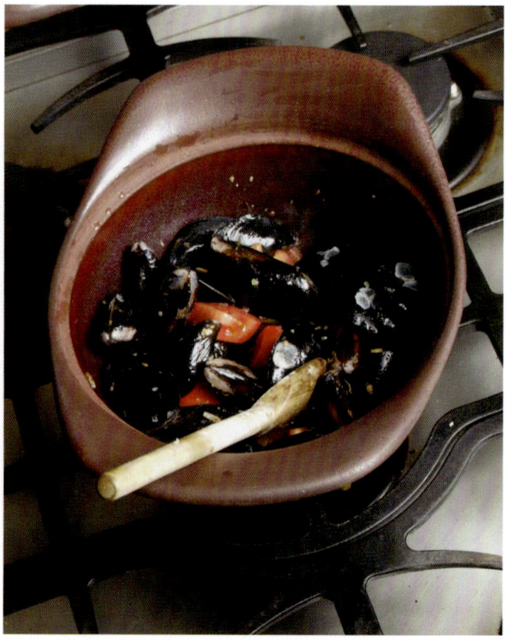

Robbie Lobell makes a variety of covered and uncovered casserole dishes and bakeware like this soda-fired flameware paella pan. Photo by Gina O. Burrill

Design Considerations

The main consideration for stovetop ware is what kind of clay to use. Most potters do not have access to a suitable flameware body, and this book isn't intended to give you the information you need to formulate your own flameware. To make earthenware pots—whether from earthenware clay or micaceous clay—you need to keep in mind the recipes you want to cook in your pots. The main concerns are similar to those for ovenware—feet, lids, and handles.

WARNING: Flameware that's improperly formulated and tested could potentially break disastrously in use, so any potter who wants to market this kind of ware must be fully aware of the risks and must test every batch. If you've done the research to formulate and test a flameware body and suitable glazes, make sure to create round pots for round burners, and to rigorously test every batch of clay. As with stoneware, avoid great changes in thickness from one part of the pot to another. The guidelines that work for stoneware are appropriate for flameware—a flat bottom with a slightly rounded corner helps protect the pot from heat shock.

Does your pot need a lid?

While not every recipe requires one, any cooking pot is more useful with a lid, and it keeps the food warm after cooking.

Should the flange go on the lid or on the pot?

Your pot will be more useful and easier to clean if the flange is on the lid. Cooking on a burner almost always produces bubbling and splattering, and having the flange on the lid tends to contain the mess. If you're cooking something that doesn't need a lid, having a gallery on the pot is inconvenient. Some potters make lids by making a completely round closed form and cutting the lid off above the half-way point with either a wavy cut or with two or three keys.

Does your pot need a foot?

In a word, NO. A pot for the stovetop should have a flat bottom without a sharp corner.

Do you want to use your pot in the oven as well as on the stovetop?

In this case, review the considerations for ovenware.

How are you going to pick up the pot?

You may want handles, although something like a bean pot is tall enough to easily pick up without handles using pot holders. For some customers handles may represent something that can easily break or interfere with other pots on the stove, or make storage more difficult. If you do make handles, any of the methods used for making handles for ovenware can also be used to make handles for stovetop ware.

If you are working in unglazed earthenware keep in mind that glaze won't help hold the handles on so they should be carefully joined—not just stuck on but blended into the body of the pot.

What will your stovetop pot be used for?

Think about what you typically cook in a pot on a burner. Soup probably springs to mind immediately. A soup pot needs to be round and generous, probably taller than it is wide. Since many soups are simmered for long periods on a low burner, a soup pot should have a lid to avoid wasting too much water or heat. A soup pot can be made from flameware or from porous earthenware; the form can be the same, though the cook will have to add water more frequently when cooking in earthenware. A soup pot calls for handles, good strong ones that are well attached. If soup is cooked in an earthenware pot it will have to be placed on a potholder or wooden cutting board when it is removed from the burner to protect the pot from contact with a cold surface. A clay pot will hold heat for a long time, and while it is hot, the small amount of liquid that seeps through will evaporate and not leave a wet spot on the table.

Similar to a soup pot is a bean pot, which is the typical use for a micaceous clay pot. Of course beans cooked on the stovetop are essentially a soup, too, though perhaps with less liquid and fewer other ingredients besides beans. So a bean pot can be smaller than a soup pot, and handles are nice but less essential. Jan Cameron's coil-built micaceous clay bean pots have handles that are fully blended into the body of the pot, and simple rounded lids that sit on a flared rim with a slight upturn at the top—no flange to clean on either pot or lid. Many of her bean pots have no lid at all, though they are all full-bellied and narrow at the top to contain the heat and the food.

Rice is another favorite that may be cooked in an even smaller pot than a bean pot. Rice cooked in earthenware comes out fluffy and evenly cooked, and it makes the pot smell wonderful. So if we want to cook soup, beans, and rice, we might need three round-bellied pots in three different sizes, with lids, but not necessarily handles. If you're working in unglazed earthenware, you might want to make separate pots for meat and vegetable dishes, since some odor may linger in an unglazed pot.

One thing to remember is that earthenware is by its nature porous—this characteristic helps earthenware resist thermal shock. While an unglazed earthenware pot is fine for liquid-based recipes that need to be simmered on low heat, any recipe that requires sautéing on high heat in oil or butter is more appropriate for a metal pan or a non-porous flameware pot. It is dangerous to an earthenware pot to put it on high heat, especially empty, so heating up oil for sautéing is hard on an earthenware pot. Perform high-heat techniques in a metal frying pan, then transfer the food to your earthenware pot when it's ready to simmer. Also, excess oil or butter may seep through a porous pot. If you use less oil than you would in a metal pot and add the vegetables before the oil gets too hot, it shouldn't seep through and the pot will be safer. It is possible to make a glazed earthenware pot that doesn't seep, and it is common practice for earthenware pots to be sealed on the unglazed foot with terra sigillata, but this is usually done to make sure serving pots won't seep and damage the table. If you don't have access to a flameware body, and you want to use glazed earthenware on the stovetop, you must make sure to use a glaze that fits the body—a crazed glaze will allow moisture through.

Many recipes need to be started on the stovetop and then moved to the oven. For this kind of recipe, something more like a casserole dish—round, relatively shallow, with a lid and handles—is ideal. The clay can be either earthenware (glazed, unglazed, or micaceous) or flameware. However, if the food needs to be sautéed in fat before it is transferred to the oven, it may be necessary to start the recipe in a flameware or non-ceramic pot before transferring it to the oven in an earthenware pot.

Tagines

If you want to try something completely different, a tagine is a traditional Moroccan pot, much shallower than a bean pot, with a tall conical lid. Traditionally this pot is made from earthenware clay, glazed or unglazed, although it can be made from flameware or

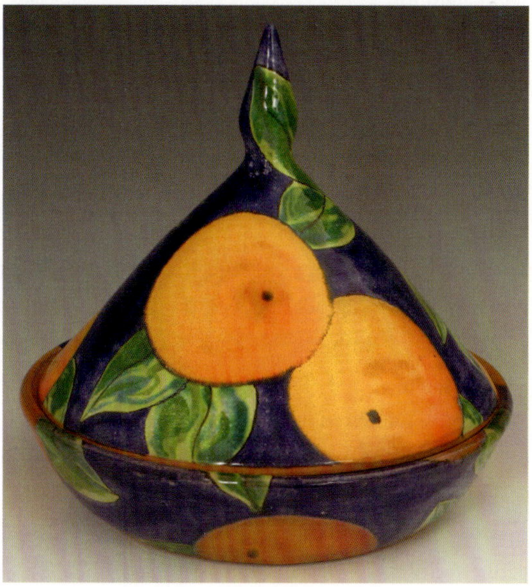

Dark blue tagine with oranges by Farraday Newsome, 13 inches in height, glazed terra cotta. Farraday does not recommend using her ware on the stovetop, just in the oven—although they are so beautiful and expensive that her customers generally use them only for serving. This is actually in keeping with Moroccan tradition—people cook in the plain unglazed earthenware tagines and use the colorfully decorated ones for serving. Photo by Farraday Newsome micaceous clay as well. Tagines can also be made from stoneware, but in that case they can be used in the oven only. This form is traditionally used to cook meat and vegetables to serve with couscous, but enthusiastic cooks have tried a wide variety of dishes in this style of pot. An earthenware tagine is suited for long slow cooking, with no high heat techniques such as sautéing. While modern Moroccan cookbooks frequently suggest cooking vegetables in oil in a tagine as a first step, traditional Moroccan cooks are more likely to layer everything in the cold tagine, allow it to come to a simmer, and add oil or butter towards the end of the cook time, for flavoring. A tagine can be used either on the stovetop or in the oven, although a large tagine may be too tall to be conveniently used in most ovens. Tom Wirt, who makes flameware tagines, says "The secret to the tagine is that as it simmers on the stovetop, the moisture condenses on the lid and bastes the dish constantly. The shape of the lid is to accommodate the traditional chunk of meat or large vegetable in the center. Vegetables cut in long strips are then stacked around that center and are more braised than steamed in cooking. Relatively little water is used in cooking the dish." Traditional Moroccan tagines often have a hole in the lid near the knob; this hole is not necessary and seems to be purely decorative. According to chef Emily Swantner, "The top of the tagine is a bit removed from the flame, which allows steam to gather at the top of the pot and drip back down on the food, which keeps it from drying out. So, you DON'T want the steam to escape, just the opposite." In fact, if the lid has a hole, some cooks stuff the hole with a bit of vegetable.

As with micaceous clay pots, earthenware tagines need to be seasoned, or "cured" with olive oil before use, or alternatively, with milk. An earthenware tagine can be glazed or unglazed and can be used in the oven or on the stovetop on low heat, with a diffuser. Note that the rather flat bottom of a tagine is a factor that is likely to shorten its life if used on a stovetop; avoid making the corner at the bottom a very sharp one.

A fun kind of earthenware pot is a potato devil, or diablo. The potato devil consists of two symmetrical shallow pots, with handles, that are placed lip-to-lip, with a handful of potatoes inside. Halfway through the cooking period the diablo is flipped over (using the handles) so the potatoes can cook on the other side. Unglazed earthenware or micaceous clay is ideal for this pot. This kind of pot can also be used in the oven, as can any stovetop ware.

If you're interested in making ware for the stovetop, you may want to start with a groggy red earthenware clay, or with micaceous clay. Your local clay supplier will have a red earthenware, but micaceous clay is only available from suppliers in New Mexico. If you want to make your own micaceous clay, you can order mica and mix it into an earthenware clay from your local supplier. You can wedge the mica right in, as much as

Unglazed earthenware potato devil by Sumi von Dassow, 5 inches in diameter. Unglazed earthenware can sometimes be used on the stovetop, but many unglazed earthenware pots are designed to be soaked in water and used in the oven to keep food moist. Photo by Sumi von Dassow

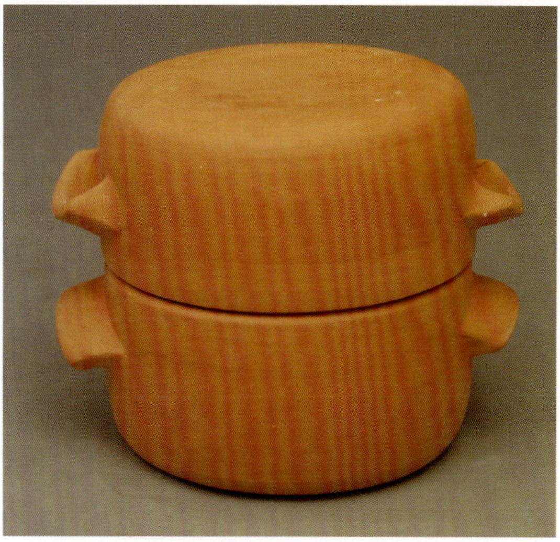

you can work into your clay (try starting with half a pound of mica in five pounds of clay. If that doesn't make the clay hard to work with, try adding more. As long as your clay remains workable there is no limit to how much mica can be added). Earthenware clay is porous even when fired to its full mature temperature. Although many potters think of earthenware as fragile and easily chipped, Vince Pitelka of the Appalachian Center for Craft at Tennessee Tech University has performed testing that indicates that the strongest clay body is, in fact, red earthenware. He found that this kind of clay resisted breaking on impact better than any other kind of clay. The common belief that earthenware clays are fragile is probably because much so-called earthenware pottery is made from stoneware clay bodies that are fired below their proper vitrification temperature. Some under-fired stoneware clays make excellent pots, but other clay bodies are fragile and easily chipped when under-fired.

Any modern potter has access to earthenware bodies from their local ceramic supplier and for most potters there is no reason to resort to under-firing a stoneware body. The simplest way to experiment with making your own stovetop ware is to use a commercial red earthenware with some grog, and leave it unglazed. (However, be aware that no clay manufacturer that I contacted has formulated an earthenware clay specifically for stovetop use, other than micaceous clay.) If earthenware pottery is not fired to the full mature temperature, it will be more fragile and more porous, but more resistant to thermal shock. New Mexico Clay, which makes micaceous clay, recommends firing to cone 017. This very low temperature approximates the temperature of the bonfires in which traditional potters fire their pots. Some potters who use micaceous clay bisque-fire their work to higher temperatures, however. The trade-off is that clay fired to higher temperatures will resist breakage due to impact better, but if fired to a lower temperature it will be more resistant to thermal shock. In practice, micaceous clay pots seem to be quite sturdy and resistant to heat shock along a wide range of temperatures. Experiment to find the best firing temperature for your own work, and test your pots by using them! If you use micaceous clay, try making slip and adding extra mica to it and coating your ware with it to reduce porosity. Rub it with your fingers to smooth it and bring out the shine in the mica particles. Burnishing it with a stone will make it smoother and reduce porosity even more.

If you use regular earthenware clay you can try coating your ware either inside or out with red terra sigillata, to reduce porosity and make it easier to clean. (Experiment—you might find the terra sigillata will scrub off if you put it inside.) If you want to make glazed earthenware pottery, use a lead-free low-fire glaze, either a commercial glaze or one you mix yourself. Like the Spanish cazuealas and Moroccan tagines that you can buy online, your handmade earthenware pottery will probably crack sooner or later in use. You may not want to try to sell earthenware pots for stovetop use because you have no control over how your customers will treat them, but it can be very satisfying to cook in them yourself for as long as they last. When they do break, they won't explode disastrously, they will just crack, and at the worst your meal will make a mess on the stovetop. (Usually cracks start at the rim and proceed slowly, so you shouldn't have to worry about this worst-case scenario.) Inspect each pot before use, tapping it to make sure it isn't cracked, use it on low heat (on a diffuser if on an electric burner) and you may get to use your pots for years.

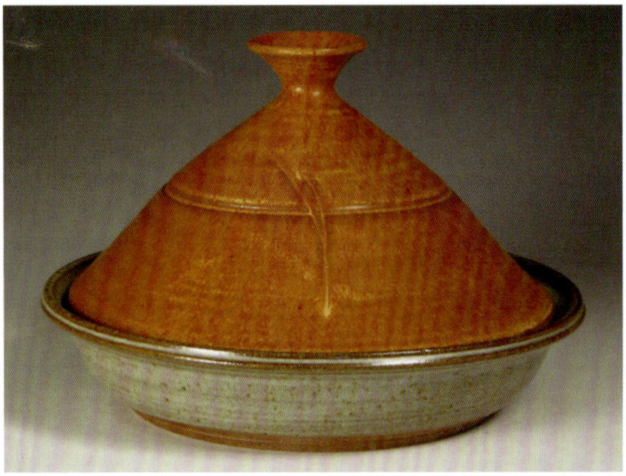

Tagine by Tom Wirt (Clay Coyote), 10 inches in diameter and 10 inches in height, flameware base with stoneware lid, both cone 10 reduction. Photo by Tom Wirt.

Seasoning a Micaceous Clay Pot (from Jan Cameron)

1. Fill the pot to just below the rim with water.
2. Place the vessel on the burner (using a diffuser on an electric burner).
3. Allow the water to come to a boil.
4. Pour out the water along with any loose clay or mica particles.
5. Heat the oven to 250°F and place the vessel in the oven for 10 minutes.
6. While the vessel is warm, coat the surface of the vessel with animal or vegetable fat, except the bottom of the pot where it will rest on the burner.
7. Allow the vessel to cool.
8. Repeat steps 5-7 until the vessel is well-oiled and shiny. When it is properly seasoned, oil beads up on the surface and doesn't soak in any more.

   Jan also says "After using them and washing them in hot water, I take a paper towel and rub oil on the inside and place them on a very low fire for a few minutes to dry them. And if the pot gets stained from use and you want to "re-boot" your pot you can preheat the pot in your oven at 400°F, then place it on a bed of coals in a barbecue pit and cover it with bark or cedar; you will return the pot to the original golden color with different fire clouds. As with a cast iron skillet, you place it in a fire to clean it. If you do this, you will need to re-season your pot."

Curing a Tagine (from www.tagine.com)

1. Submerge the tagine in water for at least 1 hour. If you can't submerge it, place it in a clean sink and slowly fill the base of the tagine with water until it stops absorbing it. Place the tagine lid upside down inside the base and fill it as well. Let stand for at least an hour to allow full absorption of water into the clay. An overnight soak is even better. Empty excess water and allow to dry for 5 minutes.
2. Spread olive oil all over the base and lid with your hand. Use 2 tablespoons of olive oil for the base and one tablespoon for the lid.
3. While the tagine is still wet with the oil, place it in the oven and set the temperature at 350°F and leave for 45 minutes. The evaporation of moisture creates a vacuum effect to pull the olive oil into the clay to seal it. Then leave the tagine in the turned off oven to cool down.

How to Seal an Earthenware Pot (from chef Emily Swantner)

1. When using an unglazed clay pot for the first time, you want to fill the bottom of the dish with milk. Milk has casein, which acts as "glue" to fill the pores and seal the pot.
2. Place the pot in a cold oven and set the temperature to 350°F, bake it for 30 minutes, then turn off the heat and let it cool in the receding heat. Drain, wash and dry; then rub with olive oil. The casein in milk might help seal the pot and keep oil from seeping through in cooking.
3. Or you can put the pot on the burner and heat it until the milk boils, then allow it to simmer for 30 minutes. Cool, drain, wash out the milk residue, and rub with oil.

PROJECT 1: Jan Cameron Making a Micaceous Clay Bean Pot

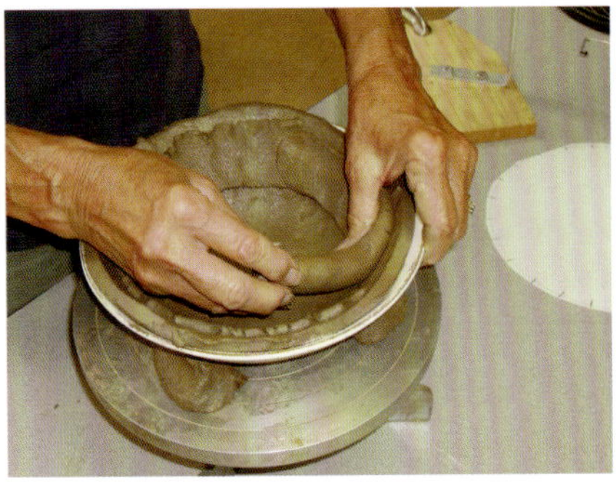

Jan lays a disk of clay in the bottom of a shallow bowl, which serves as a mold. The first coil overlaps the edge of the disk to avoid making a weak spot where the disk joins the first coil.

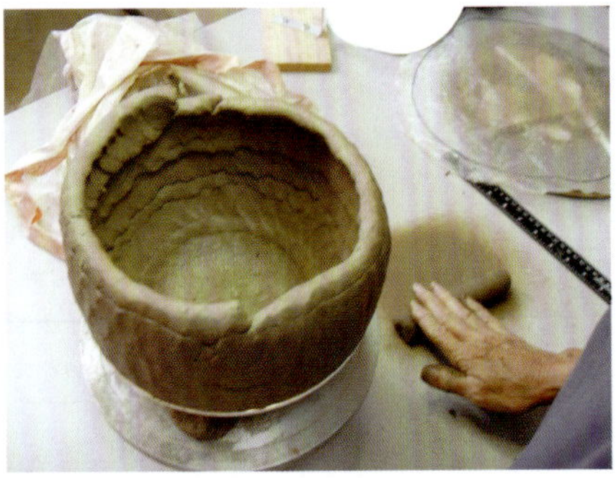

Each subsequent thick coil is pressed into place slightly overlapping the rim. Jan doesn't worry about making one coil go all the way around the pot.

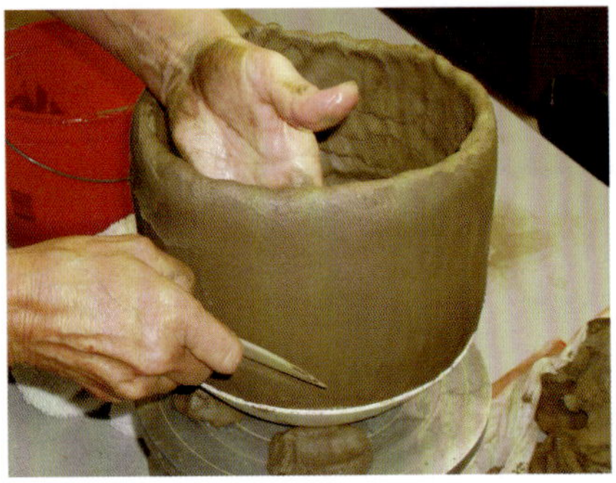

The pot is scraped inside and out with a variety of tools to smooth the surface and refine the form.

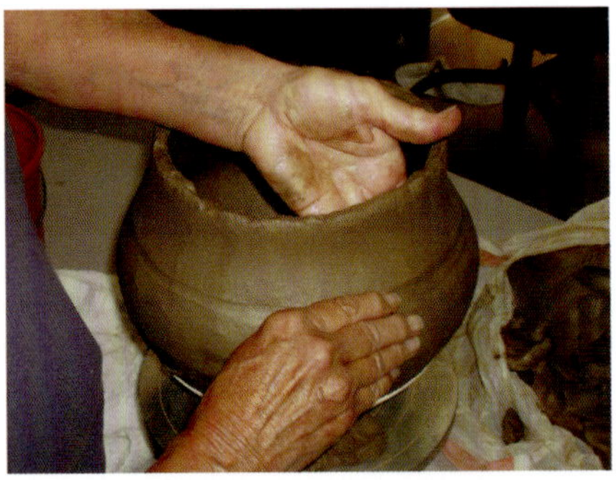

Jan uses a fingertip to put a horizontal groove in the pot. The decoration will be above this point. The form below the groove is completed.

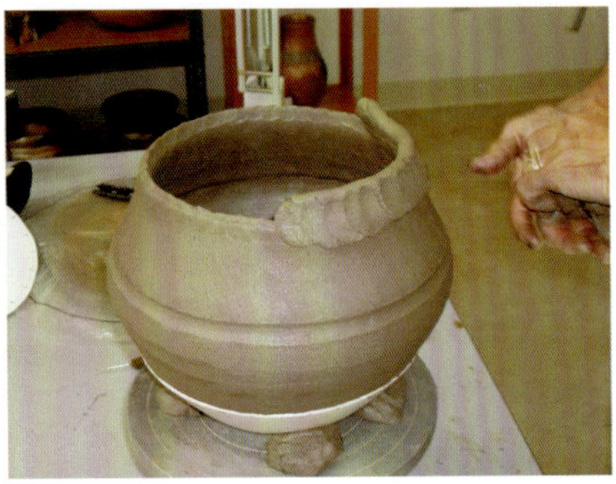

Adding a few more coils to the rim of the pot.

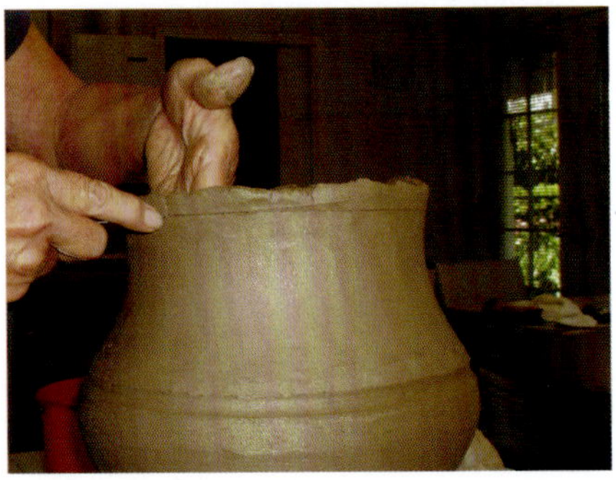

Jan cuts the rim level with a needle tool.

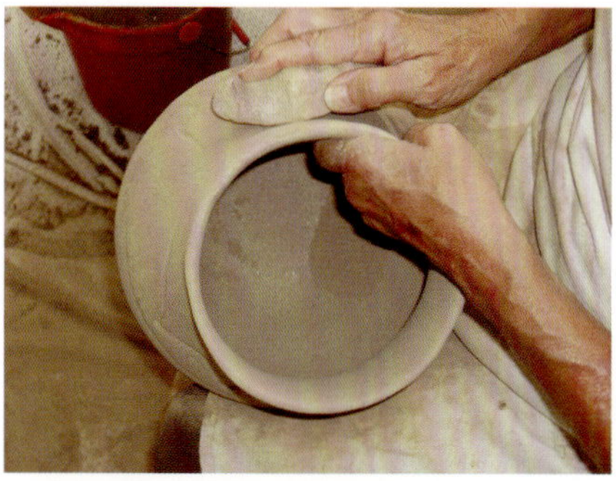

The pot is sanded with a rough stone.

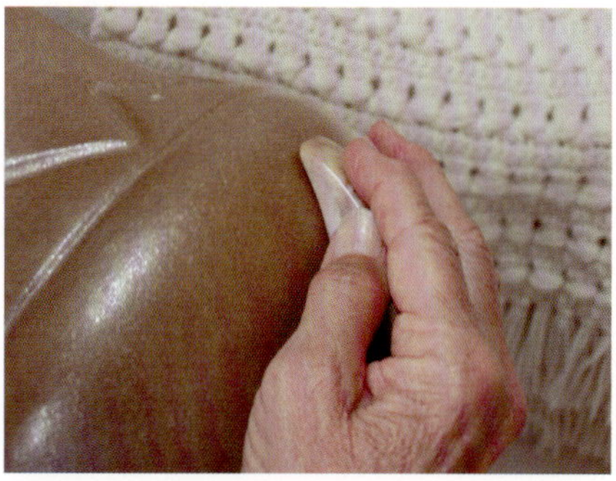

Jan applies micaceous slip and buffs the pot to a gloss with a damp sponge. She repeats this two or three times. She then polishes the pot with a stone to compress and align the mica particles.

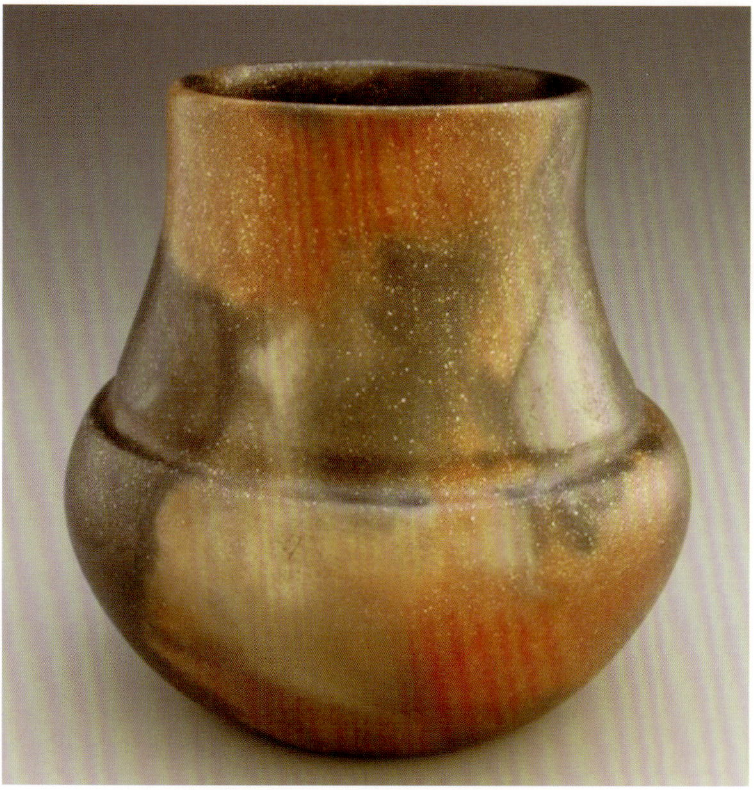

Four quart bean pot by Jan Cameron, micaceous clay, coil-built, burnished and smoke-fired. This is a very basic, very traditional form—no handles, no lid, but easy to pick up by the belly with pot holders. Photo by Walter Spohn

PROJECT 2: Making a Tagine

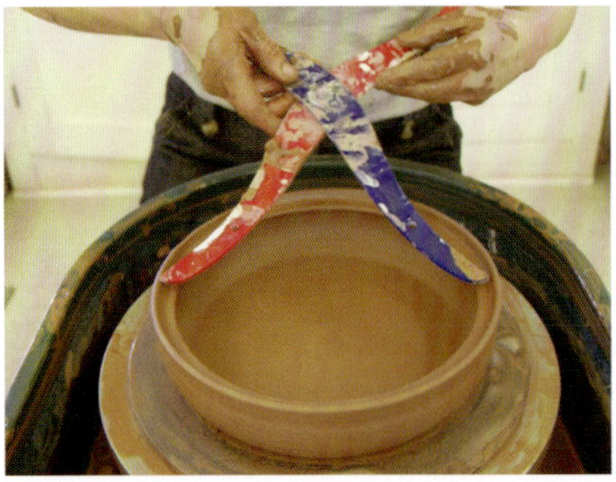

Using about 3 pounds of clay, throw the base just like you would throw a casserole dish, with a gallery for the lid, and measure the gallery with large calipers.

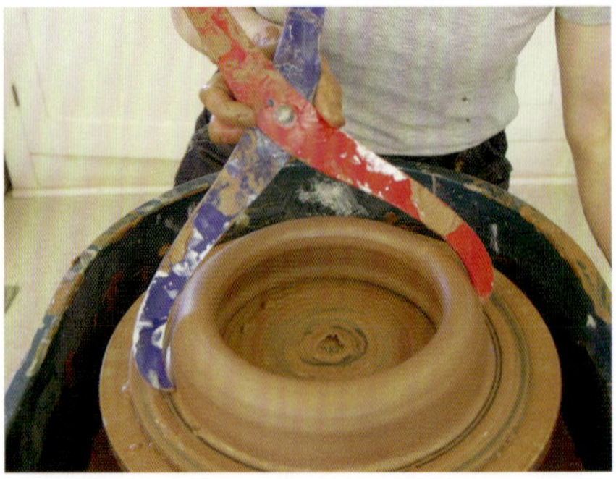

For the lid, center another 3 pounds of clay and open up down to the bat. Throw a wide cylinder, to the width of the caliper measurement, and begin pulling the walls up and in.

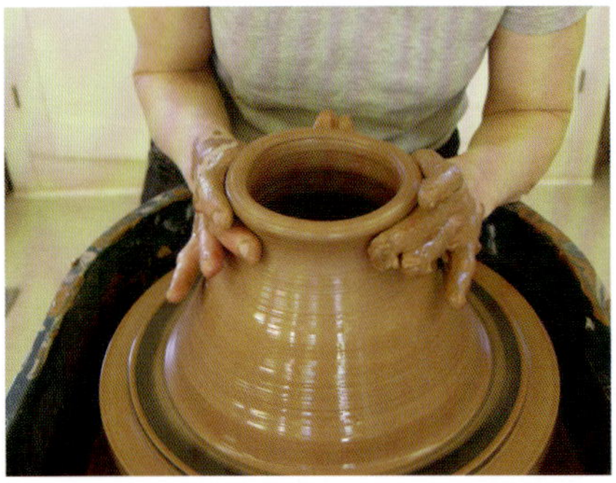

Pull the wall up, being careful to keep the top relatively narrow. Alternate pulling up with collaring in until you have pulled up as much clay as you can.

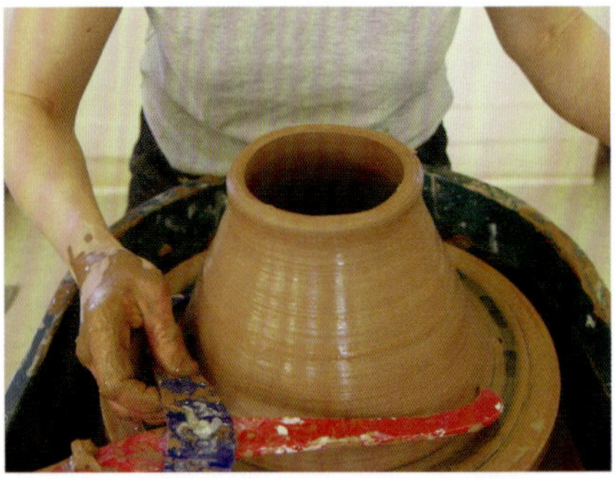

Check your measurement before you close the form to make sure you don't have to adjust it.

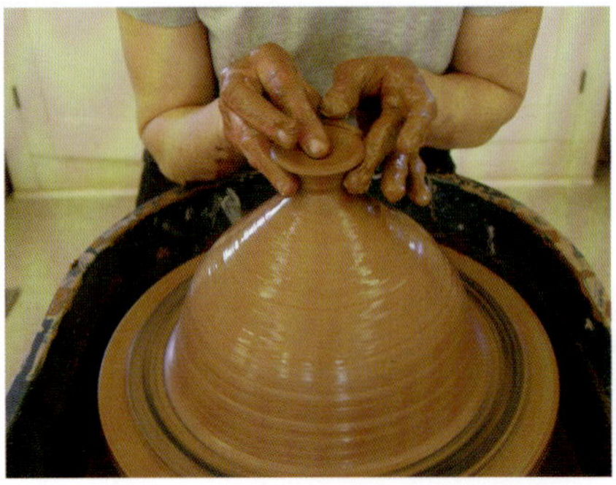

Close the top of the form, making a knob as you do so. Refine the knob into a shape you like.

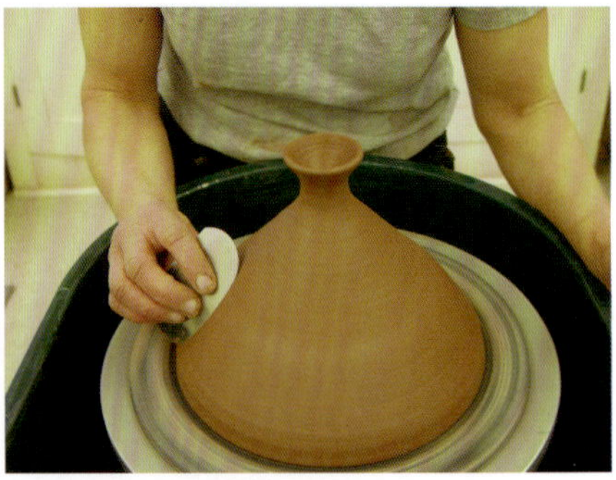

Rib the form to refine the cone.

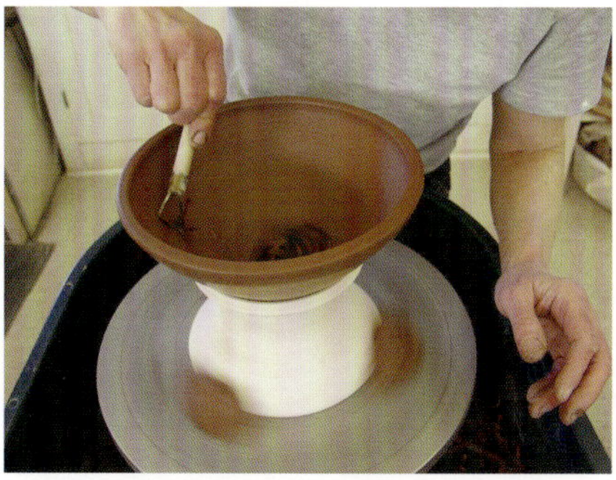

When the lid is leather-hard, turn it over in a chuck and trim excess clay from the rim. Usually you don't trim inside a pot, but in this case you might need to.

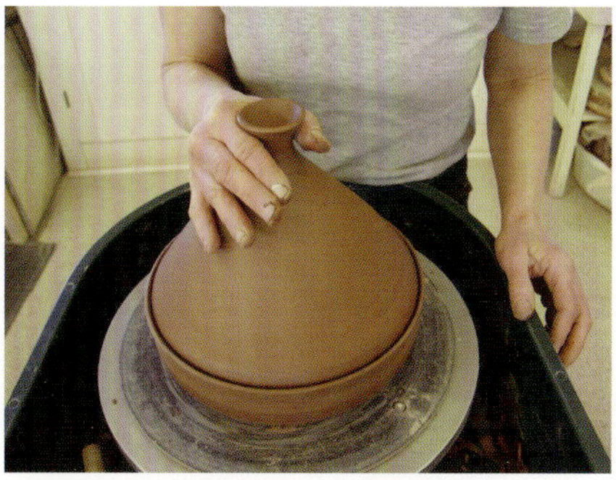

Place the lid on the pot. If it is too small, you can't do anything about it but if it's too big you can trim more away.

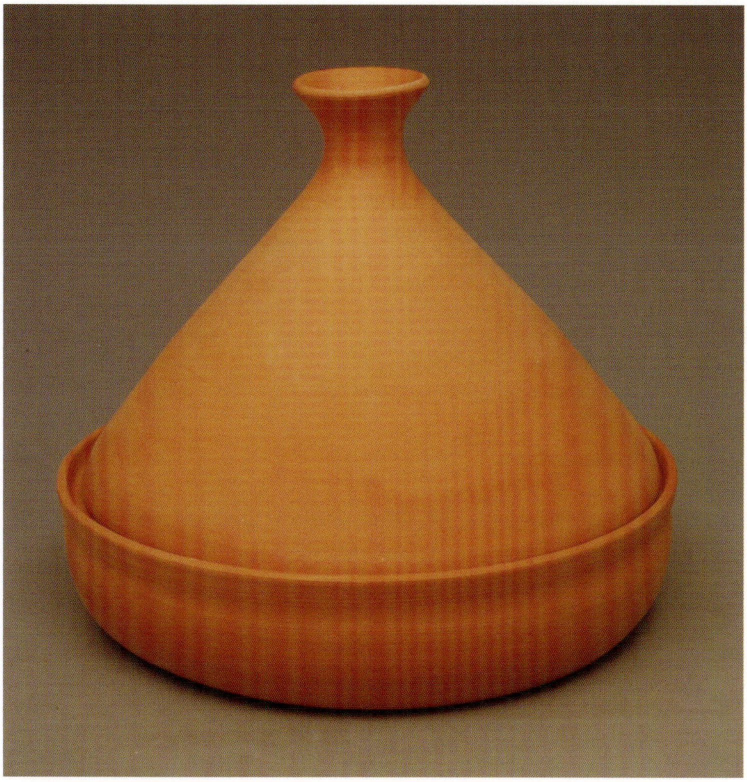

Earthenware tagine, Sumi von Dassow. Laguna R2 clay, fired to cone 06.
Photo by Sumi von Dassow

RECIPES FOR STOVETOP WARE

Spring Vegetable Risotto

by Lucia Zucconi, chef at La Meridiana International School of Ceramics, for Robbie Lobell

12 ounces rice, preferably Carnaroli or Vialone Nano, but Arborio rice is fine. Avoid long-grain rice because it hasn't enough starch.
½ fresh onion
1 glass white wine
10 asparagus spears
2 carrots
4 baby artichokes, spiky tops cut off and fuzz removed
3 zucchini or other summer squash
Handful of shelled fava beans
2 ounce Parmesan cheese
Vegetable broth, a few ladlefuls
Olive oil
Pinch of salt and pinch of pepper

Wash and cube all the vegetables. Wash, peel, and thinly chop the onion. Fry the onion slowly in a flameware casserole with 3 tablespoons of olive oil until the color is light brown. Add the rice and sauté a few minutes until it becomes transparent, then pour in the wine. Cook until the wine evaporates. Add the cubed vegetables and broth to cover about three fingers over the rice. Cook for about 20 minutes adding broth if necessary and stirring every so often. Add salt and pepper to taste and stir. Turn off the flame and add Parmesan cheese, mixing two minutes.

Cholent

2 pounds fatty beef--brisket, breast, or rib.
3 tablespoons olive oil
2 large onions, sliced
3–5 cloves garlic, peeled but left whole
2 marrow bones (optional)
2 pounds potatoes, cut into chunks, or substitute carrots
½ pound dried white haricot or butter beans, soaked for an hour
½ cup pearl barley (optional)
Salt and pepper

In flameware casserole, brown the meat in the oil. Remove meat, and fry onions till soft. Add garlic and fry till aroma rises. Add meat and bones, arranging beans, barley and potatoes around it. Sprinkle with salt and pepper. Cover with water and bring to a boil. Remove any scum and put the lid on. Set in 225°F oven and leave overnight (or start in the morning and bake for 8 hours).

Cabbage Rolls

1 large cabbage
¼ cup rice
⅓ pound ground beef
¼ pound ground pork
1 egg
½ cup milk or cream
Salt and pepper

Discard outer leaves of cabbage and cut out the stem and the heart. Steam or place briefly in boiling water till the leaves wilt and become pliable. While the cabbage cools, mix remaining ingredients together. Pull the leaves off the cabbage. Lay each leaf so it curves upward. Cut out the tough central vein. Place a small amount of the filling at the bottom of each leaf and roll up, folding the sides in. Pin shut with a toothpick or just pack them tightly together. When you've used up all the filling, cut up the remaining cabbage leaves and lay some in the bottom of a flameware casserole dish or a tagine. Pack the rolls on top of this layer. Layer the rest of the cut up cabbage on top of the rolls. Add a bit of molasses or a spoonful of brown sugar to enough broth or water to cover the rolls, or use tomato sauce. Simmer for one hour or until done, or bake in oven at 350ºF.

Beef Stew

3 pounds stew beef, or beef roast cut into chunks
3 pounds whole peeled small onions or quartered large onions
1 4-ounce can tomato paste.
¼ pound butter
Several cloves of garlic, peeled
¼ cup dried cherries and/or dried cranberries, or other dried fruit
1 teaspoon sea salt
1 teaspoon whole peppercorns
Other spices as desired: bay leaves, cloves, red pepper flakes, sage, etc.
1 cup water or broth

Put the meat into a 3–4 quart pot. Add the butter, then the onions, then the can of tomato paste. Add the rest of the ingredients. Don't stir. Put the pot on the stove on medium-high heat until simmering, then turn to low and allow to simmer 6 hours. Remove from heat, stir, and serve.

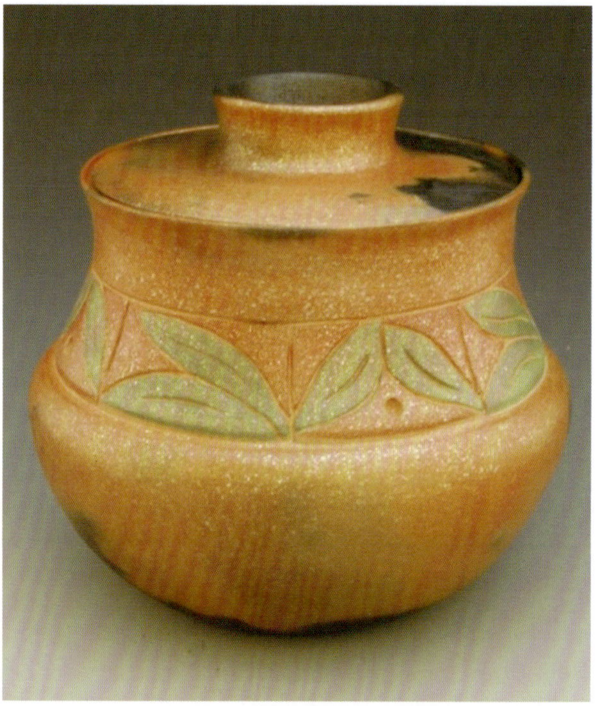

3½ quart Bay Leaf design bean pot by Jan Cameron, micaceous clay, coil-built, burnished and smoke-fired. Micaceous clay pots are typically sized by the quart, not by inches. Photo by Walter Spohn

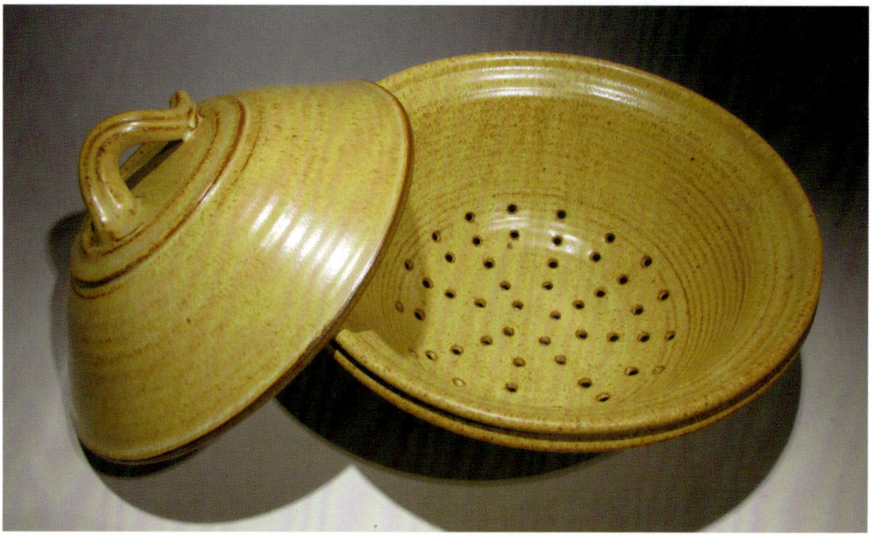

Lidded steamer by Tom Wirt (Clay Coyote), 11 inches in diameter, stoneware, fired to cone 10 in reduction. This pot is designed not to go directly on a burner but to rest on the rim of a 3-quart metal cooking pot (with water in it) to steam meat, vegetables or couscous. Photo by Tom Wirt

Green Chile Stew

1 roasted chicken, de-boned and cut into large cubes including the skin
1 16-ounce can white or yellow hominy with water
4 4-ounce cans roasted and diced green chilies with water, or 16 ounce roasted fresh
4 cups chicken broth.
12 ounces beer

Place above ingredients into mica pot and turn to medium-high heat. In a separate frying pan, heat 3 tablespoons of olive oil and 1 tablespoon of butter. Add one large sweet onion, diced, and 4 cloves of minced garlic. Sauté until the onion is soft and slightly browned.

Combine the following items and add them to the sauté mixture.
2 tablespoons Tabasco sauce
1 teaspoon oregano
2 teaspoons granulated garlic
1 teaspoon powdered onion
2 teaspoons powdered cumin
1 teaspoon dried parsley
½ teaspoon black pepper (coarse is better)
2 tablespoons red chile powder

Sauté these items with the onions for a few minutes to heat and distribute the flavors, then add the mixture to the contents of the pot. Let the stew heat up to almost boiling then turn the stove to low or medium-low. Add firm (not quite ripe) diced Roma tomatoes and a handful of chopped cilantro as soon as you reduce the heat. Allow to slow cook 1 to 2 hours.

Basic Clay Pot Beans

1 cup red beans
3 or 4 cups water or broth
1 green chile, roasted and peeled
1 onion, chopped
5 garlic cloves, minced
2 strips bacon, chopped (optional)
Salt, pepper, and other seasonings as desired

Soak beans overnight in a bowl; drain. Put beans in a 2-quart micaceous cooking pot and add water or broth, chile, onion and garlic. Bring to a boil and then turn down to simmer. Cook uncovered 2 hours or until beans are soft. Add bacon and simmer until bacon is cooked through. Add salt, pepper and other seasonings (cumin, dried chile pepper, oregano, etc.) to taste. Add other vegetables as desired.

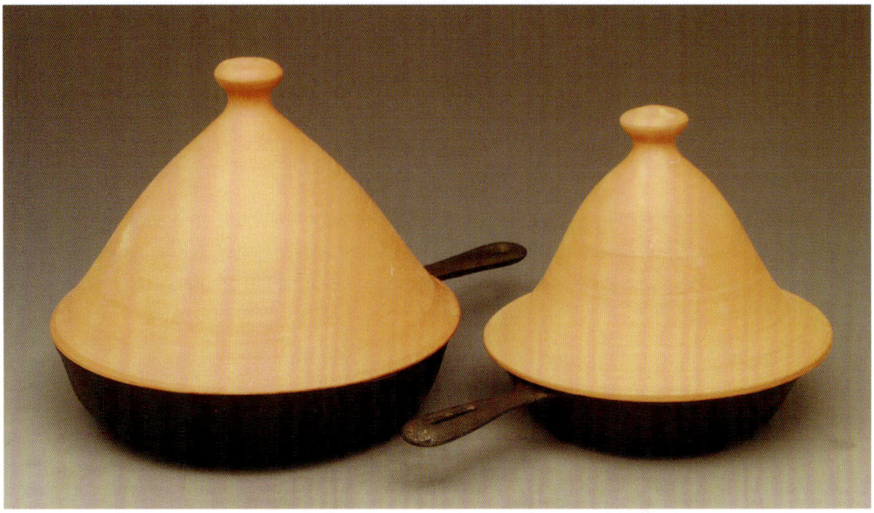

Cast iron skillets with tagine lids by Sumi von Dassow. If you want to try a tagine but you're nervous about using clay on the burner, simply make an earthenware lid to fit a cast iron skillet. This emulates modern tagines which consist of enameled cast-iron bases with clay lids. Photo by Sumi von Dassow

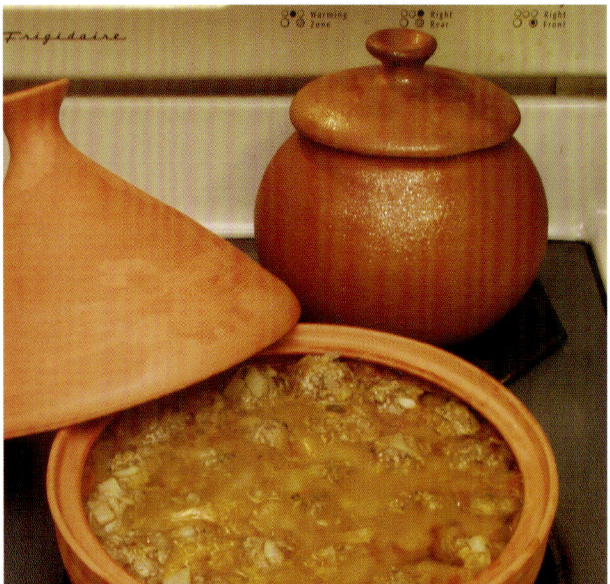

Earthenware tagine by author on glass-topped electric cook-stove on a diffuser. Behind it is a micaceous clay pot cooking rice on another diffuser. Laguna R2 clay, fired to cone 06. Photo by Sumi von Dassow

Tagine of Potatoes and Cod

¼ cup olive oil
Juice of one lime or lemon
¼ cup chopped parsley or cilantro
2 or 3 cloves garlic, minced
1 teaspoon salt
1 teaspoon cumin
1 pound cod fillets
2 small onions, sliced
1 pound small potatoes, sliced
2 tablespoons olive oil

Mix first six ingredients and purée in a blender. Pour half of this sauce over the fish and marinate for 1–2 hours. Heat olive oil in a skillet or flameproof tagine and sauté onions until soft. Transfer to earthenware tagine and top with sliced potatoes. Mix ¼ cup of water with remaining sauce and pour over onions and potatoes. Cover tagine and simmer for an hour or until potatoes are soft. Place marinated cod on top and simmer for another 20 minutes or until cooked through.

Spicy Kefta Tagine with Tomato Sauce

1½ pounds ground meat—beef, buffalo or lamb
1 onion, finely chopped
1 small bunch of parsley, finely chopped
1 teaspoon each cinnamon, cumin, ground coriander and paprika
1 teaspoon salt
1 28-ounce jar of your favorite tomato sauce (or homemade)

Mix meat, onion, parsley and spices. Form into golf-ball sized meatballs. Pour sauce into tagine base and place on burner (on diffuser if electric burner) set on medium heat. When sauce begins to simmer, place meatballs in sauce in a single layer. Cook 30 minutes until done through. Serve with couscous, rice or quinoa.

Rice Cooked in a Tagine or Micaceous Clay Pot

2 cups brown rice
4 cups water
1 teaspoon salt
1 tablespoon butter

Soak rice overnight in a non-porous bowl or pot. Transfer to earthenware pot, add salt and butter, and cover. Place pot on a diffuser on medium heat and bring to a boil. Turn heat down and simmer for 1–1½ hours until rice is done. Brown rice cooked in an earthenware pot is fluffy and evenly cooked. Rice can also be cooked in an earthenware pot in an oven set to 450ºF.

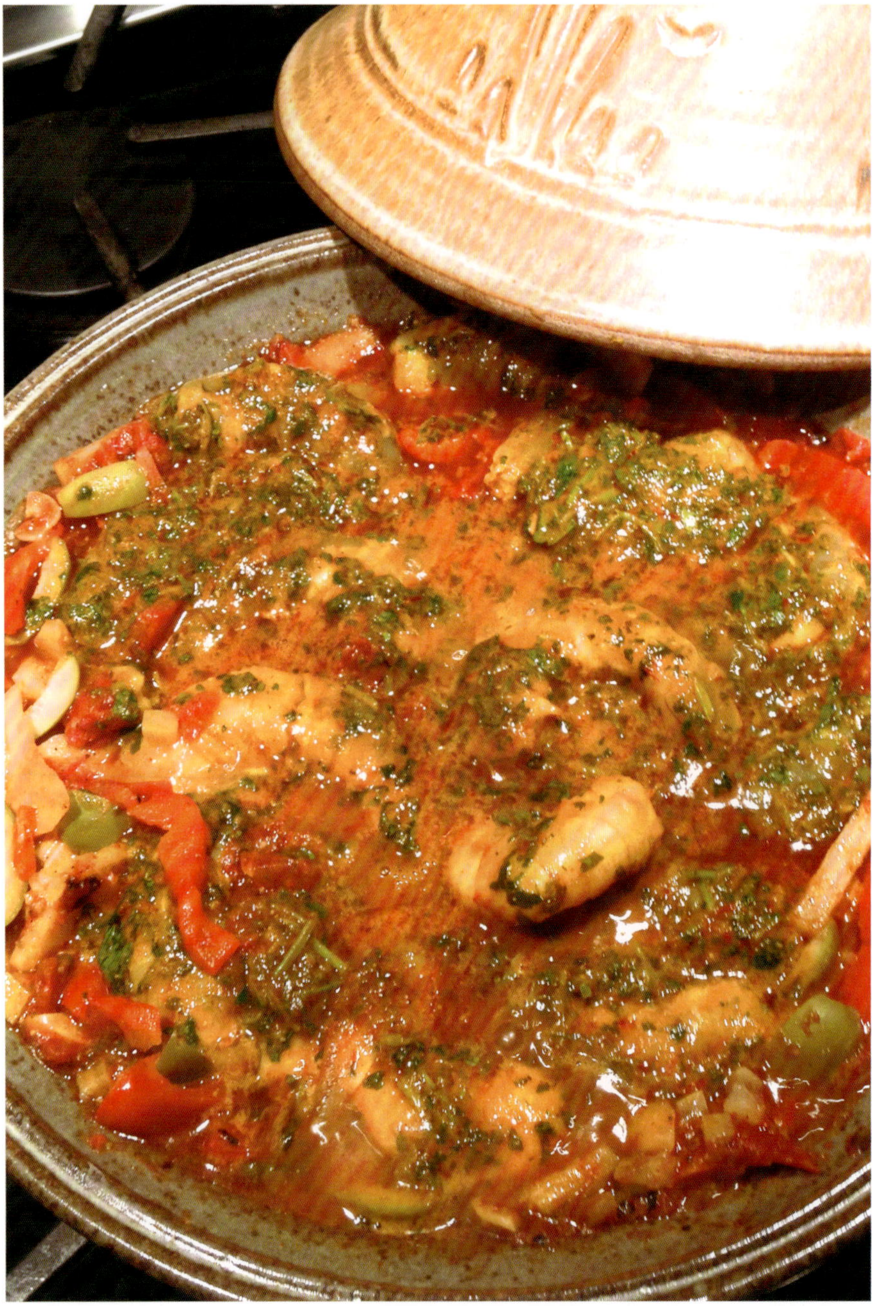

Shrimp tagine cooked in a Clay Coyote flameware tagine. Recipe from chef Emily Swantner. Photo by Emily Swantner

Shrimp Tagine with Vegetables and Preserved Lemons

by Emily Swantner, Adapted from Paula Wolfert in Couscous and Other Good Food from Morocco *via Mourad Lahlou in* Food and Wine 2009.

1 large garlic clove, peeled, roughly chopped
⅓ cup cilantro, including stems
⅓ cup flat-leaf parsley, large stems removed
2 teaspoons sweet paprika
1 level teaspoon Spanish smoked paprika
Large pinch cayenne
Small pinch saffron threads, crumbled
2 tablespoons fresh lemon juice
½ cup extra-virgin olive oil
1½ pounds large shrimp, shelled and deveined, tails left on
2 14½-ounce cans fire-roasted tomatoes, preferably Muir Glen
3 large garlic cloves, minced
1½ teaspoons toasted and ground cumin
Kosher salt and freshly milled black pepper
1½ pounds assorted baby potatoes, halved
3 large carrots, thinly sliced on the bias
1 large sweet onion, julienned
1 red bell pepper, julienned
1 yellow bell pepper, julienned
⅓ cup chicken stock or water
½ preserved lemon, peel only, small dice, homemade or store-bought (search Internet)
¾ cup pitted green olives, halved lengthwise
Cilantro sprigs for garnish

In a food processor, pulse to combine, leaving a little texture, the garlic clove, cilantro, parsley, sweet and smoked paprikas, cayenne, saffron, lemon juice and olive oil. Transfer to a bowl, add the shrimp, toss to coat and refrigerate for 2 hours. Meanwhile, in a medium saucepan, combine the tomatoes with the garlic and cumin and season with salt and pepper. Simmer over moderate heat, stirring occasionally, until the tomatoes are broken down and slightly thickened, about 10 minutes. In a mixing bowl, toss together the potatoes, carrots, onion and red and yellow bell peppers. Season with salt and pepper. In the bottom of a tagine or enameled cast-iron casserole, spread half of the tomato sauce. Top with the vegetables, then the remaining tomato sauce. Drizzle the stock or water down the sides of the tagine. Cover and simmer over moderately low heat until the vegetables are just tender, about 20 minutes. *Note: At this point, the tagine can be refrigerated overnight. Bring to room temperature and gently rewarm before proceeding.*

Add the preserved lemon and olives to the casserole and arrange the shrimp on top in a single layer. Season with salt and pepper. Cover and cook over moderately low heat until the shrimp are pink and curled, about 3 to 5 minutes. Garnish with cilantro sprigs and serve in the tagine.

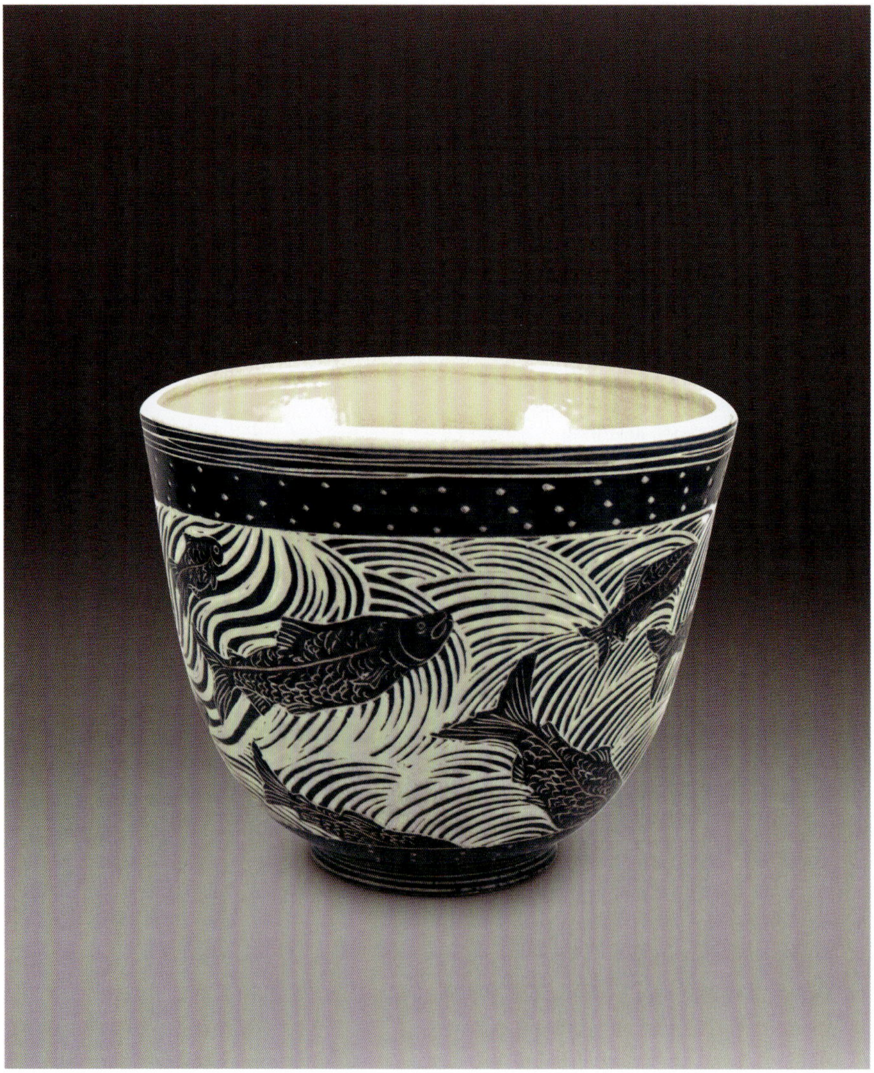

CHAPTER 6

Ware for the Microwave

You might think any piece of pottery can be used in a microwave oven, but that isn't the case. Although some earthenware potters recommend using their ware in the microwave, in fact, if a piece of pottery is porous, it should be used with care in a microwave. Once the pot has been out of the kiln and in use long enough to soak up and retain moisture, that moisture gets hot when exposed to microwaves. Handles and rims will get hot, causing potential burns to the user when removing the dish from the microwave. If the piece has glaze on it, this process of heating retained water causes the clay to expand and contract every time it's used in the microwave, and eventually the glaze will craze. This action is also likely to shorten the life of a pot. Once crazed, the porous ware retains moisture more easily. As a recommendation, if the glaze fits the clay very well, and the foot is sealed with terra sigillata, an earthenware pot might be relatively safe to use in the microwave. And if you don't mind using pot holders to remove the pot from the microwave, you might be comfortable using porous ware in the microwave anyway.

Some cooks like to cook in unglazed porous ware in the microwave oven—they even soak the pot in water before baking in it, just as they might do before using it in a conventional oven. The absorbed water heats up and helps to steam the food inside. This may help keep food from becoming excessively dry in microwave cooking. Micaceous clay pottery can also be used in the microwave without soaking it. Though this clay is sparkly, the bits of mica are not metal but a form of silica, so the clay won't damage the oven.

Many potters advise against using dark iron-bearing clays, or glazes with a great deal of metallic oxides in them in the microwave. This is not generally the case. While we all know metal should not be used in a microwave, the metallic oxides and compounds that occur in clay and glazes do not cause sparking when microwaved; however, any pottery decorated with metallic luster overglazes will cause sparking.

As long as they are actually vitrified, stoneware, porcelain and flameware should be quite safe to use in the microwave. The test for whether a piece of pottery is microwave-safe is quite simple. Fill a microwave-safe mug with cold water and place it

Salmon Bowl by Gayle Bair, 6½ inches in diameter, cone 6 porcelain. Photo by Gayle Bair

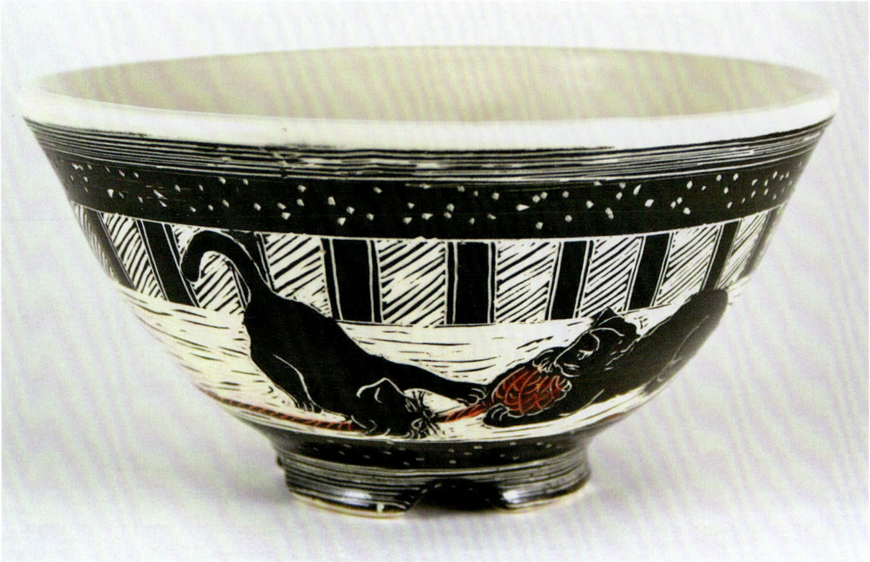

Oatmeal bowl by Gayle Bair, cone 6 porcelain, 4½ inches in diameter. Photo by Gayle Bair

in the microwave alongside the empty piece of pottery that you wish to test. Run the microwave long enough to heat the water to boiling and then touch the empty piece. If it is cool, it hasn't retained any water and it can be considered microwave-safe. Of course, if the piece has just come out of the kiln it won't have retained any water, so to test a brand-new piece of pottery, boil it in a pot of water first, then allow it to air-dry completely before testing it. If you sell pottery that is expressly designed for use in the microwave, then you must be sure to test it for vitrification according to the instructions in chapter 2.

One caveat about using pottery in the microwave is that if you heat a small portion of food on a wide shallow bowl or plate, you are subjecting the pot to very uneven heating. You are creating a small very hot spot in the center of the dish where the food is, while the rim remains cool. This is very likely to cause the dish to crack eventually. It is a good idea to completely fill a dish with food when using it in the microwave, just as you would for oven use, and avoid putting favorite plates in the microwave at all. Deeper bowls and mugs are not as subject to this kind of thermal shock as wide plates, because generally they will be more completely filled, and also because the shape is more resistant to thermal shock.

Having said all this, it is likely that a high percentage of pottery of any sort gets used in a microwave. Cooking in the microwave is so quick and easy, especially when reheating leftovers, that it could be difficult to sell pottery if it carried a warning against such usage. If you sell your ware, test it yourself, and be honest with your customers. You might want to suggest they avoid cooking in a very special piece, but recognize that any mug is going to end up in there occasionally—and in fact, mugs usually survive the experience just fine as long as a hot handle doesn't make the user drop it.

Mugs and bowls are favorite forms for daily use, and for many people daily use definitely includes cooking or reheating food in the microwave. Tea or hot chocolate drinkers heat up their water in the mug they intend to use; many an oatmeal eater will make his breakfast in his cereal bowl; and a can of soup (or leftover homemade soup!) is easy to divide between two soup bowls and reheat. If you are making soup bowls for use in the microwave, you might want to consider putting handles on them. A bowl of hot soup can be difficult to remove from the oven otherwise. The traditional type of handle for a soup bowl is a cylinder that protrudes from the side of the bowl, although bowls can be made with a pulled handle such as you might use on mug, or even two handles like a casserole dish.

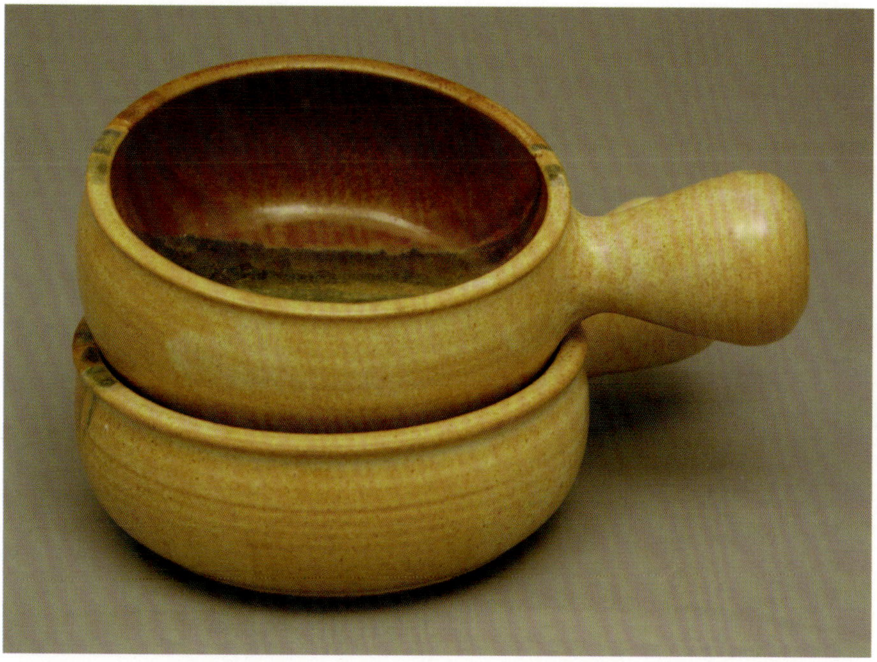

Soup mugs by Catherine Schroeder Abelson, 5 inches in diameter. These are the classic "French Onion Soup mug," easy to take out of oven or microwave full of steaming hot soup. Stoneware, cone 6 oxidation. Photo by Sumi von Dassow

Any form of baking dish might be used in the microwave as well as in the oven, especially if it is small enough for a couple of servings of leftover casserole. Any baking dish that is sized for one or two people is begging to be used in the microwave, and a recipe that can be easily and quickly made and shared by a couple will help a small baker sell.

Many potters make Brie bakers, a simple dish that can be made with or without a handle at the rim to allow for easy removal from the oven or microwave. If you want someone to buy a Brie baker, it should come with a recipe. The recipe is just a suggestion for this sort of baking dish, which could be used for other purposes. Brie can be baked in the oven or the microwave, depending on which is most convenient. On the other hand, apple bakers are a single purpose form, designed to hold a cored apple upright for baking in the oven or a microwave. A baked apple is a quick and easy dessert or snack, something you don't want to heat up the whole oven for, so it is a perfect candidate for microwave cooking. This form really has to be sold with a recipe, or people will think it is a very large ring holder!

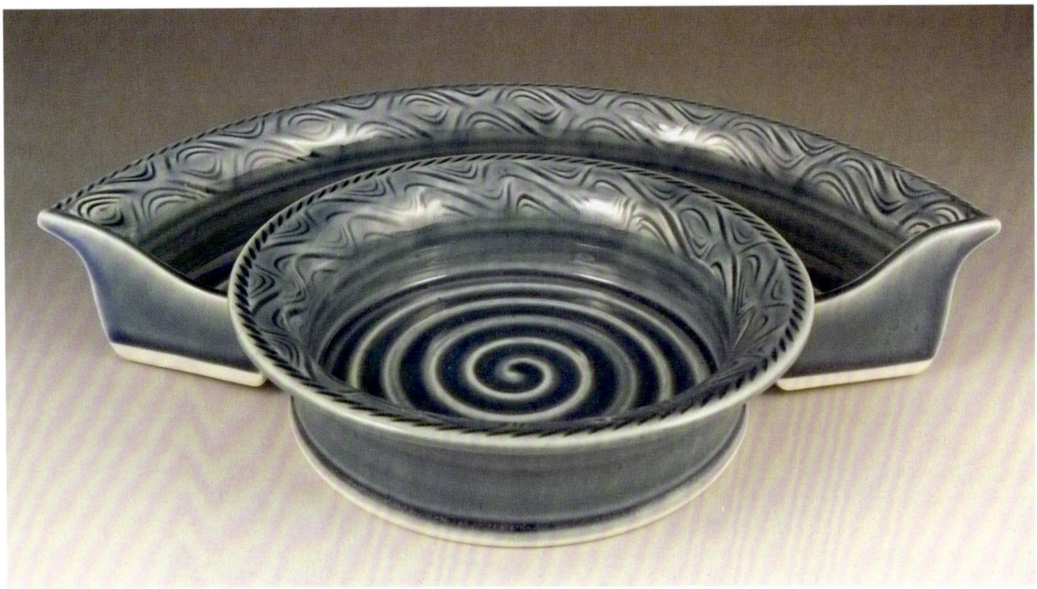

Brie baker with cracker dish, Gregory A. Johnson. Cracker dish is 15 inches in diameter while the Brie baker is 8¼ inches in diameter. Gas fired to cone 10. Photo by Gregory A. Johnson

PROJECT: Making an Apple Baker

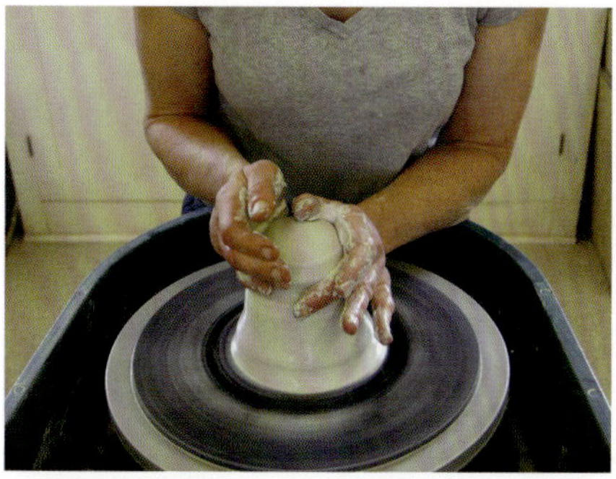

Center about 5 pounds of clay and make a groove at the bottom of a doorknob-sized portion of clay at the top of the hump. The groove marks the bottom of the pot.

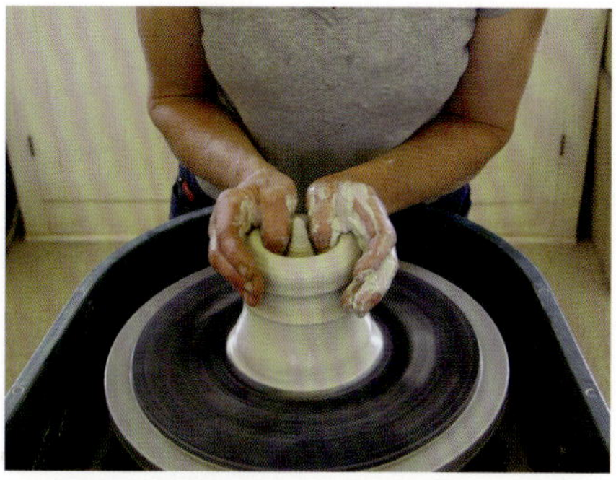

With pinkie fingers resting in the groove, open up with your thumbs but keep the thumbs an inch apart to allow a "finger" of clay to protrude from the center of the pot.

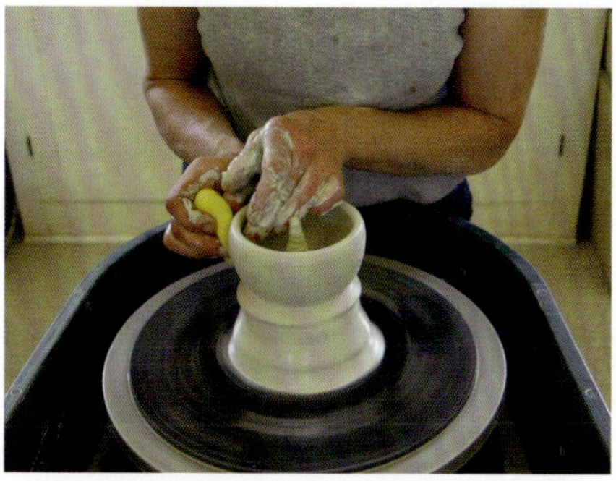

Pull up the walls from the groove to the rim.

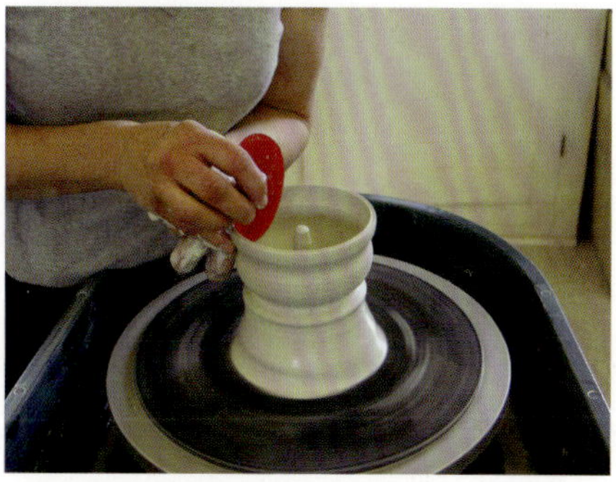

Use a soft rib to pull out the top of the rim to make it more interesting.

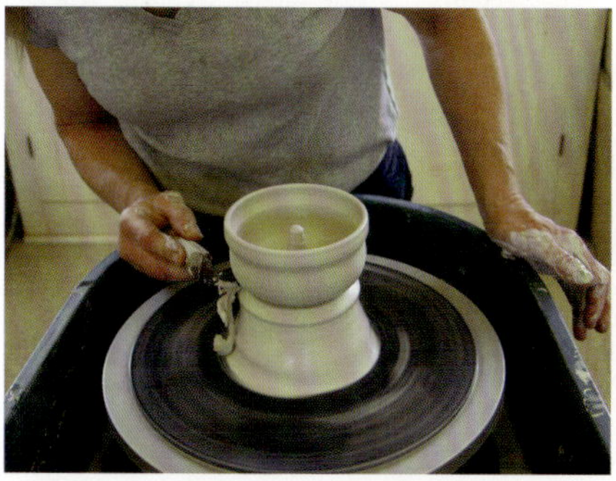

Put the point of a wood or metal tool into the groove and cut away excess clay. This makes it easier to cut cleanly with your cutting wire.

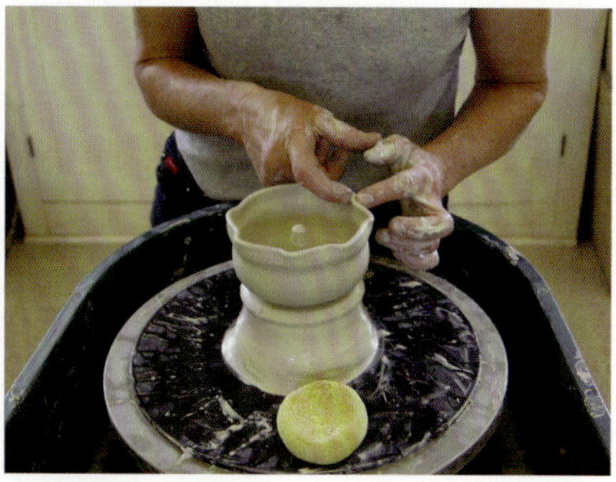

Use your index fingers to flute the rim. Place the finger tips slightly offset, one inside the rim and one outside, and gently push toward each other.

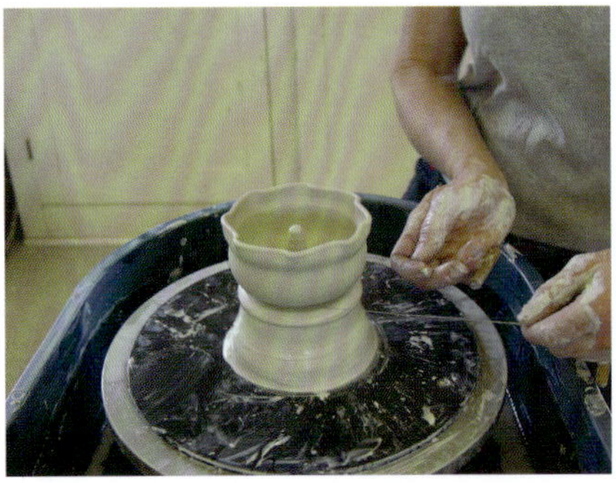

Wrap a cutting wire ¾ around the bottom of the pot in the groove you cut. Turning the wheel slowly, hold your left hand steady and pull quickly with your right hand.

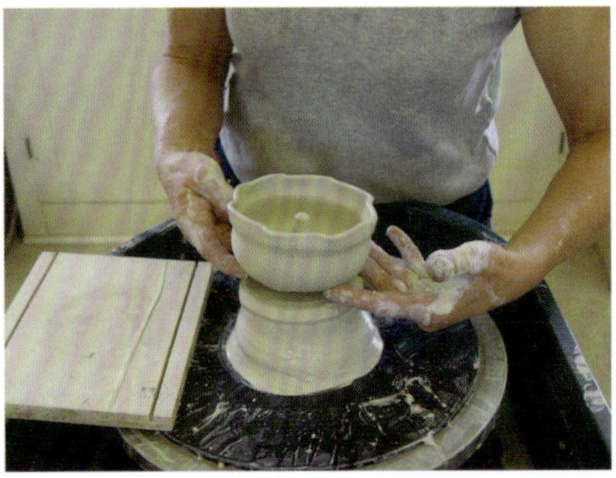

With dry fingertips, lift the pot off and put it on a board. Now throw another apple baker off the rest of the hump.

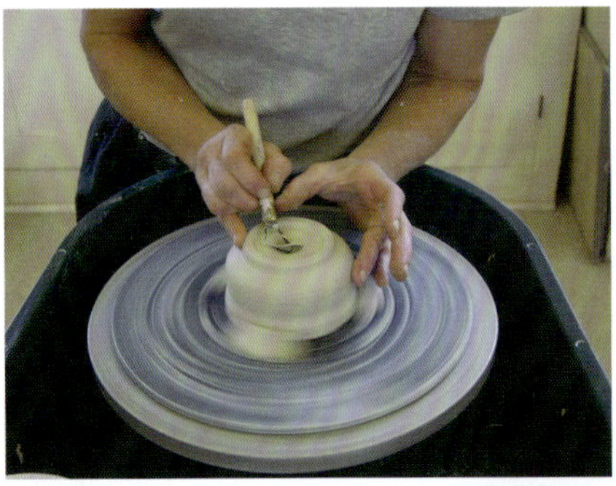

After throwing several bakers off-the-hump, let them set up. Trim the feet. In the center where the "finger" sticks up, trim down into the "finger". This keeps the baker from cracking across the bottom, and allows them to be stacked.

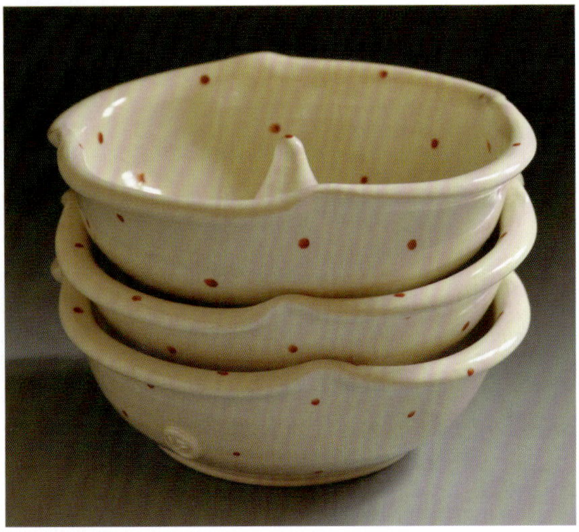

Apple bakers by Lucy Fagella, 6½ inches in diameter, porcelain, cone 6 oxidation. Photo by Lucy Fagella

RECIPES FOR MICROWAVE WARE

Fruity "Packs a Wallop of Flavor" Oatmeal

Thick cut oatmeal (not instant)
Milk or milk substitutes, for example, coconut, almond, or soy milk
Grated apple (can substitute applesauce) reduces the amount of liquid needed
Cranberries or raisins
Sliced almonds or crushed walnuts
Sliced Strawberries
Blueberries—add after cooking to prevent it coloring the oatmeal
Chopped pears or peaches
Maple syrup or honey
Pat of butter

Place in microwave-safe bowl, cover with wax paper, and microwave on high until oatmeal absorbs moisture and is the preferred texture.

Baked Apple

Core an apple and place it in the apple baker. Dot with one tablespoon butter and pour in one tablespoon water. Top with raisins, nuts, brown sugar, honey, maple syrup, cinnamon, or other spices. Bake in 350°F oven for 20 to 30 minutes or in microwave for 2–4 minutes until apple is cooked through. Serve with cream, whipped cream or ice cream.

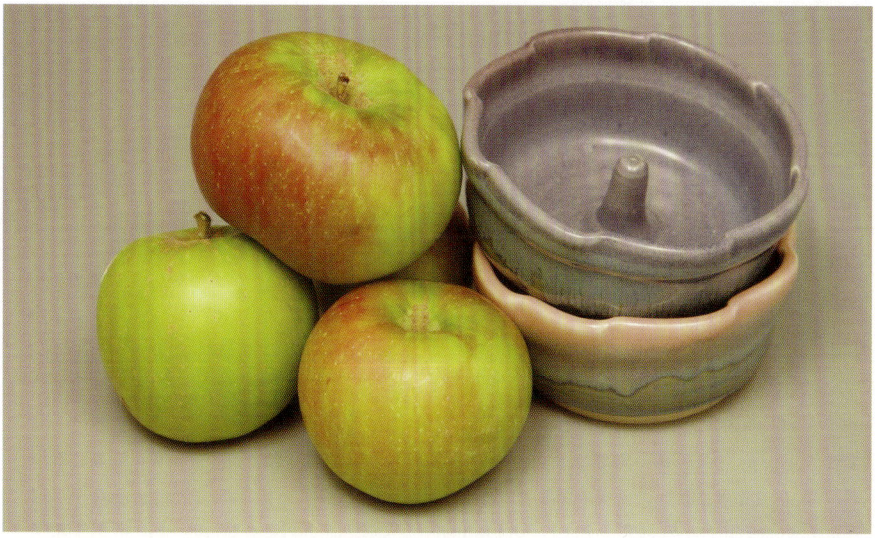

Apple bakers by Sumi von Dassow, apple bakers, 4 inches in diameter and 2 inches in height. Stoneware, cone 6 oxidation. Photo by Sumi von Dassow

Mexican Hot Chocolate

1 cup milk
1 ounce Mexican chocolate

Place milk in microwave-safe mug and heat until steaming but not boiling. Place milk and chocolate in blender and purée. Return to mug and serve.

Baked Brie with Kahlua and Pecans

¾ cup crushed pecans, lightly salted
¼ cup Kahlua (a coffee-flavored liqueur)
2 tablespoons brown sugar
1 13–15-ounce package Brie cheese

Spread pecans in a small dish; salt lightly. Microwave on high for 2 to 3 minutes, stirring every minute until toasted, or toast in toaster oven 300°F for 10 minutes. Remove from oven or microwave and add Kahlua and sugar; stir well. Remove rind from top and sides of Brie with cheese cutter or potato peeler; discard rind. Don't worry if a few spots of rind remain. Place the Brie in Brie baker and spoon pecan mixture over the top. Microwave uncovered on low setting until Brie softens to spreadable consistency. Serve as an appetizer with crackers, French bread or pear wedges.

Hot Brie or Camembert with Chutney

Place a small round of Brie or Camembert in Brie baker and microwave on high for one minute or until sides begin to bulge. Top with mango or peach chutney. Alternate toppings: Blend brown sugar, cinnamon, allspice and walnuts with cranberries for a holiday treat!

Hot Crab Dip "The Real Thing"

4-ounce package cream cheese, softened
½ cup mayonnaise
¼ cup finely chopped onion
1 tablespoon fresh lemon juice
½ teaspoon hot pepper sauce
½ teaspoon Old Bay seasoning or other seasoned salt
6 ounces fresh or canned lump crab meat, drained

Place all the ingredients except the crab in a bowl and blend together. Stir in the crab. Place in the top part of your dip chiller/warmer and bake in oven or microwave, uncovered, until heated through. Put tap water in bottom dip bowl and heat until boiling in microwave. Set filled dip bowl on the bottom bowl to keep warm. Makes 1⅓ cups.

Baked Brie with Caramelized Onions and Herbs

1½ large onions, cut in thin slices, not rings.
2 tablespoons butter plus 2 tablespoons olive oil or oil from sun dried tomatoes
½ jar (7–8 ounce) of oil-packed sun-dried tomatoes drained, cut in small pieces (very easy if you use a scissors)
1 13–15-ounce package Brie cheese
2 tablespoons fresh snipped basil
2 tablespoons minced parsley
Pepper to taste

For caramelized onions, cook in butter and olive oil in a frying pan uncovered, over very low heat about 35 minutes until tender and golden, stirring 3–4 times so onions don't get too brown. Use low flame so onions will turn golden and sweet.

Combine remaining ingredients in small bowl. Using a potato peeler or cheese cutter, cut off white rind from the top and sides of the Brie. Don't worry if a few spots of rind remain. Discard rind. Place Brie in Brie baker (ungreased). Top with caramelized onions, then tomato herb mixture. Bake uncovered in oven at 325°F for 10–12 minutes until Brie is softened, or microwave on low power for about 1 minute. Serve with crackers or baguette slices.

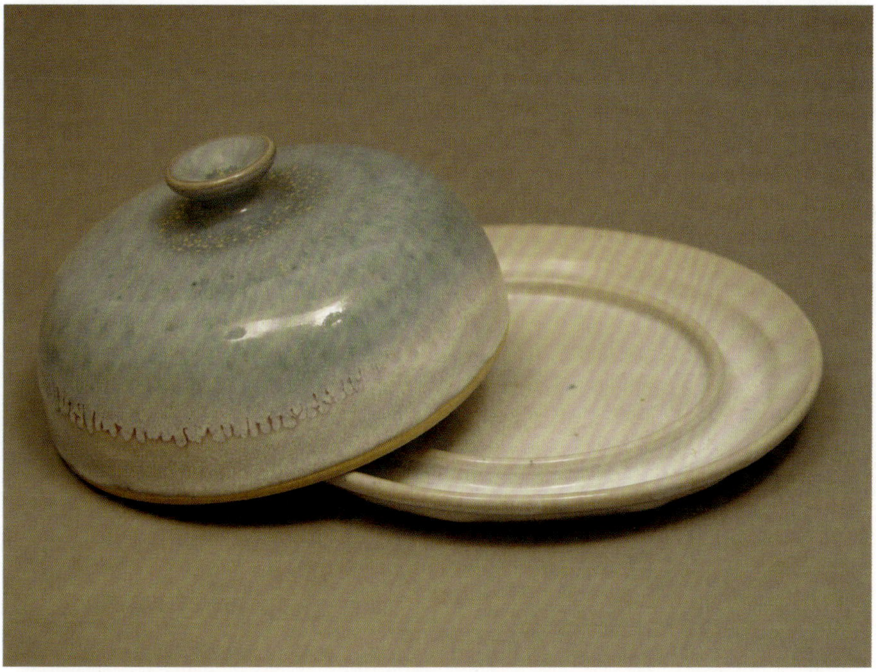

Covered Brie baker/cheese bell by Sumi von Dassow. 9 inches in diameter, stoneware, reduction-fired to cone 7. Photo by Sumi von Dassow

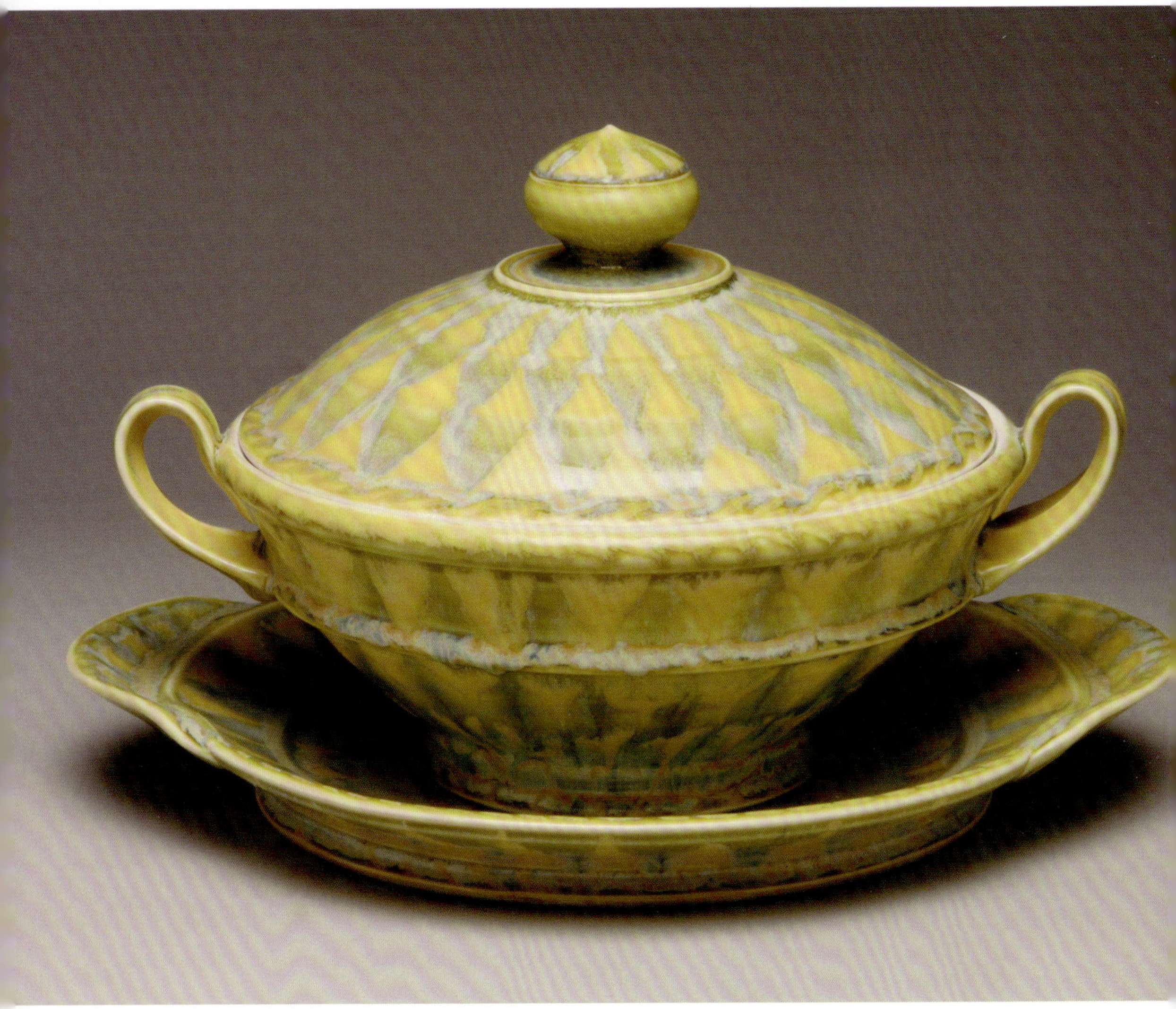

CHAPTER 7

Serving Ware

Much of what most potters make can be classified as serving ware. Almost anything that is put on a table can go in a platter, bowl or pitcher, and many potters specialize in these forms almost exclusively. These forms can be simple and basic, or creative and artsy. There's no particular correct way to make a useful bowl or platter, and most customers don't need a recipe to know what to do with them. Therefore, this book is not concerned with these forms. This chapter will focus on ware that is designed to serve particular foods—in other words, ware that a customer might not know how to use if you didn't tell them.

Serving ware is not subjected to as much stress as ware for baking or cooking in, and can be made from a variety of clays. If it is intended to hold liquid for extended periods of time, vitrified stoneware is most convenient, although some earthenware potters use terra sigillata to seal the bottoms of their ware. Farraday Newsome makes earthenware serving dishes, and she has a different method for sealing earthenware clay that she feels is even more effective than terra sigillata. She bisque fires to the highest temperature her clay will stand without slumping (cone 01) so that it is strong and dense although still porous. The low-fire (cone 05) lead-free glaze she uses fits the clay body best when the clay is bisque-fired to this temperature, so she gets less crazing.

Crazed glaze is a major reason earthenware often seeps. She glazes the entire pot, including the bottom, if possible. This means the pot is fired on stilts. While a large stoneware platter would undoubtedly warp if fired on stilts, her large pots don't warp because she has already bisque-fired the clay to a higher temperature than the glaze firing. If the pot has a trimmed foot ring, it can't be fired on stilts, but she seals the clay with a bit of extra work. First she glazes all of the bottom except the foot rim. Then she brushes thinned glaze on the foot rim and sponges most of that off with a slightly damp sponge. This pushes some of the glaze into the pores. Then she rubs it with a damp finger, pressing even more glaze into the pores and removing most of what is left on the surface. When the piece is dry there is a very slight film of glaze visible on the foot rim. There is never enough left to stick to the kiln-washed shelves, and it is much better sealed than if the foot is entirely unglazed.

Yellow tureen and tray by Sarah Jaeger, 10½ inches in height, gas oxidation fired to cone 10. Photo by Tom Ferris

Other than making sure your pot will hold liquid if it needs to, there is no general list of "rules" for what makes serving ware useful. It can have a trimmed foot or a flat bottom, and a lid or handles if it needs them. The primary function of handmade serving ware these days is to look beautiful on the table. Perhaps the only general guideline that covers serving ware is the simple common-sense admonition to be sure the foot is wide enough to be stable in use. You shouldn't have to worry about tipping a full gravy boat over while reaching for the mashed potatoes, or knocking a salad off the buffet table.

Liquids

What do you serve food in besides bowls, platters and pitchers? For liquids you have cruets for oil and vinegar and boats for gravies and sauces. A cruet is a very small pitcher with a narrow opening—actually more like a bottle with a small spout, to pour a small amount of oil or vinegar. The small size makes a handle unnecessary, though many potters choose to add them for visual balance with the spout. These may be used to store oil and vinegar in between meals, so a stopper or cork is helpful. Many potters make cruet sets with a tray to hold two cruets, one for oil and one for vinegar. On the other hand, since gravy is thick and hot, a gravy boat or sauce boat needs to have a

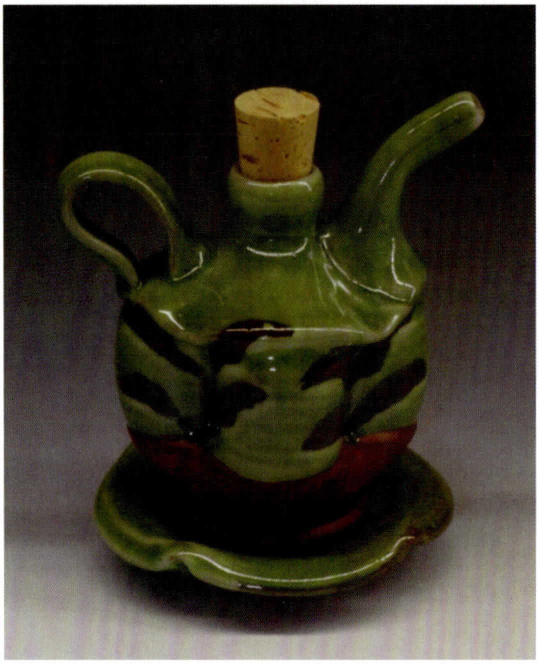

Cruet by Elise Delfield, 5½ inches in height, glazed, with wax resist, lightly burnished red terra sigilatta on the bottom to make it watertight. The brick red color on the bottom of this piece is the terra sigillata. Terra sigillata is a slightly glossy surface, almost waxy to the touch, that is frequently used on earthenware to seal the foot of the ware. Photo by Elise Delfield

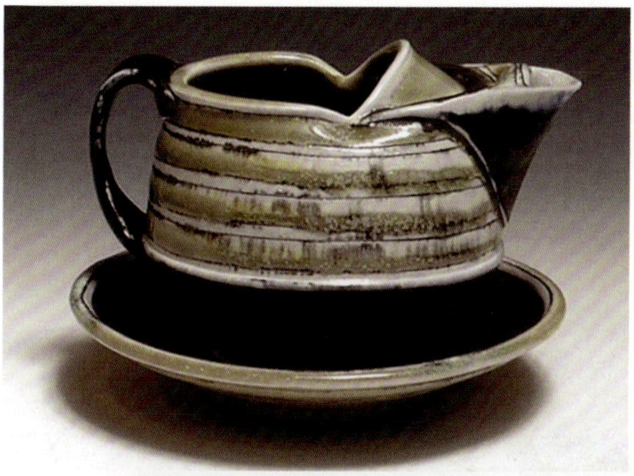

Gravy boat with saucer by Lorna Meaden, 6 inches in height, wood/soda fired. Photo by Lorna Meaden

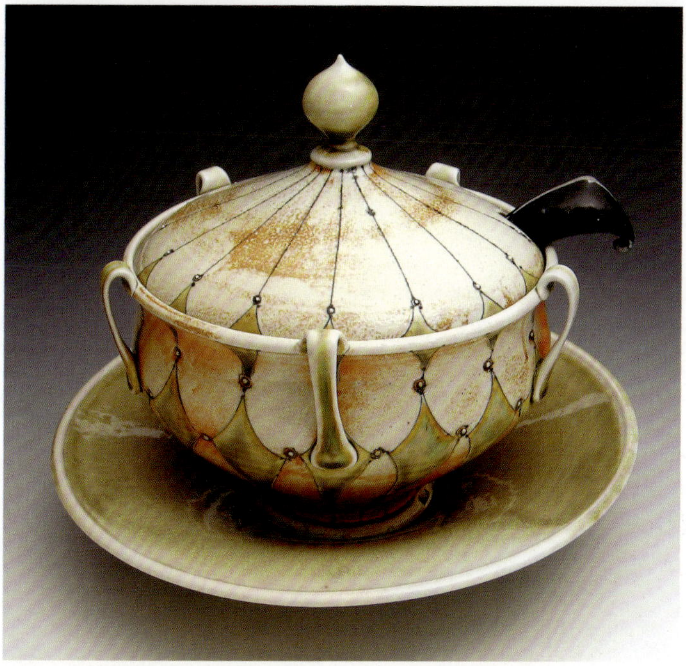

Soup tureen by Lorna Meaden, porcelain, 10 inches in height, wood/soda fired. Photo by Lorna Meaden

wide pouring spout and a handle. It is usually short and wide, to allow for easy filling. You don't need to make a saucer for a gravy boat, but you might want to use it with one. Also, of course, there are soup tureens, for soup. Usually these have a hole in the lid for the ladle, and some potters even make ladles to go with their tureens. A tureen may come with a platter or tray to catch drips.

Chip and Dip

One very popular form that has many variations is the chip and dip server, ubiquitous at potlucks and buffet dinners. The iconic chip-and-dip set is a large platter or shallow bowl form with a small bowl stuck in the center, but this may not actually be the most useful form. A large platter or shallow bowl with a small bowl that *isn't* stuck in the center might be more useful—easier to store, easier to clean, and more versatile. Even more useful is to make an extra small bowl for each set, so the dip can be refreshed in a clean bowl as necessary. There are many possible ways to make the dip bowl sit above the chip bowl so bits of chip don't fall into the dip—put it on a pedestal, build the pedestal into the chip

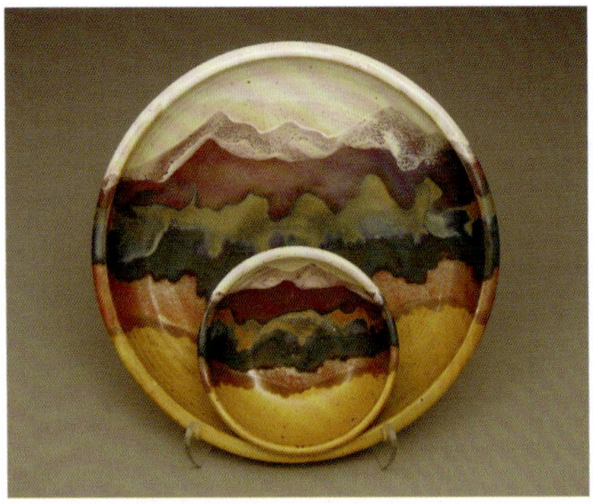

Two piece chip and dip set by Anita Garfein, reduction fired stoneware, 12½ inches and 6 inches in diameter. A chip and dip set is more versatile and easier to store when the two pieces are separate. Photo by Sumi von Dassow

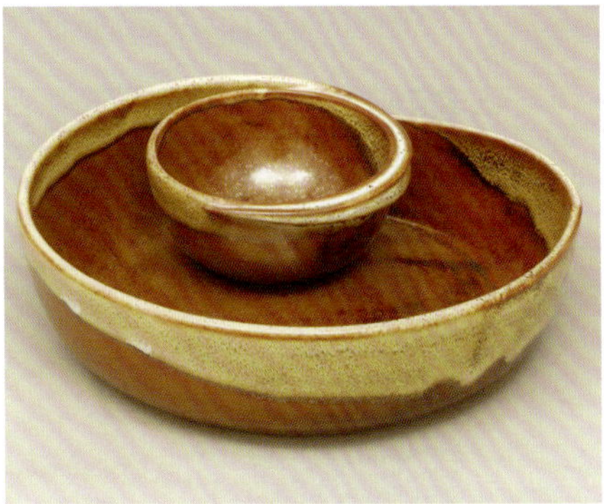

Chip and dip set by Sumi von Dassow, 10 inches in diameter, thrown and altered stoneware. Chip and dip sets offer lots of options for having fun and making something a bit different but still useful. Photo by Sumi von Dassow

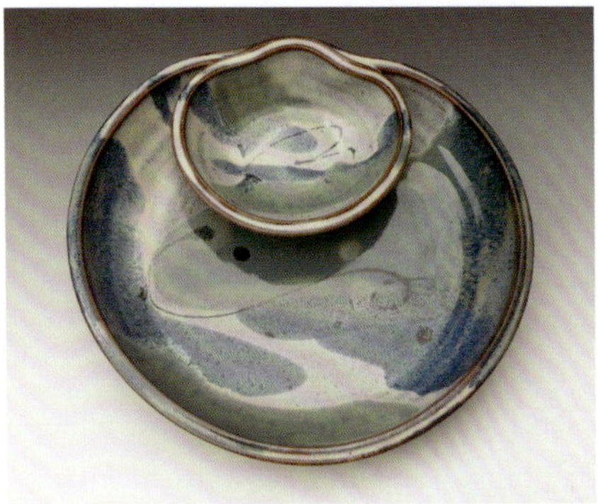

Chip and dip set by Dana Lehrer Danze, 11 inches in diameter, wheel-thrown and assembled red stoneware, oxidation fired to cone 6. Photo by Lehrer Danze

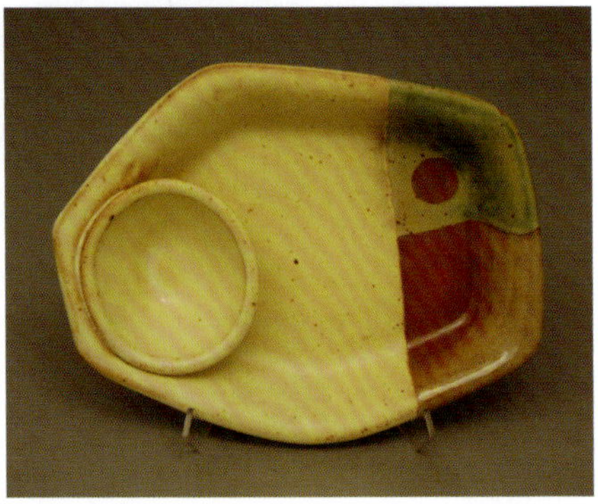

Chip and dip set by Lynn Hull, 9 inches in length, reduction fired stoneware. There's no reason a chip and dip set has to be round! Photo by Sumi von Dassow

Crocus Sauce Bowl and Plate by Joan Bruneau, 12 inches in diameter. Wheel thrown and assembled earthenware with slip, sgraffito decoration and polychrome glazes. Photo by Joan Bruneau

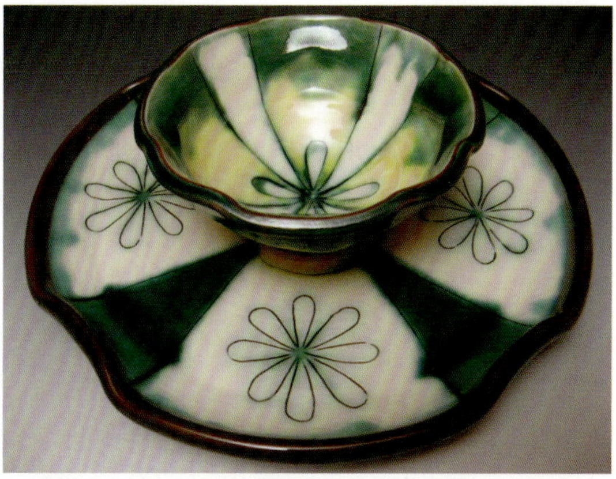

bowl, or even perch the dip bowl on the rim of the chip bowl. Lora Rust goes one step further, making a handmade handle on a stainless steel knife blade to go with her appetizer set (see p. 26). And while no customer needs instructions or a recipe to know what to do with a chip-and-dip set, it seems like everybody always likes to get a new dip recipe, so it can't hurt to attach your favorite dip recipe to every set you give away or sell.

Double Bowl

Something that ought to be more common on buffet tables is a double bowl set for keeping cold foods cold. The lower bowl holds ice, the upper bowl holds perishable foods such as shrimp salad. A lid for the upper bowl insulates the food even better. A small version can be made for perishable dips.

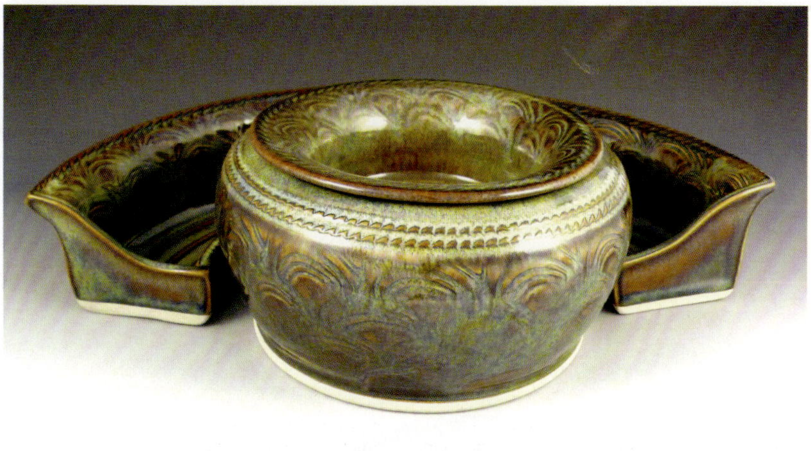

Dip chiller with cracker dish by Gregory A. Johnson, stoneware, cone 10 reduction-fired stoneware. Photo by Gregory A. Johnson

Butter/Cheese Dishes

Other items of serving ware include butter dishes and cheese bells. These are covered dishes intended to keep butter and cheese from drying out or attracting insects while they sit out on the table. A butter dish typically reflects the rectangular shape of a stick of butter, while a cheese bell is usually round, although there isn't any reason butter couldn't be served on a round dish and cheese on a square one. You might include a recipe for herb butter or cheese balls with these items.

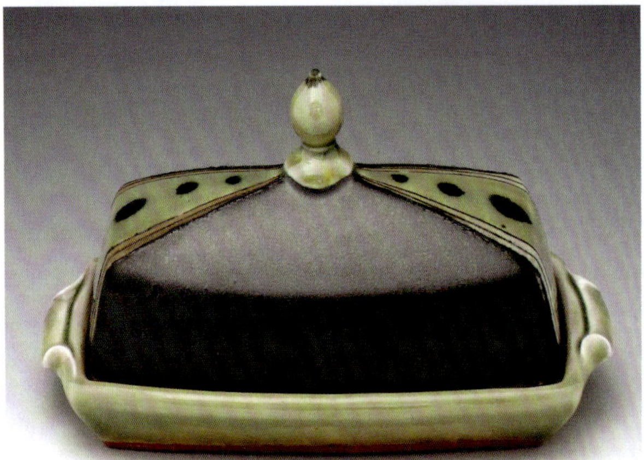

Butter dish by Lorna Meaden, 5 inches in length, slip-cast porcelain, wood/soda fired. Photo by Lorna Meaden

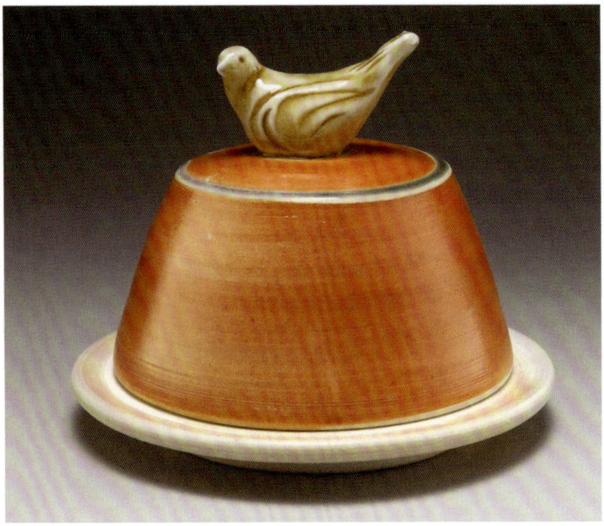

Butter dish by Pat Burns, 5½ inches in height, soda-fired porcelain, cone 10. Photo by Courtney Frisse

Cake Plates/Stands

One more serving piece that is probably most often used at wedding receptions is the cake stand or cake plate. A cake stand elevates a cake above its surroundings to show off the artistry of the cake decorator, and the cake and cake stand together become the decorative centerpiece of a table. It needs to be big enough for a standard 9-inch cake, and it may or may not have a small lip around the edge. A lip keeps frosting from dripping off the edge of the cake stand onto the table; but too much of a lip makes it difficult to serve a slice of cake.

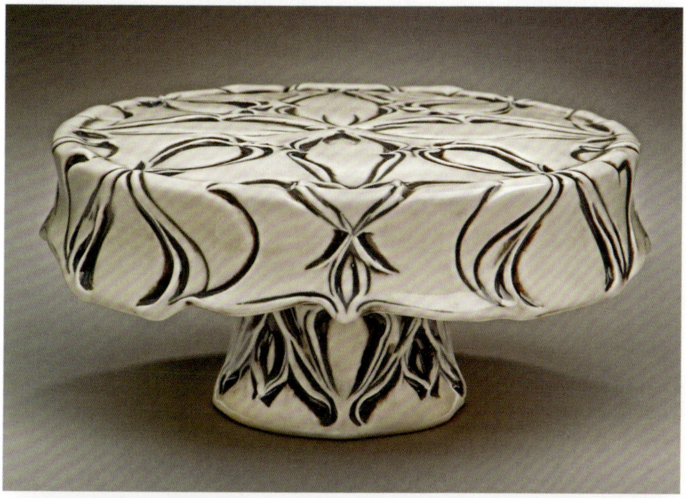

Cake stand by Lora Rust, 9 inches in diameter, thrown and altered porcelain, cone 6 oxidation, clear glaze with black engobe wash, Photo by Walker Montgomery

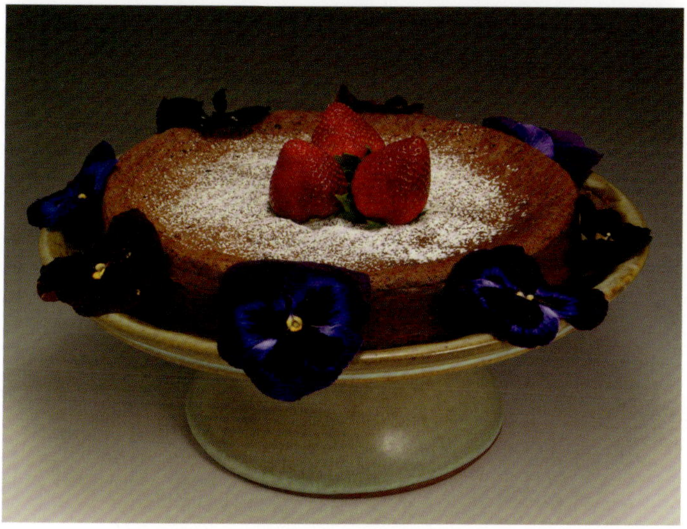

Cake stand with cake, by Steve Rolf. Stoneware, fired in reduction. Photo by Robert Paul

Olive Trays

Another buffet table item is the olive tray. This is something nobody needs—there's no reason you can't put olives or other small hors d'oeuvres in a bowl or small plate. But it's fun to arrange your olives, or pickles or peppers, in this little canoe-shaped dish, and it squeezes between other dishes nicely, too. This is an item that might need a label to tell customers what it is, and if you have a favorite canapé recipe, you could include that as well.

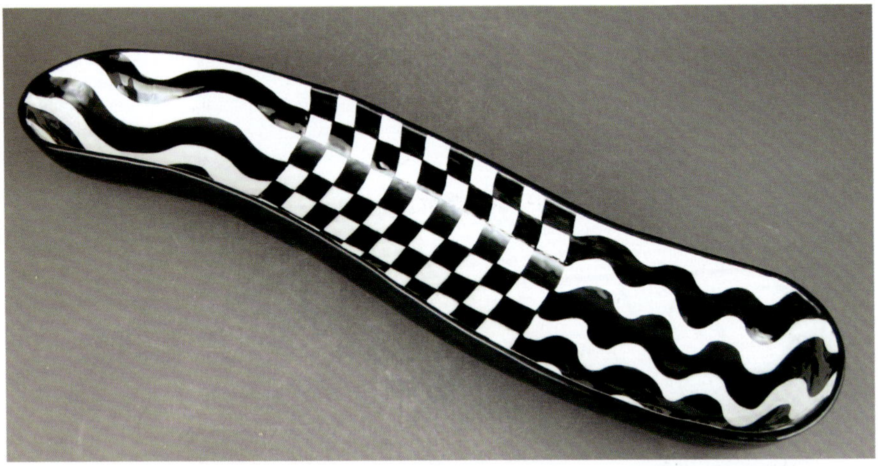

Curvy Olive Dish by Eleonora Eden, slip-cast earthenware, 13¾ inches in length. Photo by Eden

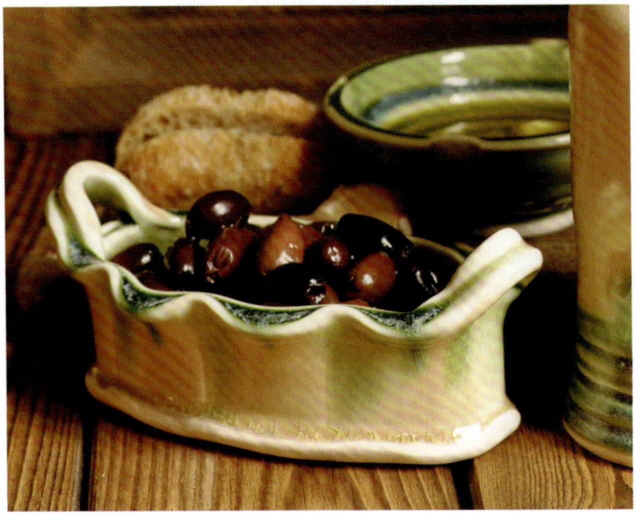

Olive dish and garlic grate dish by Lucy Fagella, porcelain, oxidation fired to cone 6. Photo by Lucy Fagella

PROJECT: Making an Olive Tray

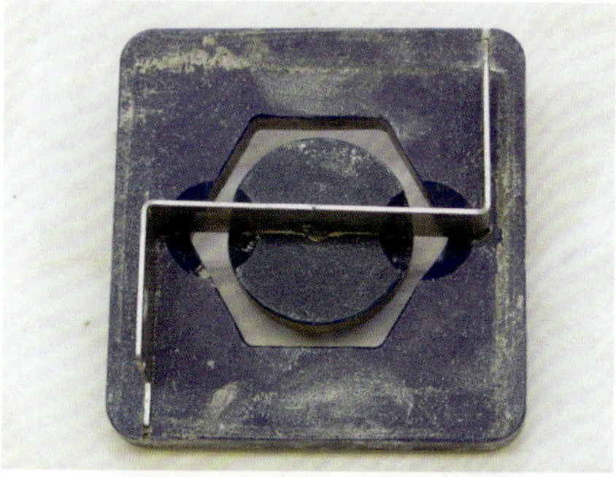

The North Star Extruder die used is a hollow hexagon with the round center instead of the hexagonal center.

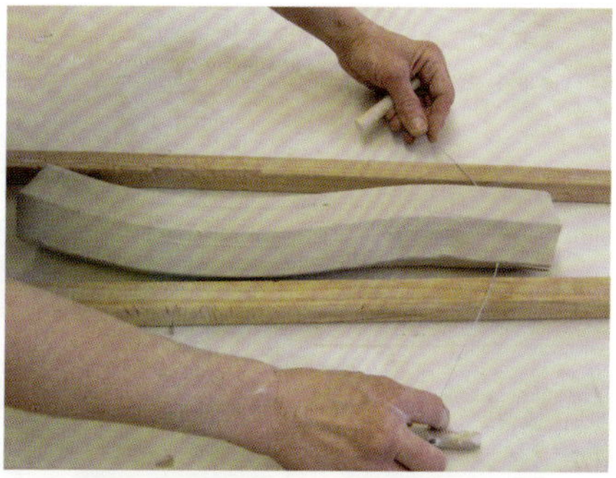

Lay the extrusion flat between two 1x1 sticks that are exactly half the height of the extrusion so they line up with the corners of the hexagon. Bisect the extrusion with a cutting wire.

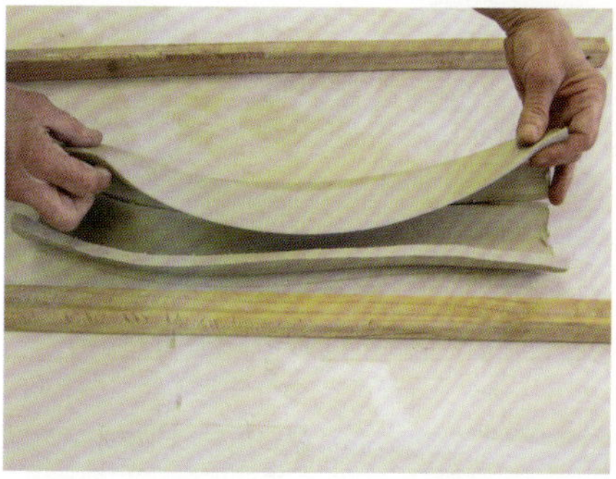

Peel apart the two halves of the extrusion.

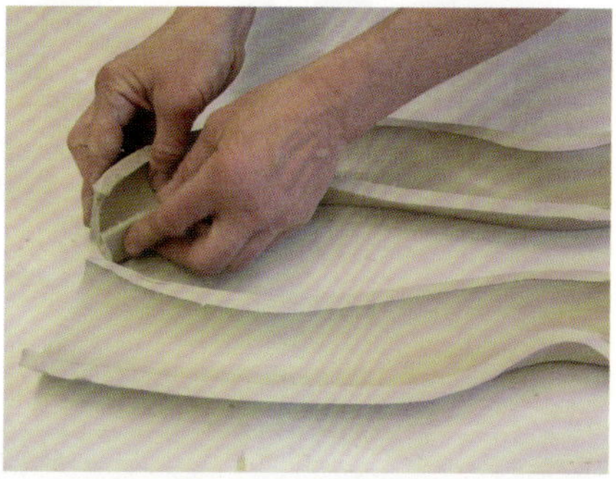

Cut the ends straight, curve the trays however you want them (they will tend to have a natural curve) and pinch the ends together.

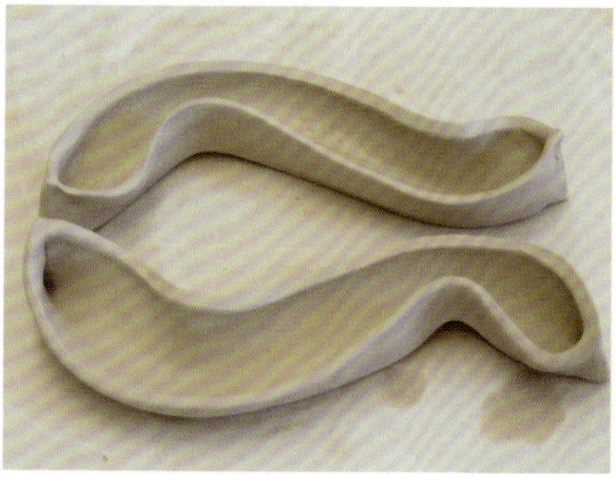

After smoothing the ends and the cut edges, you have two symmetrical olive trays.

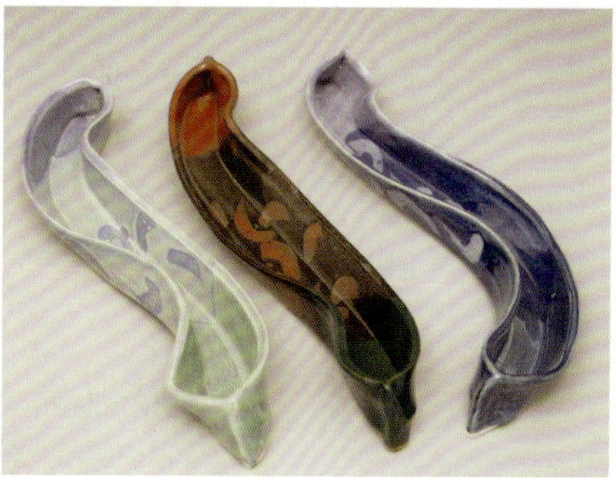

Three olive trays by Sumi von Dassow. Oxidation fired stoneware. Each about 15 inches long and 1½ high. Photo by Sumi von Dassow

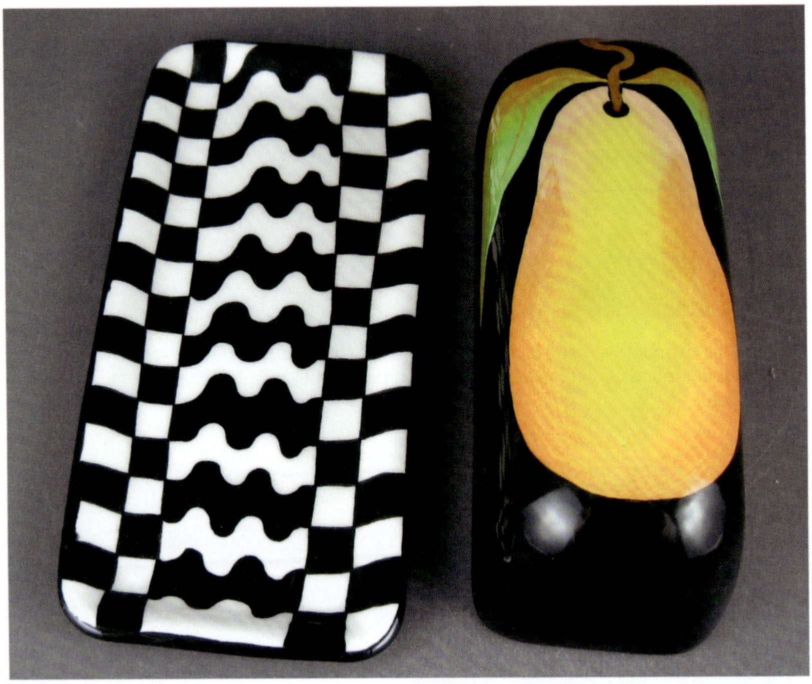

Pear Butter Dish by Eleonora Eden, 7 inches in length, slip-cast earthenware. Photo by Eden

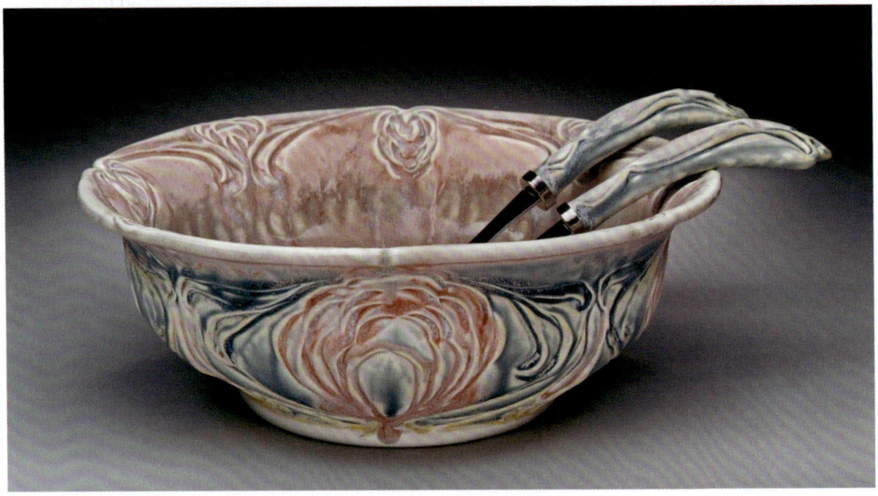

Salad bowl with utensils by Lora Rust, 11½ inches in diameter, porcelain Clay (stainless steel inserts), cone 6 oxidation. The decoration on Rust's work is neither impressed nor carved, but formed in the wet clay with handmade wooden tools. The addition of utensils makes this a special-occasion bowl. Rust even includes a salad recipe with it. Photo by Walker Montgomery

RECIPES FOR SERVING WARE

Edamame Dip

1½ pounds shelled edamame, cook per instructions on bag
1 cup sour cream, yogurt, or Greek yogurt
5 ounces fresh goat cheese or feta cheese, crumbled
1 chipotle chili, chopped, plus 1 tablespoon adobo sauce (from can)
4–5 tablespoons fresh lemon juice
1 small garlic clove, chopped
1 teaspoon salt (less if cheese is very salty)
1 tablespoon chopped oregano

Drain edamame and transfer to food processor. Add the rest of the ingredients and purée until smooth. Add water to thin if necessary and adjust seasonings to taste. Refrigerate at least 1 hour. Serve with pita chips or crackers.

Spring Pea Dip

2 cups of freshly shelled peas
¾ cup of water
3 tablespoons fresh tarragon (or fresh mint)
¼ cup cream (or 2 tablespoons tahini for vegans)
1 tablespoon butter
Salt and black pepper to taste

Gently simmer peas in water till just tender (approximately 5 minutes). Drain peas and put in food processor along with other ingredients. Delicious dip or spread with pita chips, toasted baguette rounds or serve with seared scallops.

Hummus

2 cans chick peas (drain, but save liquid)
⅓ cup tahini (sesame seed paste)
Lemon juice
Salt
Garlic
Cumin

Combine ingredients in food processor. Season to taste with lemon juice and spices. Add reserved liquid as needed to thin to desired consistency. Serve with chips or raw vegetables.

Spinach Artichoke Dip

10 ounces spinach
1 14-ounce can artichoke hearts
4 cloves minced garlic
8 ounce cream cheese
½ teaspoon red pepper, optional, or black pepper
¼ teaspoon salt
½ cup shredded Parmesan cheese
½ to 1 cup grated mozzarella, white cheddar, or jack cheese

Cook spinach until soft; drain and place in food processor. Add artichoke hearts, garlic, cream cheese, salt and pepper. Process until just slightly chunky. Place in saucepan on low heat and add cheeses, heating and stirring until melted. Serve with bread or crackers.

Lavender Goat Cheese with Cherries

from Anderson Turner of Lucky Penny Farm
8 ounces goat cheese (chevre), room temperature
2 tablespoons dried culinary lavender
4 ounces dried cherries
2 teaspoons honey

Mix goat cheese with lavender in small bowl. Chop dried cherries into small pieces and combine with honey in another bowl. Roll goat cheese/lavender mixture into two equal balls and slightly flatten them. Compress the cherry/honey mixture, divide into two parts, and place on top of cheese balls. Add lavender sprigs for garnish. Chill if not serving immediately. Will keep refrigerated for a week.

Flavored Chevre or Cream Cheese

8 ounces chevre or cream cheese
Few sprigs of tarragon and chives, or other herbs such as rosemary; or
½ teaspoon cumin, some diced jalapeno peppers, and some cilantro; or
Finely diced carrots, celery, parsley, and red onion

Mix 8 ounces softened cheese with chosen flavoring. Roll or pat into a ball and chill. Serve with baguette slices, crackers, or raw vegetables.

Easiest Guacamole Ever

Avocado
¼ teaspoon lemon or lime juice
Salt and pepper to taste

Mash avocado in a bowl. Add other ingredients and stir. Variations are limitless—adding a little chopped onion, tomatoes or jalapeno. Serve with tortilla chips.

Spiced Pumpkin Dip

8 ounces cream cheese, room temperature
2 cups confectioners sugar
1 can solid-pack pumpkin (or 2 cups puréed cooked pumpkin)
3 teaspoons pumpkin pie spice
1 teaspoon vanilla extract
½ teaspoon ground ginger
Apple and pear slices

In a large bowl, beat the cream cheese and confectioners sugar. Gradually add the pumpkin, spices, and vanilla; beat until smooth. Serve with fruit.

Summer Salsa

1 cup diced fresh tomatoes
1 clove minced garlic
Juice of one lime
1 chopped avocado
½ teaspoon salt
2 tablespoons chopped cilantro (reserve 1 tablespoon for garnish)

Combine ingredients and garnish with cilantro. Serve with blue corn chips.

Baba Ghanouj (Eggplant Purée)

1 large eggplant
1 clove garlic
⅓ cup tahini (sesame seed paste)
Juice of 1 lemon
⅓ teaspoon ground cumin
Salt and pepper
1 tablespoon olive oil

Broil eggplant whole by turning side to side until skin is charred and eggplant is soft to the touch. Depending on size of the eggplant and broiler, this takes 20–30 minutes. Remove eggplant from broiler, allow to cool, then peel. Cut eggplant into chunks, place in food processor and purée. Add other ingredients and blend thoroughly. Correct seasoning and serve as dip with crackers or vegetables.

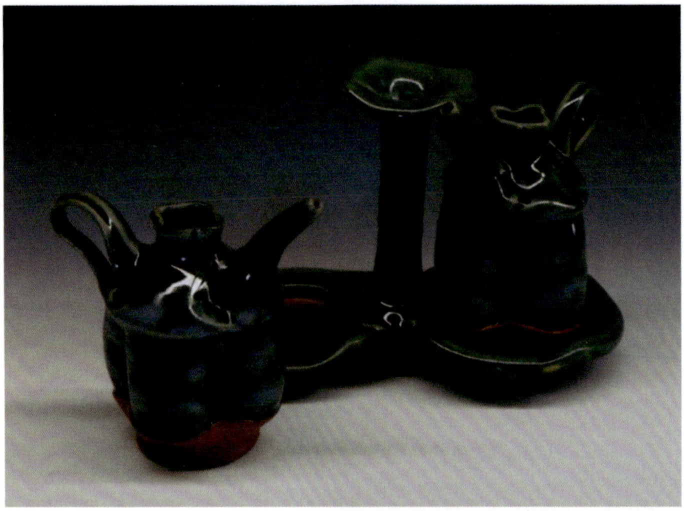

Oil and vinegar set by Elise Delfield, 9 inches in length, glazed and lightly burnished red terra sigilatta on the bottoms to make them watertight. Fired to cone 3–4. Photo by Elise Delfield

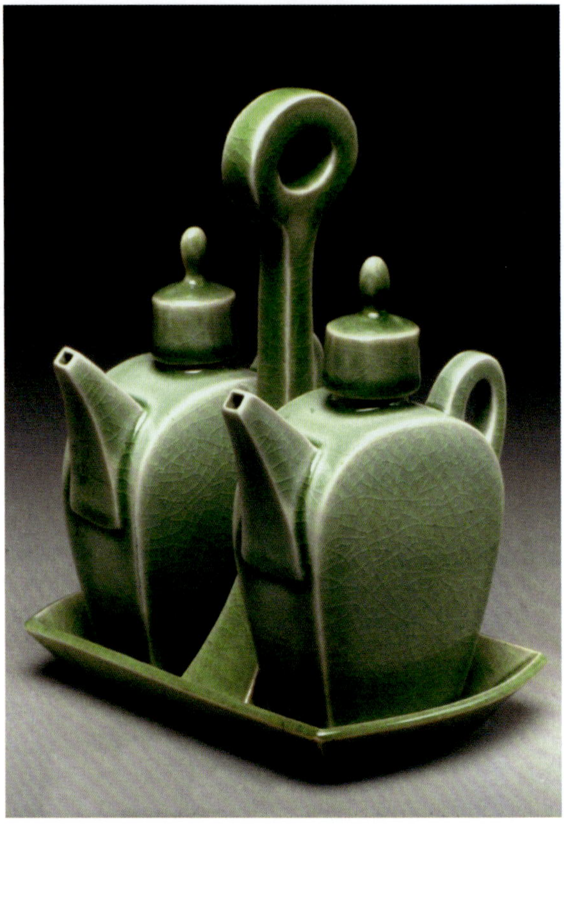

Celadon cruet set by Margaret Bohls, slab-built porcelain, 8½ inches in high, fired to cone 10 reduction fired. Photo by Margaret Bohls

Favorite Family Salad

Spring mix greens
¼ cup dried cranberries
¼ cup slivered almonds (lightly toasted)
2 ounces goat cheese or crumbled feta
¼ cup balsamic vinegar
⅓ cup light olive oil
⅓ cup extra virgin olive oil

Mama's Oil and Vinegar Dressing

1 teaspoon dry mustard
1 teaspoon sugar
1 teaspoon salt
½ teaspoon pepper

Combine in jar, adding olive oil slowly.

Summer Herb Salad Dressing

½ cup olive oil
½ cup apple cider vinegar
½ cup fresh herbs: parsley, oregano, basil, chives, rosemary, and thyme, any combination, whatever you have. In winter, use 2 tablespoons dried herbs or 1 tablespoon fermented mixed herbs
1 clove garlic, minced
¼ teaspoon each salt, pepper, mustard powder, and turmeric

Place all ingredients into blender and blend until smooth. Taste and add salt if necessary.

Miso Ginger Salad Dressing

2 tablespoons white miso
2 tablespoons rice vinegar
1–2 teaspoons dark sesame oil
2 teaspoons finely grated ginger (or ginger juice)
1 scallion, thinly sliced
3–4 tablespoons grapeseed oil
½ teaspoon sriracha sauce (optional) for spicy version
1 teaspoon honey (optional)

Mix briskly until emulsified. Toss with mixed greens; include bits of fruit and/or nuts for texture.

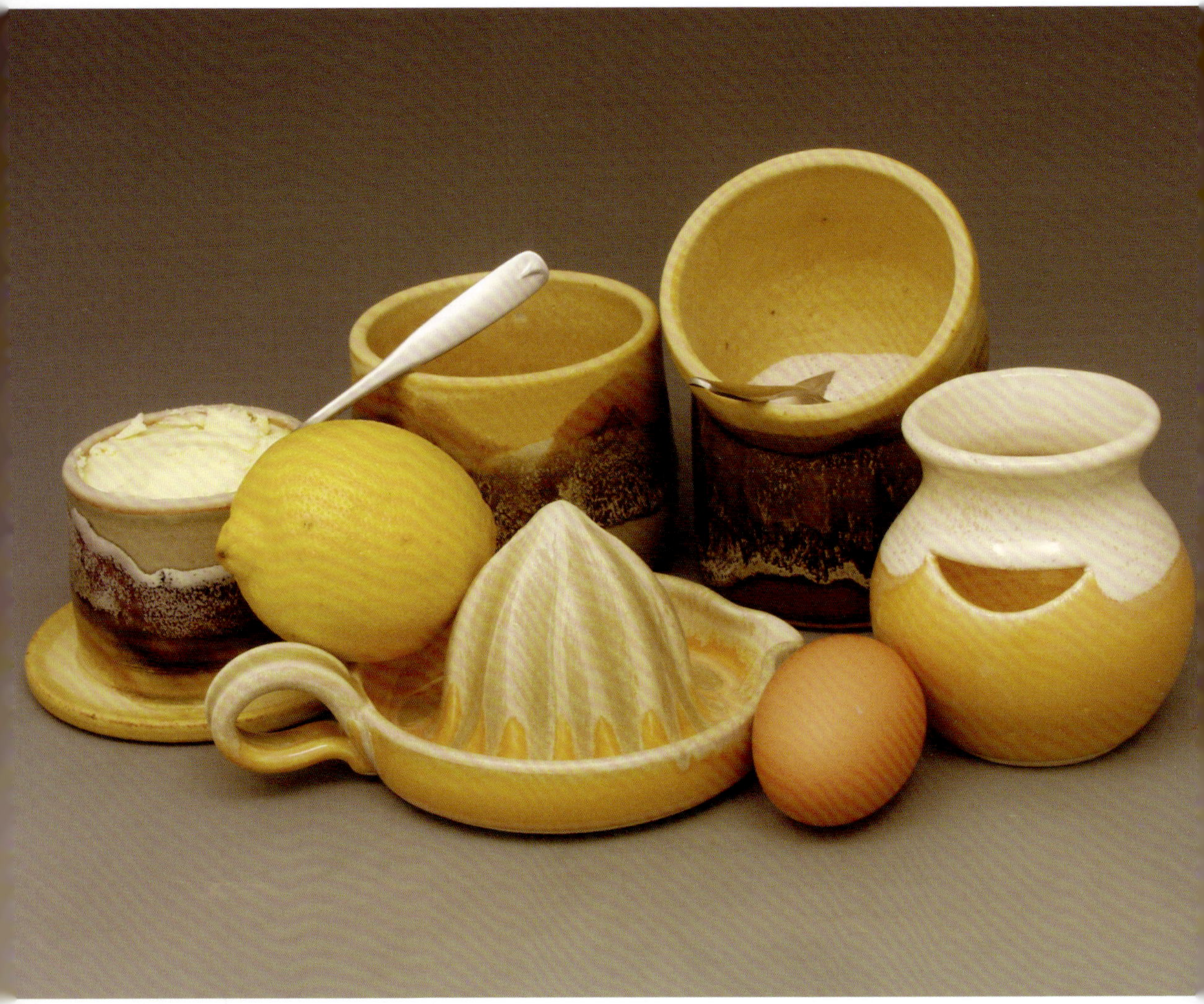

CHAPTER 8

Preparation Ware

As with serving ware, almost any pot can be used to prepare food. A cook will grab a bowl to grate cheese into, a mug to whisk corn starch into broth, a saucer to mince a clove of garlic on. But some kinds of pots are designed to make certain preparation steps easier, and those pieces are what this chapter is about.

Mixing Bowls

In times past when every household had to bake bread every week, a standard item for every potter was a bread mixing bowl. A bread mixing bowl was big and heavy and sized in gallons, and while we aren't likely to need a bowl sized in gallons, there are still some cooks who mix batter by hand and want a big sturdy bowl. A plain sturdy bowl might be a mixing bowl, while a bowl with a pour spout is a batter bowl.

A smaller version of a batter bowl is an omelet bowl, for whisking up an egg or three for breakfast. An omelet bowl or a batter bowl can have a handle, though some potters simply bend a portion of the rim in to allow the cook to grab the bowl with the thumb and a finger. This thumb grip is placed a quarter or a third of the way around the rim from the spout, keeping in mind that a right-handed cook will want it a quarter of the way clockwise from the spout (assuming that she is grasping the bowl in the left hand and using a whisk or spatula in the right hand). If you want to be egalitarian, make two thumb grips. A simple way to make a bowl easy to grasp is to put a thumb hole opposite the spout.

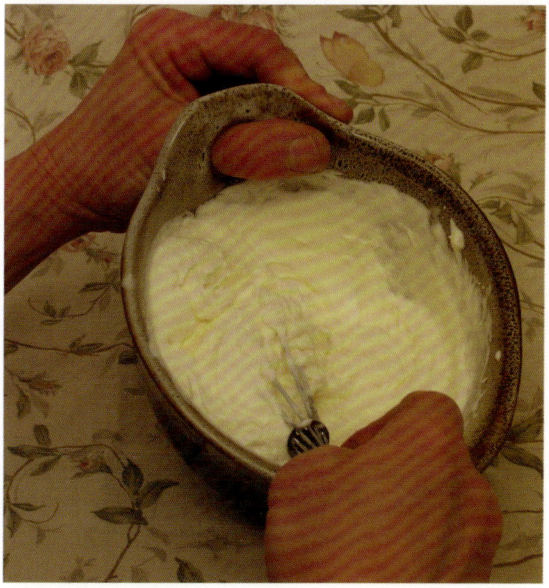

This simple batter bowl is easy to hold steady while whisking cream or eggs.
Photo by Sumi von Dassow

Useful pots to keep in the kitchen while baking: a butter crock, a salt pig, a citrus juicer and an egg separator. To 4 inches high, fired to cone 6/7 oxidation and reduction. Photo by Sumi von Dassow

Egg Separators

If you want to separate your egg yolk and white before whisking them, you might need an egg separator. This is shaped like a small vase with a half-moon shaped hole cut out of the shoulder—you crack the egg into the vase and pour the white out the hole. When you make an egg separator you need to make sure the opening is not so big that the yolk slips out along with the white, but not so small that the yolk simply blocks it completely. To accomplish its purpose, the vertical dimension of the opening needs to be narrower than an egg yolk, while the horizontal dimension must be wider. Of course the edges of the opening must not be sharp enough to break the yolk.

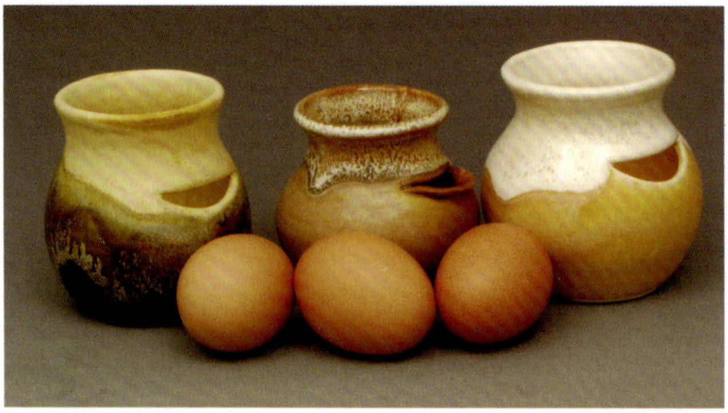

Egg separators by Sumi von Dassow, to 4 inches in height, cone 6 oxidation and reduction. There are two basic ways to make the opening for the egg whites—cut a crescent or half-circle shape out, or cut a slit and pull a spout from the bottom of the slit. Either way, the opening should be at the top of the belly of the pot. Photo by Sumi von Dassow

Graters

Another useful tool that is exceptionally easy to make is a garlic or ginger grating dish. Simply make a small saucer and use a tool to make sharp-edged cuts in the bottom, or use a slip-trailer to create sharp pointed drops of slip in the saucer. This can be used to grate garlic or ginger for recipes, or to make garlic-infused olive oil. Grate the garlic, pour some oil over it, and let it sit for half an hour—then dip bread into the oil for an appetizer, just like in fancy restaurants.

Citrus Juicers

A citrus juicer is another staple of the potter's art. A basic juicer is a dome with several grooves cut into it, with a rim to catch the juice and a spout to pour it out. A juicer can have a handle, and some potters build in a way to catch the seeds (although lemon seeds can be quite tiny and impossible to catch.) You can even put slits in it and make a bowl to go under it. If you like to squeeze oranges or grapefruits, you can make a larger sized juicer. If you make juicers, make sure the grooves are pronounced enough to function well, and that the dome is neither too big for a lemon to fit on it, nor so pointed that the tip will push through the bottom of the lemon. Look at the shape of a lemon and make the juicer match it, and then test your juicers on real lemons.

PROJECT: Dannon Rhudy Making a Juicer

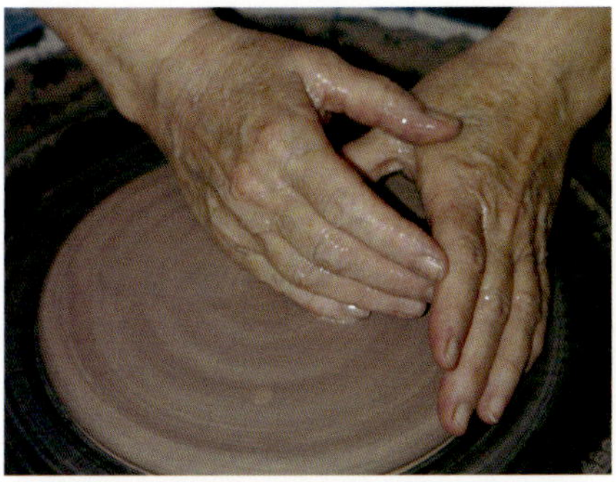

To make a juicer approximately 6 inches in diameter, start with about 1½ pounds of clay, or a bit more. Center the clay and flatten to approximately a 7- to 8-inch circle on a bat.

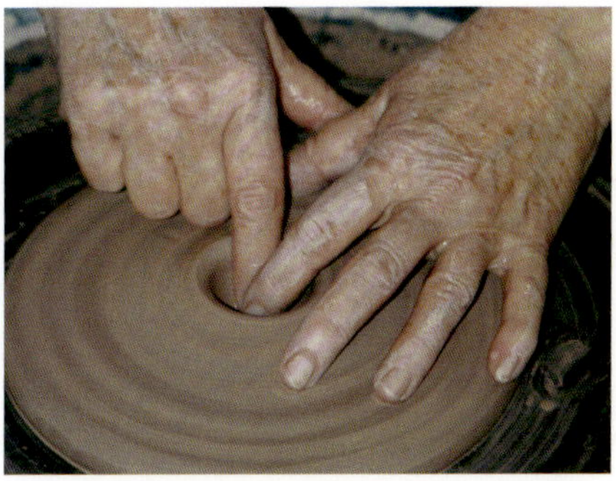

Open the center to the bat, making the opening 2–2½ inches wide at the bottom.

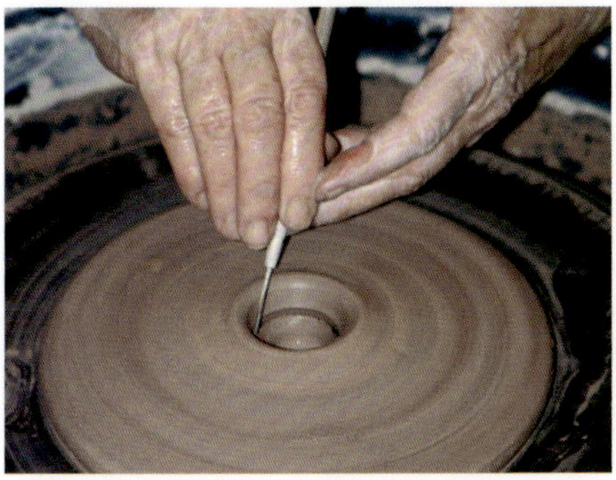

Raise the wall of the opening slightly (an inch or two) and use your needle tool to trim the inside of the opening. Bevel the opening leaving the trimmed part in place (it pops off later).

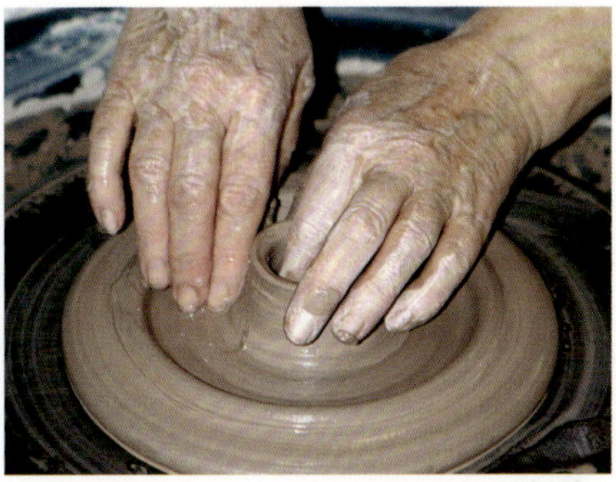

Finish pulling up the center wall.

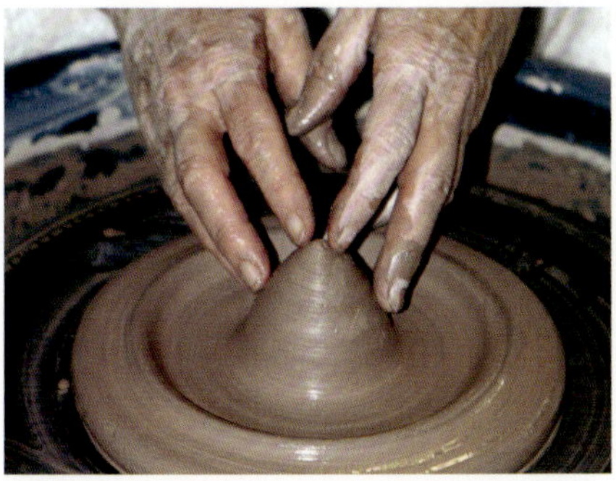

Completely close it. Leave a barely blunted point on the tip of the closed part The walls of this closed form will be slightly thick; but you will need this thickness later.

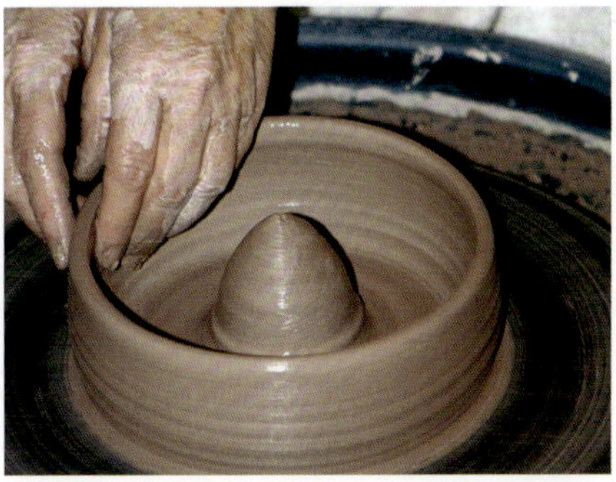

Move to the outside edge of the piece. Pull up the outside wall to a height of about 3 inches.

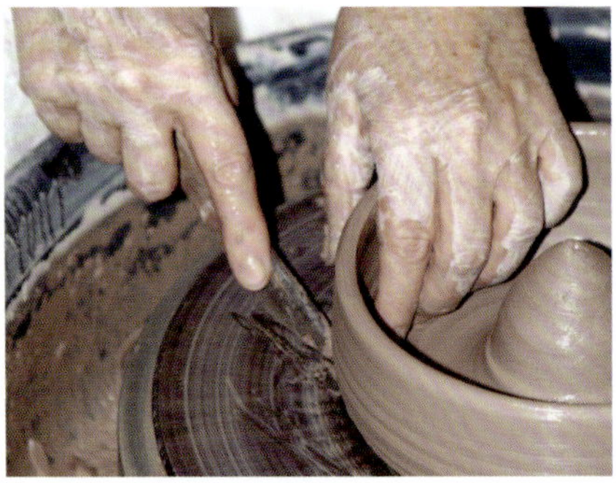

Keep the space between the inner closed portion and the outer wall flat and smooth. Using a 45° stick or metal tool, trim the outer bottom edge of the form.

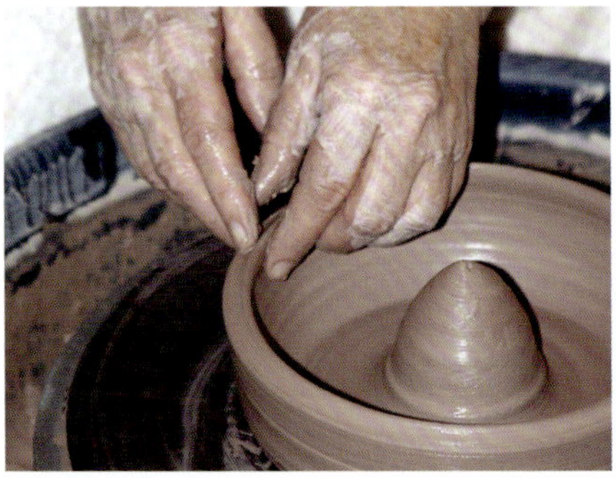

Set the rim of the outer wall. Make a good thick rim, no matter the shape, because thin rims chip.

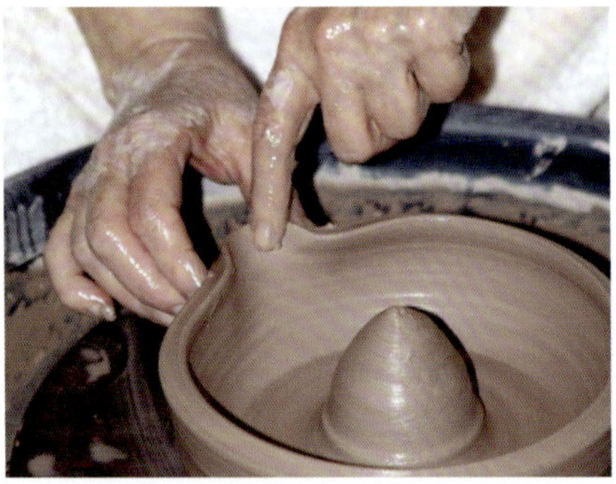

Pull a nice spout, just as you might pull a spout on a pitcher. It can be simple or elaborate, but keep in mind the end use of the juicer.

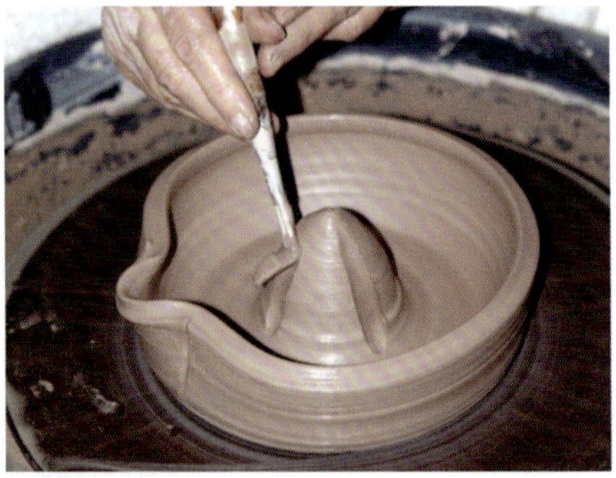

Flute the closed form in the center of your juicer. The rounded end of a small loop tool is ideal. Start at the bottom of the closed center form and pull up steadily. Space grooves evenly.

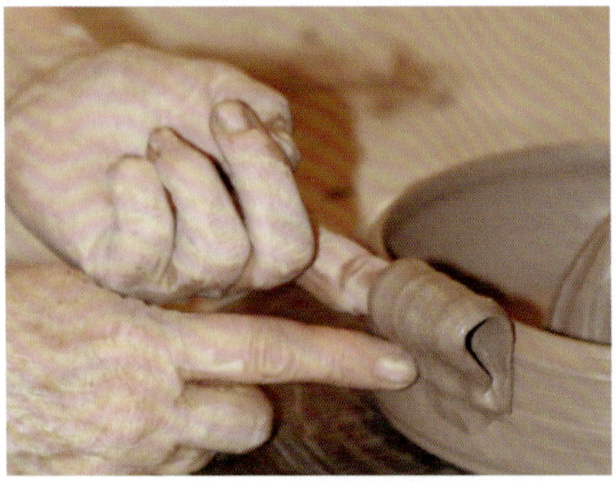

When you have fluted the entire closed portion, pull a wire under the whole piece. Lift the bat off the wheel. When soft-leather-hard, attach a handle opposite the spout.

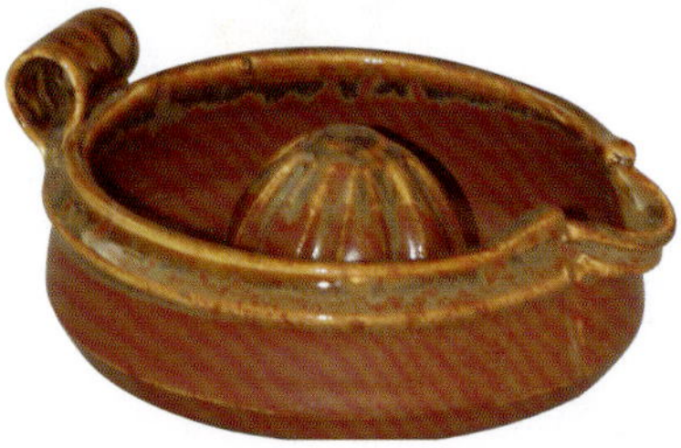

Finished juicer by Dannon Rhudy, 6 inches in diameter, fired to cone 6 with iron red glaze.

RECIPE

Unbaked Cheesecake (Gluten-free)

1 cup almonds
½ cup dates
½ lemon, grated rind and juice
½ tablespoon plain gelatin
1 cup cream cheese
1 farm-fresh egg*
¼ to ½ cup raw honey*

Grind almonds in food processor; add dates and process into tiny crumbs. Press date/almond mixture into 8-inch buttered pie dish. Put lemon juice into small bowl and sprinkle with gelatin. Allow to dissolve, then place bowl into a pot of simmering water until gelatin mixture warms and melts. Separate egg. Place cream cheese, egg yolk, grated lemon rind and ¼ cup honey into bowl of food processor and process until smooth, then pour in gelatin mixture and process again. Taste and add honey if needed. Beat egg white until stiff with a pinch of cream of tartar; fold in cream cheese mixture. Pour into crust and chill several hours. Double this recipe for a 10-inch pie dish. May use a baked pie crust instead.

*Since the egg will be raw it must be a farm-fresh egg from a trusted source! And you might as well use local raw honey since it won't be heated.

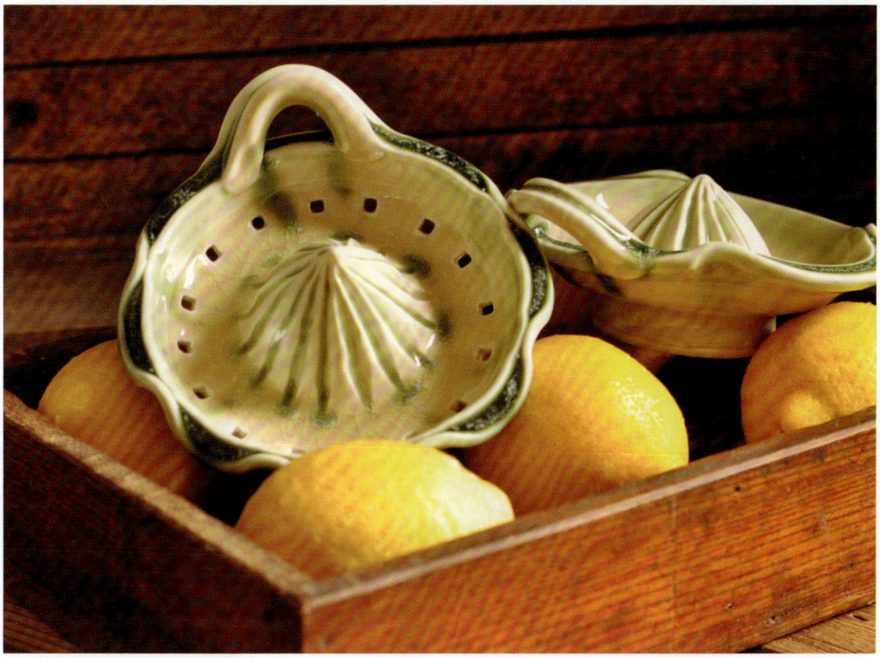

Citrus juicer by Lucy Fagella, 5 inches in diameter, porcelain, cone 6 oxidation. Photo by Lucy Fagella

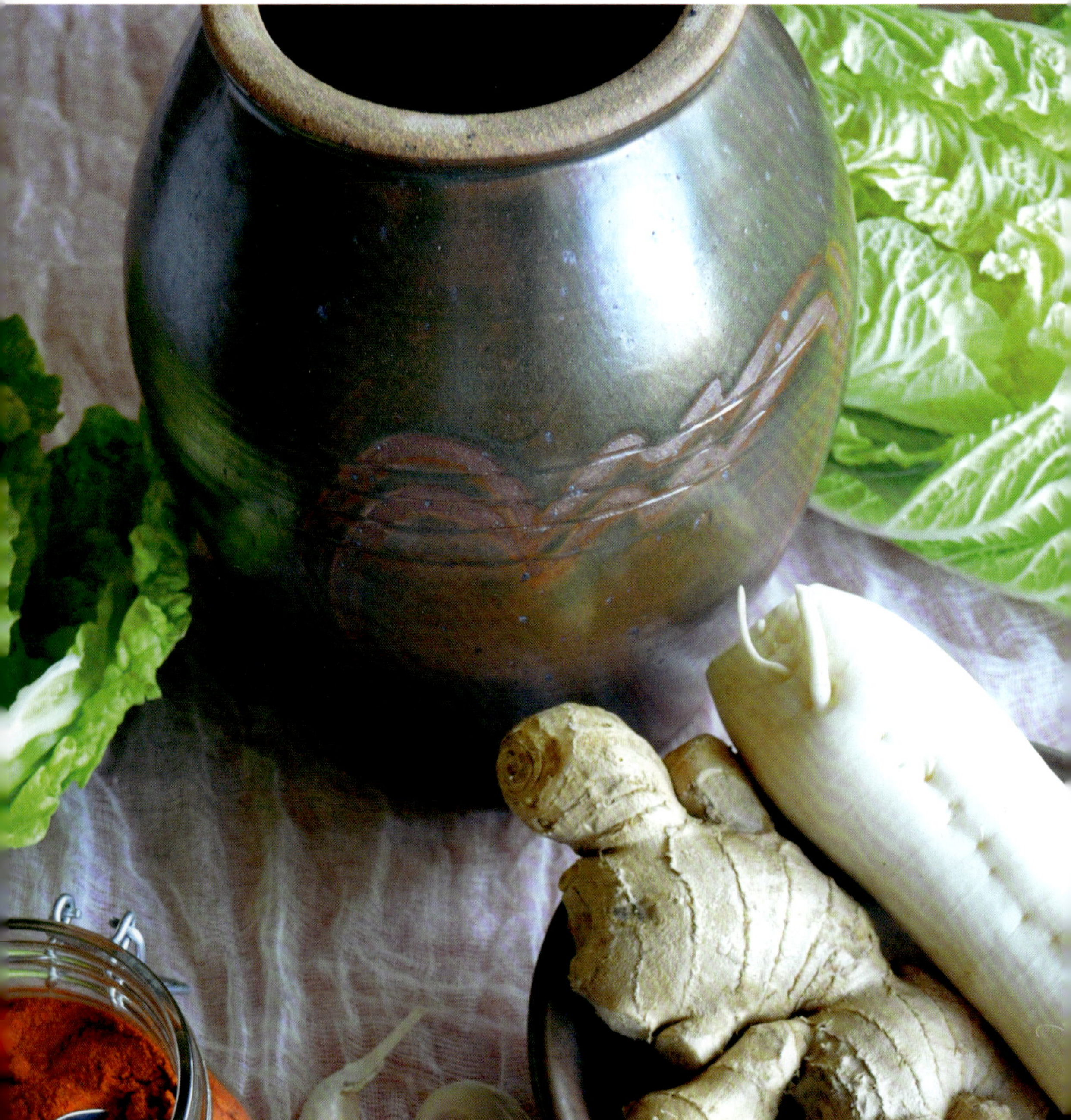

CHAPTER 9

Storage Ware

Pots for storing food need lids. For many lidded containers it doesn't matter what kind of clay they are made from; and if they will be holding dry foodstuffs it doesn't really matter whether they are vitrified or porous.

Cookie Jars

Probably the most ubiquitous pot for storing things in is the cookie jar. Every household has one, and it should be pretty or cute because it sits on the kitchen counter, and also sturdy because kids reach into it. About the only criterion to judge a cookie jar by is this: is the opening big enough to get your hand in—and back out—with a cookie in it? Usually a cookie jar has a slightly domed lid without a flange. This matters. The gallery should be on the jar and the lid should be a simple dome, because if there is a flange on the lid, the user will have to leave space above the cookies for the flange to fit in. This means filling the jar, putting the lid on, then taking a couple of cookies out to get the lid to sit right.

Canisters

Other basic storage forms are canisters, usually made as sets in graduated sizes for storing flour, sugar, coffee, or other dry goods such as herbs or salt. Canisters are usually fairly tall and straight-sided to use counter space efficiently, with any kind of lid. Just be careful they fit on the counter underneath the cupboards. A special category of canister is the tea caddy for keeping loose-leaf tea or tea bags. A tea caddy needs to be smaller than a flour canister since tea is used in small quantities and loses flavor if stored too long.

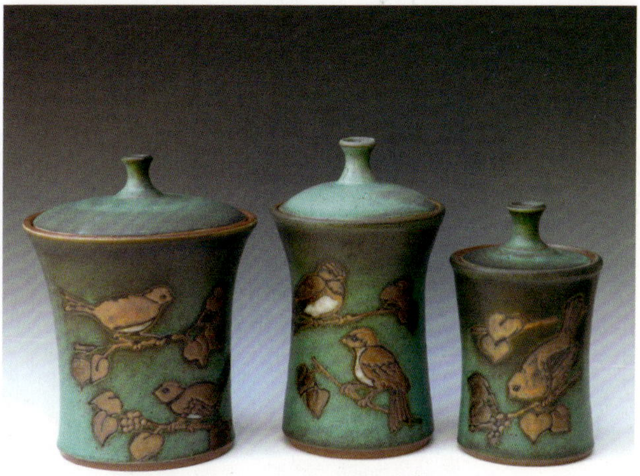

Canister set by Dana Lehrer Danze, 10, 9, and 8 inches in height. Stoneware, oxidation fired to cone 6. Photo by Dana Lehrer Danze

Onggi jar by Adam Field with kim chi ingredients—napa cabbage, daikon radish, ginger, garlic, and red pepper. Photo by Jani Uusi-Pantti

Butter Crocks

If you make and sell lidded pieces you usually don't have to tell your customers what to do with them—if they are looking for a cookie jar or canister, they'll know what they want (although it can't hurt to put a favorite cookie recipe in a cookie jar). But there are some special lidded forms that do need instructions. One of these forms is the French butter crock. These crocks are for households that use butter on a daily basis, say for spreading on your morning toast and your mashed potatoes at dinner. Rather than getting the stick of butter out of the refrigerator and waiting for it to soften, you keep the butter in the butter crock and it stays fresh and spreadable. The butter crock is a simple cylinder with a special kind of lid. The lid has a flange on it that is almost as deep as the crock, and the butter is packed into this lid. What keeps the butter fresh is a small amount of water in the crock, just enough to touch the lip of the lid to seal it from air circulation. In most climates, water is enough to keep the butter fresh, but if the temperature is hot enough to melt butter, chipped ice can be added to the water.

The butter-holding portion of the lid should taper in just slightly, to keep the butter from sliding out, and you may also want to avoid using a very glossy glaze in the butter portion to help keep the butter in place. Some users in warm climates report that the butter keeps better if there are a couple of small holes in the sides of the butter chamber. When the crock is full, the butter covers these holes but as the butter is used, the holes allow the water level to rise inside the butter chamber. This way there is less air in the butter chamber to cause the butter to go rancid. Two or three holes at ½–1 inch vertical intervals are all that is needed. Some potters also put holes in the top of the butter chamber to help keep air pockets from forming as the butter is packed in.

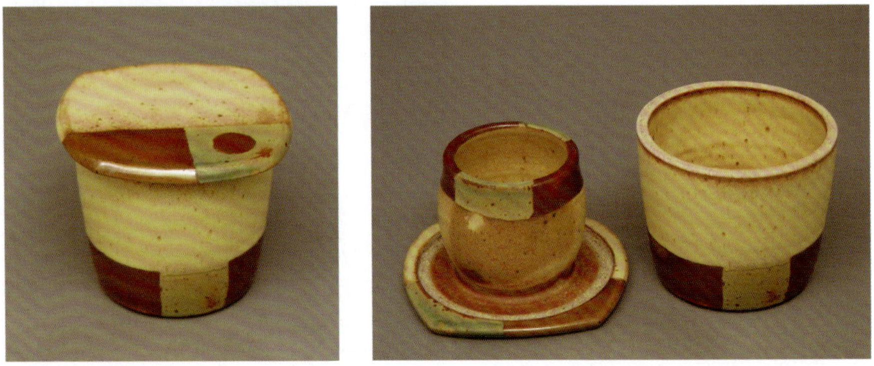

French butter crock by Lynn Hull, 4½ inches in diameter, reduction fired stoneware. Lynn fires the two pieces together, waxing the rim of the base as well as around the flange of the lid.
Photo by Sumi von Dassow

Butter crocks should be made of vitrified stoneware for two reasons: butter may seep into earthenware and go rancid eventually; and of course the base section of the crock must be vitrified or the water will seep through. Earthenware can be used for a butter crock if care is taken to make sure the glaze fits the clay well so it doesn't craze, and if the bottom is either glazed or coated with terra sigillata to make it leak-proof.

Pickling Crocks

Another very special kind of lidded form is the sauerkraut crock, or pickling crock. Traditional pickles are made by pouring brine over cucumbers and spices in a crock and placing a weight on top of the pickles to keep them under the brine until they ferment. Sauerkraut is made by shredding up cabbage and adding salt. The cabbage releases water and makes its own brine, but just like pickles, sauerkraut also needs to be held under the brine with a weight. This process takes days to weeks, depending on the ambient temperature and the desired degree of sourness. In the 21st century, of course, fresh, frozen and canned vegetables are easy to come by in the winter, but for thousands of years, before canning and refrigeration were invented, and before vegetables could be transported halfway across the world to be enjoyed out of season, fermenting was the only way people could preserve vegetables through the winter. Many modern fermenting enthusiasts use plastic buckets for this process, using a plate with a rock on top to weigh down the contents; but until the 20th century, the ceramic pickling crock was an important piece of kitchen equipment.

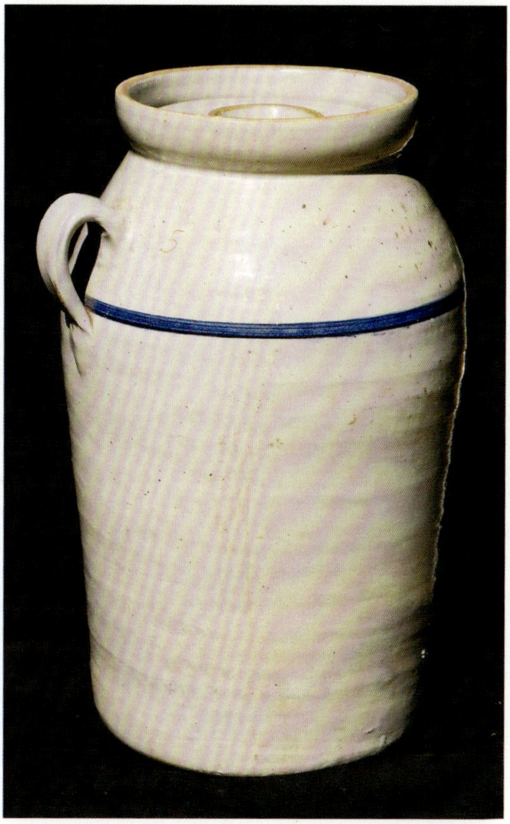

This is an image of a butter churn/pickling jar made by Jerry Brown sometime early in the 20th century. This is a five-gallon churn used for making butter or for pickling and preserving food. There is a hole in the lid to insert a dasher for butter-making; for pickling a cloth would simply be tied over the rim. Wood-fired stoneware. Photo by Jim Brown

Fermenting has become wildly popular lately among foodies and health nuts, and the production of ceramic pickling crocks is potentially a great business opportunity for potters. Vitrified stoneware clay with a carefully chosen non-crazing, food-safe liner glaze are the perfect materials for this purpose.

A pickling crock is a very simple form. It needs to be straight-sided, with walls slightly tapering out towards the top. This allows a weight such as a suitably sized plate or a disk of clay made to fit the crock, to be placed on top of the contents to keep the fermenting vegetables under the brine. This weight can be a heavy disk of clay, or sometimes two half-circles. The crock doesn't need to be covered with a lid in order for the contents to ferment properly, and many people whose grandparents kept a fermenting crock remember the crock in the pantry with a cloth tied over the rim to keep insects out. However, a simple lid is easier to use and clean than a cloth. The weight or disk should fit inside about half-way down, to allow the user to press down on the shredded cabbage as the crock is packed. Pressing hard on salted cabbage causes it to release liquid, and the weight must be sufficient to keep the shredded cabbage underneath this liquid. It can take quite a bit of weight to keep the developing sauerkraut submerged; and if it doesn't stay submerged, the part exposed to air will mold. If the ceramic weight isn't heavy enough, the user can weigh it down further with a rock, a jar of water, or a plastic bag full of brine. If the crock is stored between shelves in a cabinet, the disk can be held down with any suitable object and then actually wedged in against the shelf above!

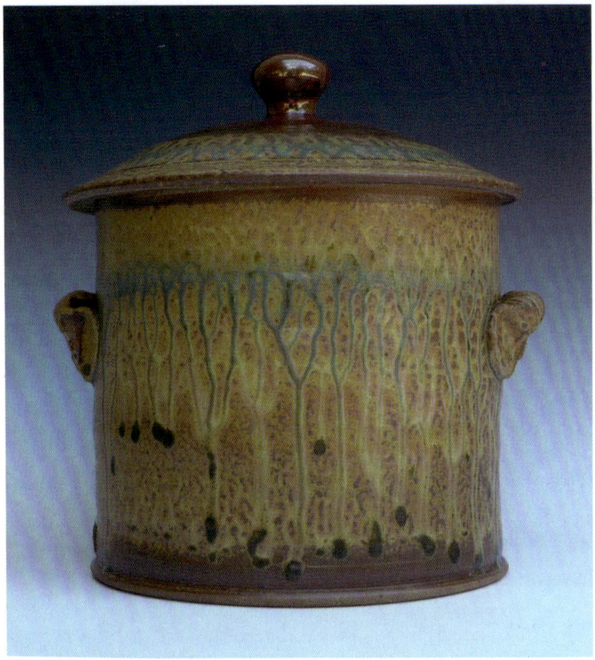

Sauerkraut crock by Mark Issenberg, 10 inches in height, reduction fired to cone 10 with layered sprayed ash glazes. Photo by Mark Issenberg.

Pickling and fermenting are arts as old and widespread as pottery, and the types of jars and crocks used for this process are many and varied. European and American picklers use crocks with a wide mouth and a weight that fits below the mouth. Korean pickling crocks, known as onggi pots and used to make kim chi, have a round shoulder with a slightly narrower neck and mouth. They are covered with a lid of the sort that might be referred to as a ginger jar lid—shaped like a toque hat or like a bowl turned upside-down. Koreans don't usually use a weight inside (maybe a clean rock) to keep the kim chi beneath the brine, but the narrow neck and wide shoulder ensures that the contents can't rise too far above the brine. It is also possible to weigh the ferment down in this kind of crock by using two matching semicircular pieces that can be maneuvered into position below the constriction of the neck. Once they are in place, the neck will keep them from floating up.

An ancient Chinese form of pickling crock uses an air lock to keep the fermenting vegetables from being exposed to air. This is a very simple and clever concept—the rim of the jar features a deep groove that the lid sits in. This groove is kept filled with water, so that carbon dioxide from the fermenting vegetables can escape but air can't get back in. As long as the groove is kept filled with water, the vegetables will keep fermenting without molding. Weights inside the crock are still used on top of the contents to keep the fermenting vegetables submerged in the brine. This form of crock is the gold standard for pickling crocks, allowing a ferment to be kept safely for many months without much attention other than keeping the groove in the rim filled with water.

The only really challenging aspect to making fermenting crocks is that they tend to range from large to very large. While it is perfectly possible to ferment in any size jar, in practice it is most useful to have a jar of at least half a gallon capacity. One average-sized cabbage fills a quart-sized jar, but if you are going to bother to shred cabbage and keep it in a jar for days or weeks, you really want to be able to prepare several cabbages at a time. With a large crock you can make lots of sauerkraut when cabbages are in season and keep it for months. While the basic form of a fermenting crock is very simple, just a wide-mouthed cylinder, making a large one may require eight or more pounds of clay. However, because the form is so simple, it is easy to throw it in multiple sections. A grooved rim, if desired, can be added as the last section.

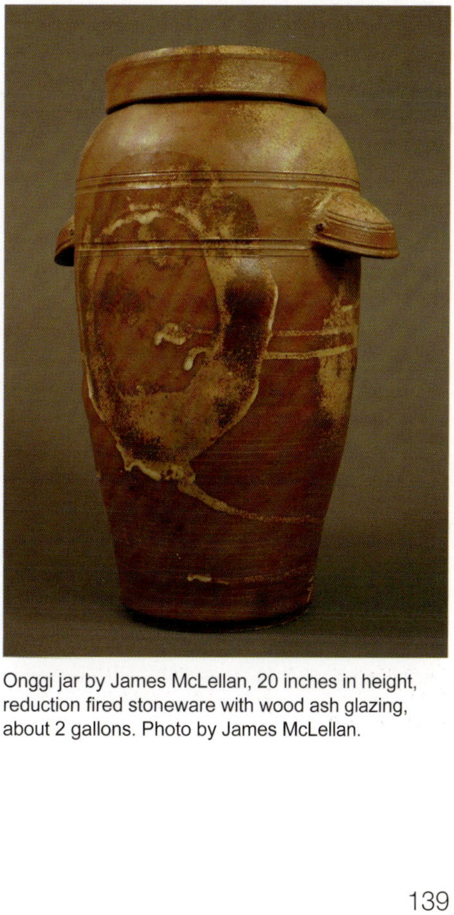

Onggi jar by James McLellan, 20 inches in height, reduction fired stoneware with wood ash glazing, about 2 gallons. Photo by James McLellan.

Adam Field specializes in extremely large onggi jars, which he makes on a kick wheel, building up the form with coils and using the wheel to smooth and shape the pot. He spent most of 2008 in Icheon, South Korea, studying traditional Korean pottery-making techniques

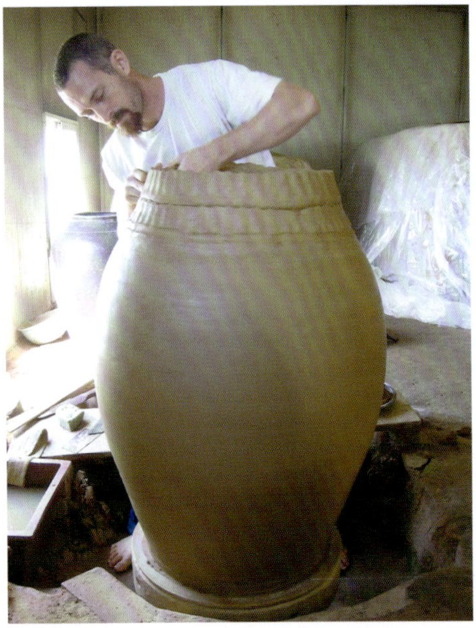

Adam Field adding coils to the top of a large onggi jar. The form is coil-built on the wheel, starting with a slab base. Coils are added a few at a time. Paddles and ribs are used as the wheel spins, to shape and smooth the pot inside and out. Photo by Adam Field

under 6th generation Onggi master Kim Il Mahn. He has since returned to the United States and makes large onggi jars for American connoisseurs. His jars vary from the size of an apple up to 125 liters—but one to three gallon jars are the most popular.

Not all pickle recipes require long-term fermenting. Many vegetables can be pickled in vinegar in a few hours to a few days. For this type of quick pickling, a relatively small jar with a well-fitting lid that can easily fit in your refrigerator is all you need. These recipes don't require salt and don't rely on lactic acid fermentation to develop flavor; the acid in the vinegar, and whatever herbs and spices are added, is all that is needed to flavor the vegetables.

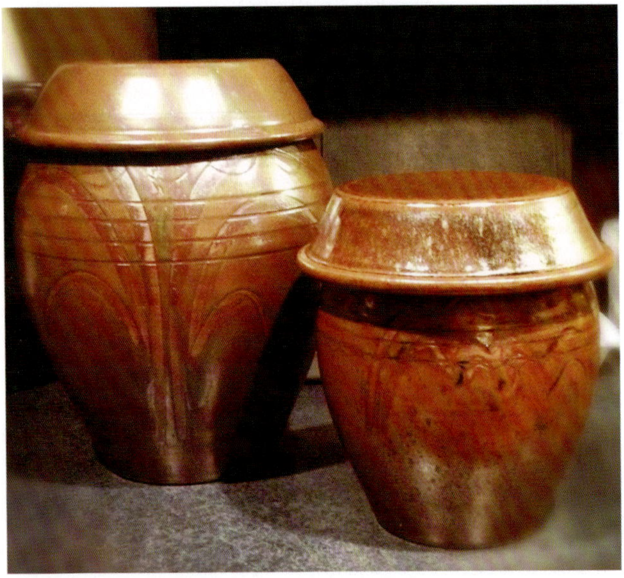

Onggi jars by Adam Field, cone 10 reduction. 2 to 3 gallon jars, 14 to 18 inches tall. Onggi jars are the traditional fermenting jars found in Korea. Photo by Adam Field

Salt Pigs

One commonly used kind of storage pot doesn't require a lid. This is the salt pig, which is very popular among cooks. Stored on the kitchen counter, next to the stove, it allows a busy cook to spoon salt into recipes with one hand. Though many potters make stoneware salt pigs, traditionally this form is made from earthenware and the interior is left unglazed to allow the porous clay to absorb moisture and keep the salt from clumping. Perhaps this feature is not necessary with regular table salt which contains anti-caking agents, but sea salts often do form clumps in a shaker. There isn't any one correct form for a salt pig, but the traditional one is shaped like a bent chimney-pipe. Another popular style is shaped like an egg standing on end, with a hole cut in the side. The opening faces forward instead of up, allowing the salt to be spooned out conveniently, and helping to keep dust and cooking debris out of the salt. A salt pig is a very handy pot to have nearby while you are making sauerkraut.

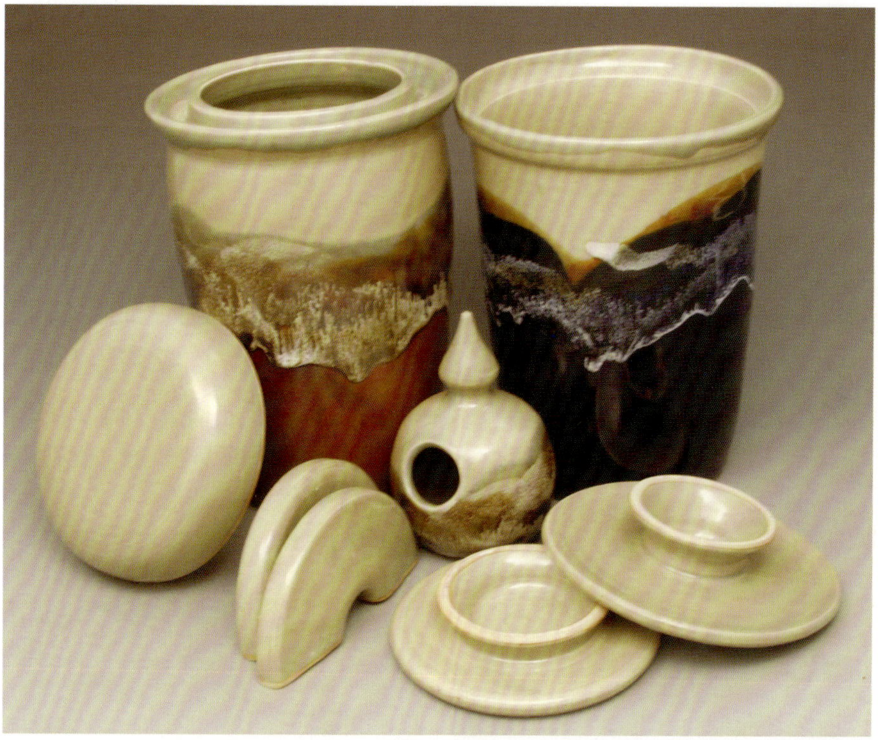

Two fermenting crocks with a salt pig by Sumi von Dassow showing lids and weights. The crock on the left has an air-lock rim. The lid fits in the channel that is filled with water during fermentation to allow carbon dioxide to escape and prevent oxygen from getting in. The contents are weighed down with the two semi-circular pieces. The other crock has a simple disk for a weight, which is used to press the contents down under the brine. Extra weight is often added by placing a clean rock or other heavy object such as Baggies filled with salt water on top of the disk. Crocks about 11 inches in height, reduction-fired to cone 7. Photo by Sumi von Dassow

PROJECT 1: Making a French Butter Crock

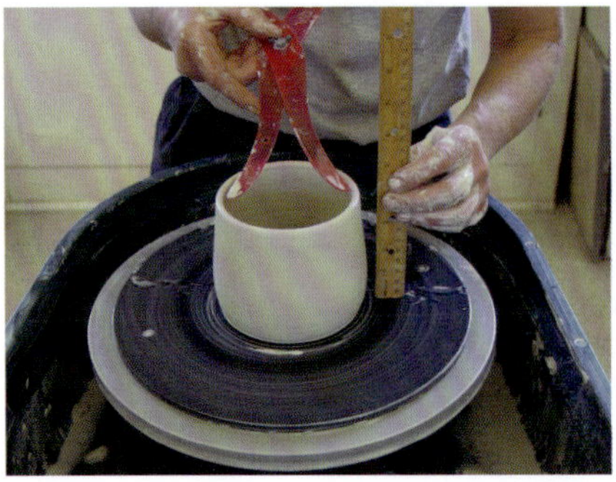

Using 1 to 1½ pounds of clay, throw a cylinder leaving ¼ inch of clay on the bottom, no need to trim a foot. Measure inside the rim and the height using Lid Master calipers.

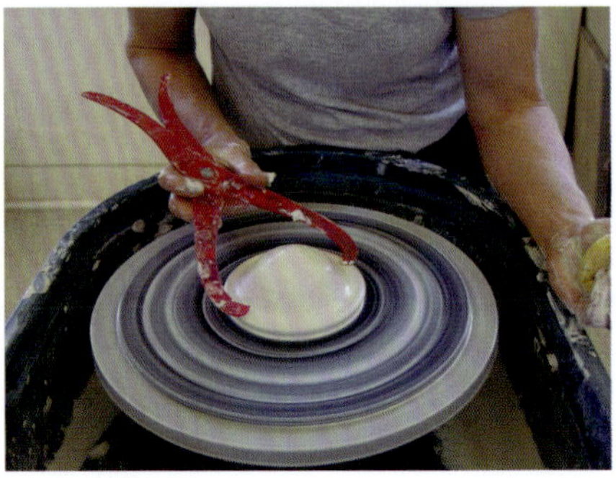

Use a little less clay for the insert. Open it wider than your caliper measurement. Push the edge of the clay flat and start pulling up a cylinder from the rest.

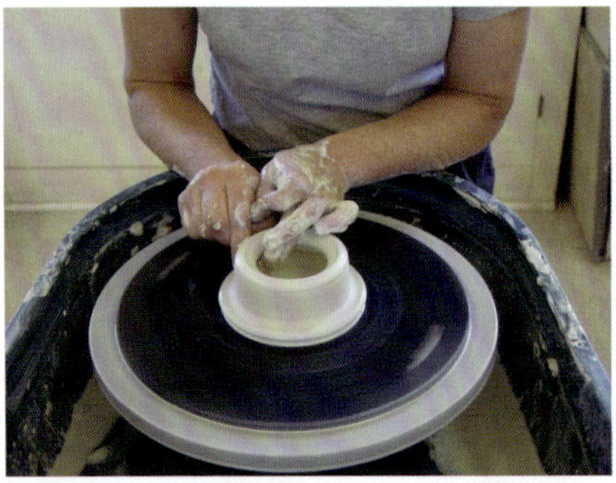

Leaving the outer edge flat, pull the central cylinder up to slightly less than the height of the base section. The top of the crock should end up about ½ inch shorter than the base.

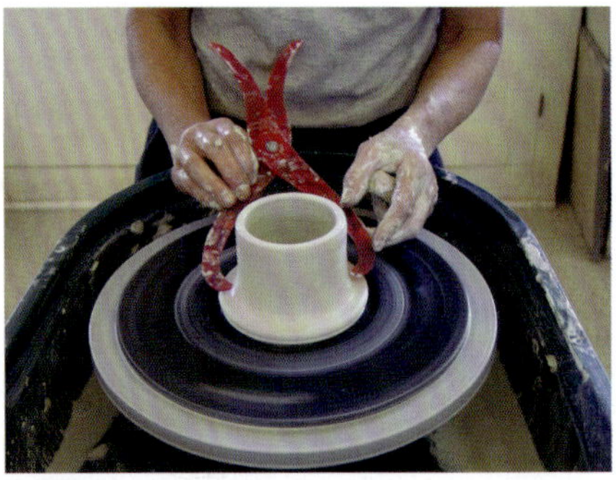

Measure the lid and make sure one end of the caliper set fits inside the rim of the base, and the lid fits inside the other end of the caliper set. Make sure the lid is ½ inch shorter than the base.

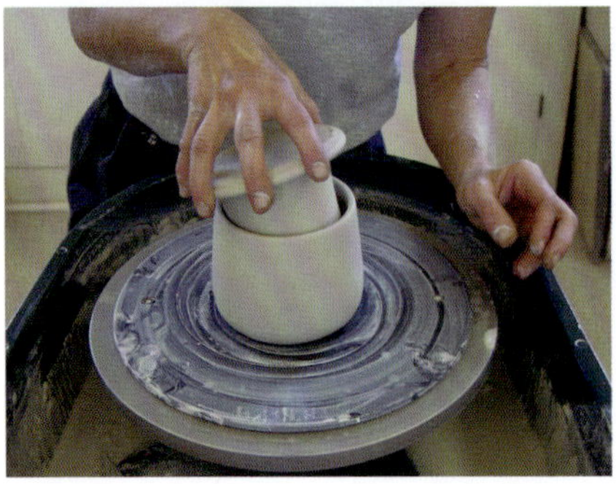

When the two pieces are leather hard, try them together. The lid should fit snugly inside the base, and it should be about ½ inch shorter.

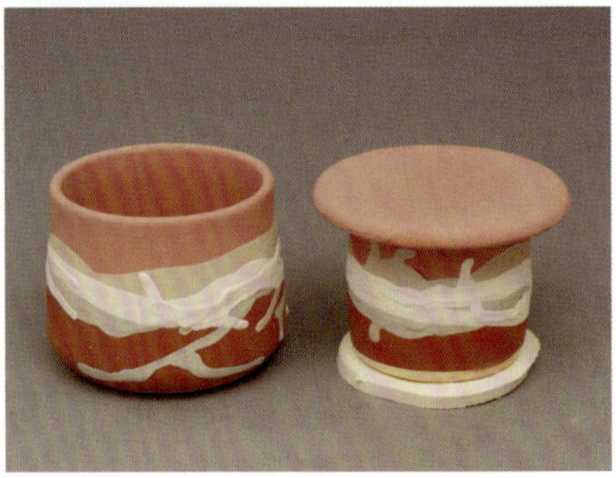

The glazed butter crock ready to be fired, showing the top on a "sacrificial slab."

Firing Note: The two pieces will be fired separately to avoid leaving the rim of the base and the corresponding area on the top unglazed. This requires firing the lid on a "sacrificial slab" so that the long flange won't be deformed by shrinking in the firing. A "sacrificial slab" is a bisque-fired disk of clay that the piece is placed on for the glaze firing. The disk shrinks evenly in the firing, allowing the piece placed on it to shrink with it and avoid deformation. Without this disc, the lid will tend to become oval or irregularly shaped in the firing and might not fit properly into the base after firing.

How to Fill Your Butter Crock

from Gayle Bair

1. **Allow a stick of butter to get almost to room temperature.**
2. **Remove wax paper from butter.**
3. **Place stick vertically into butter chamber.**
4. **Place wax paper on top of the stick of butter.**
5. **Placing the heel of your hand on the wax paper, mash the butter into the chamber. If necessary use your fingers (keeping wax paper in place) to push butter more tightly into the chamber. The chamber doesn't need to be full to the brim.**
6. **Put ¼ to ½ inch cool water in the base of the butter crock.**
7. **If it is very warm, add chipped ice to the water.**
8. **Put the top on the crock. Don't worry about the butter getting wet—the water will be displaced by the butter chamber but it won't go inside.**

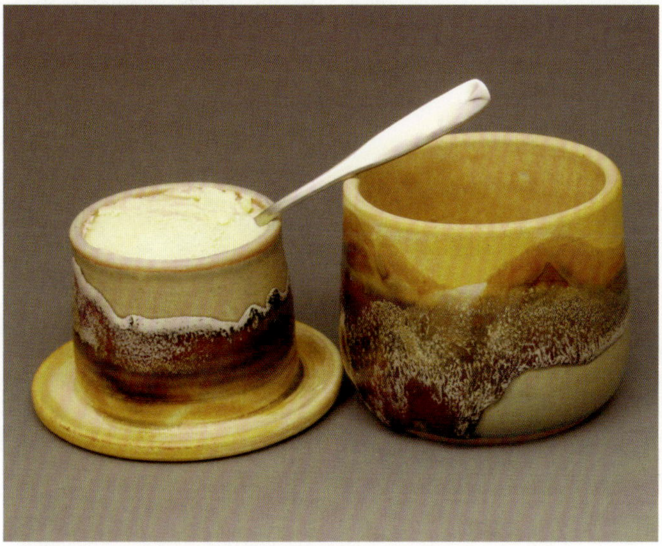

Butter crock with butter by Sumi von Dassow, stoneware, cone 7 reduction-fired. Photo by Sumi von Dassow

PROJECT 2: Making a Salt Pig

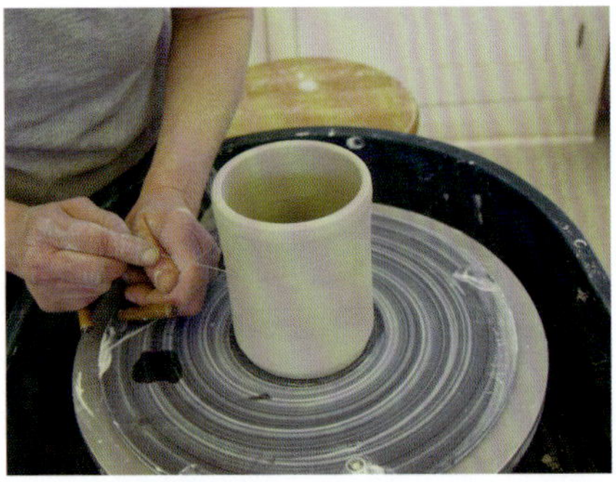

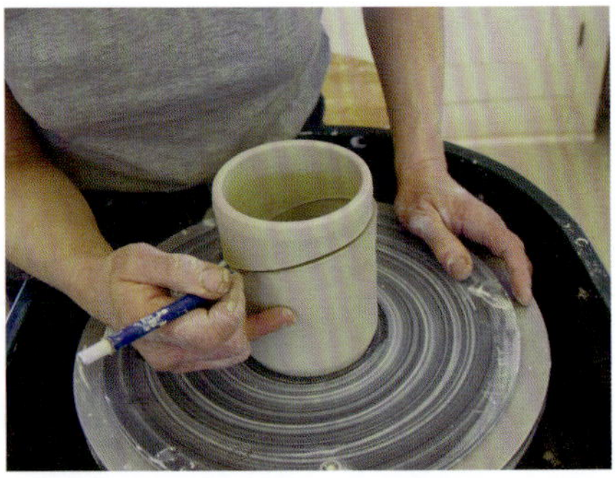

Throw a simple cylinder from 1¼ lb of clay. When the cylinder has set up a bit, but before it is fully leather-hard, use a cutting wire to mark a slanted line around it, from about ½ inch below the rim on the side away from you down to about an 1 or 1½ inches below the rim on the side close to you. Press the wire (don't cut) so you can see the mark. Cut rim at a 45° angle, angling up.

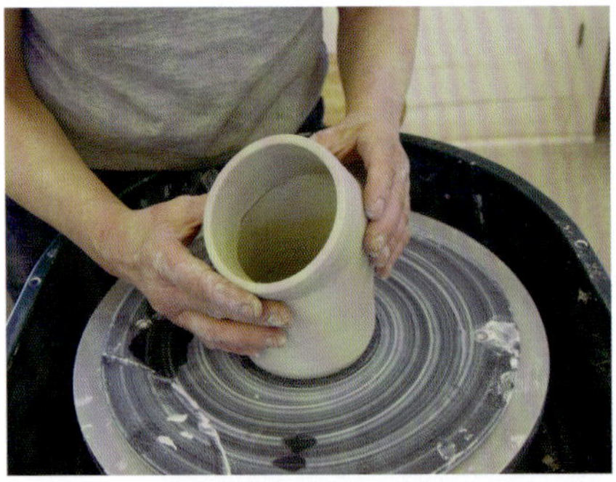

Turn the top section 180° and set it back on to see how it fits.

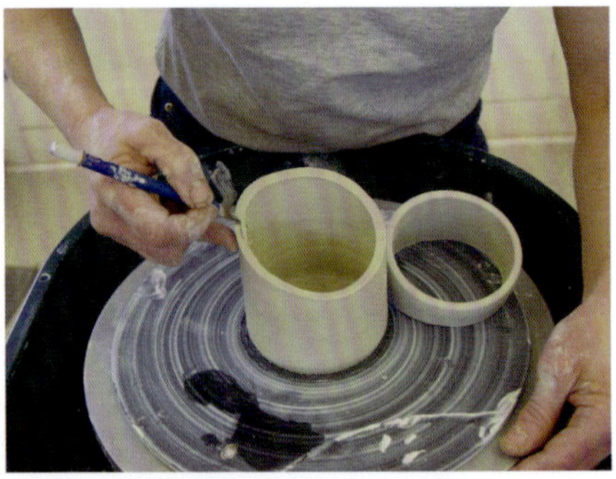

Bevel the inside edge of both pieces. Use magic water to join them then add a small coil in the joint if necessary. You might not need a coil if the clay is soft enough and the cut is very accurate.

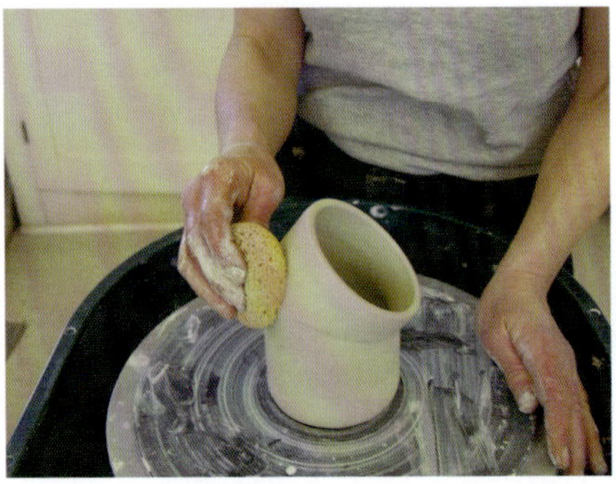

Smooth the join carefully inside and out with fingers, a soft rib, and a sponge.

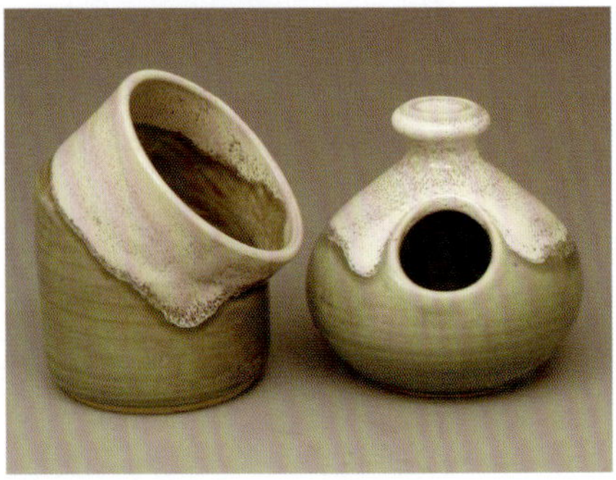

These are two common designs for salt pigs. The one on the right is preferred by cooks who like to use a spoon for salt and the one on the left by those who add salt with their fingers.

PROJECT 3: Making a Sauerkraut Crock

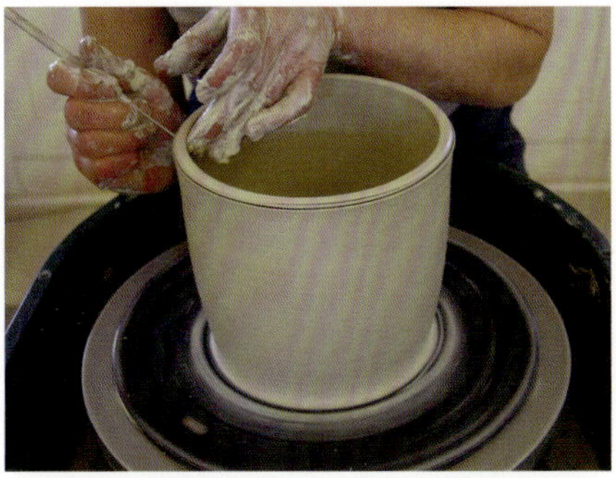
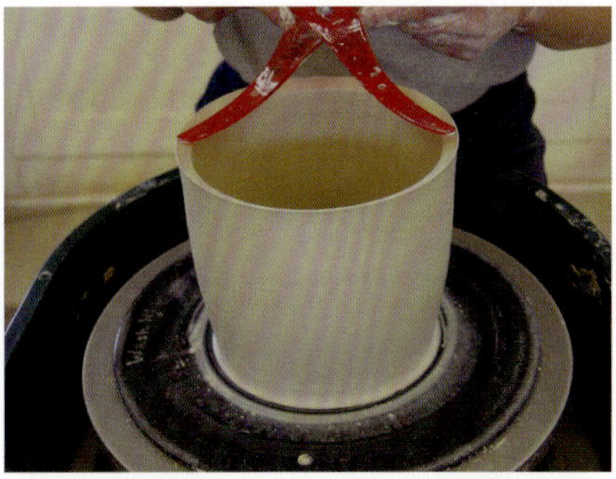

Using three or four pounds of clay, throw a cylinder. Leave only ¼ inch on the bottom—no need to trim a foot. Cut the rim of the cylinder at a 45° angle, angling down, with the outer edge higher than the inside edge. Set aside to dry, wrapping the rim with plastic to keep it from drying too much. Use calipers to measure the outer edge of the rim after cutting.

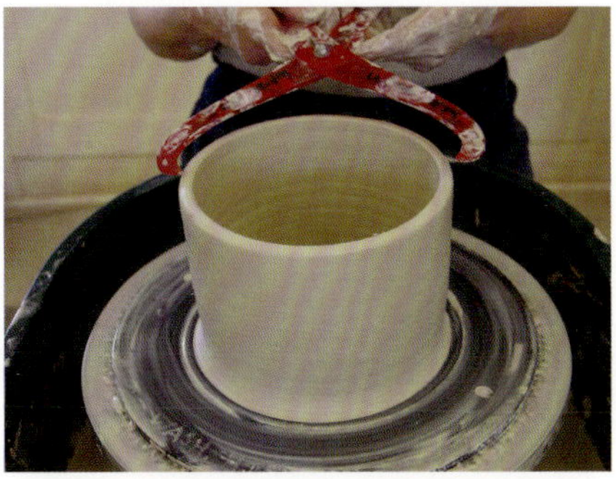
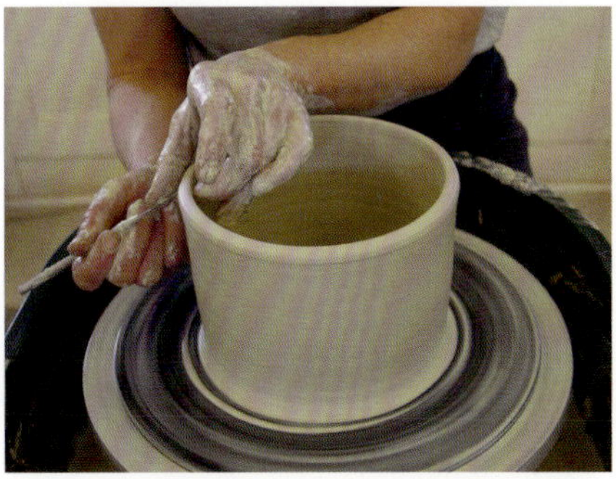

Using slightly less clay than for the first section, throw a second cylinder, opening all the way to the bat. This will be the top section. Measure the rim of this section to match the first section. You should try to make sure the rim of this section is about the same thickness as the rim of the first section so they will join together without trouble.

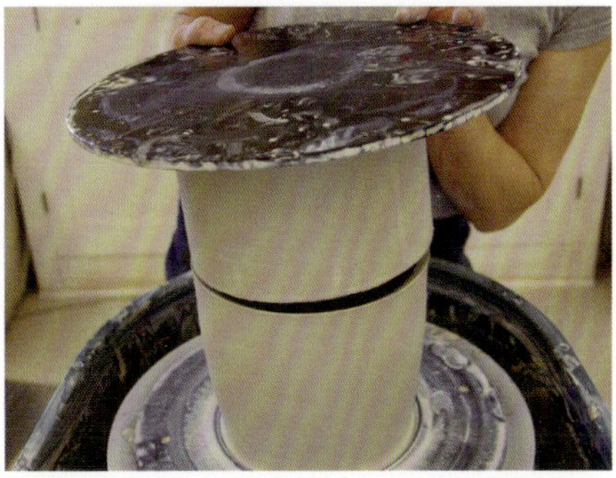
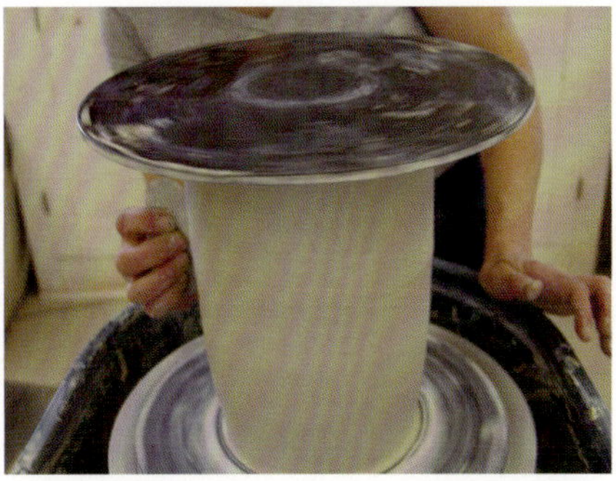

After both sections have had a chance to set up briefly (they should be nowhere near leather-hard yet) use a toothbrush to generously scrub both rims with magic water. Lift top section, flip it upside-down, and set it in place on top of the bottom section. Use a finger and a metal rib to smooth over the join.

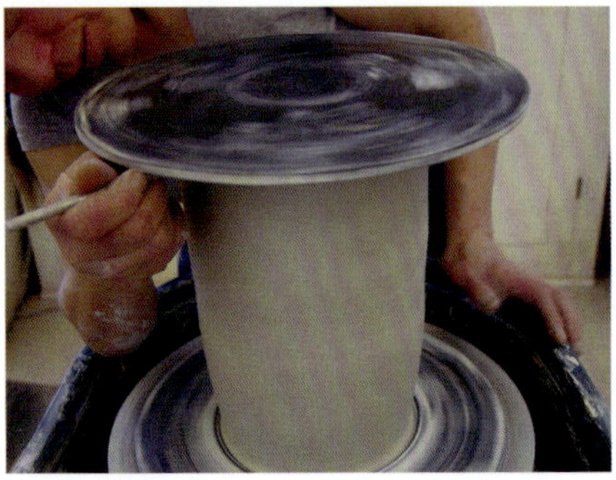

Use a needle tool to cut the bat away from the upper section.

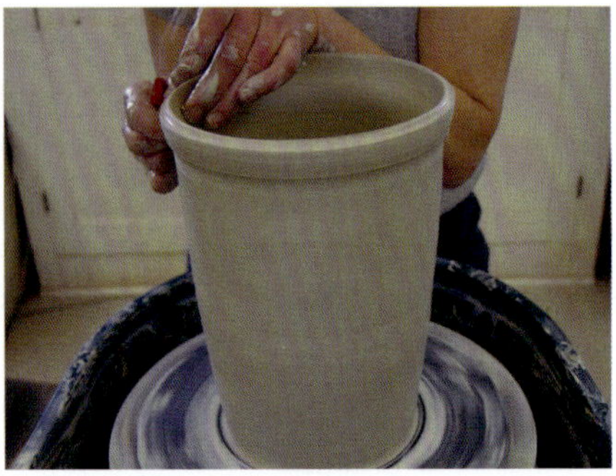

Smooth the join on the inside, then make a couple of pulls to make this section a little taller to create a slightly tapered cylinder, Use fingers and a rib, pull the rim out to make a simple gallery.

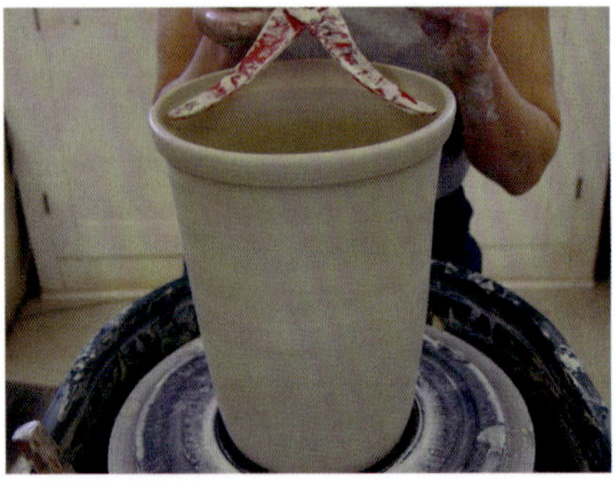

Use calipers to measure inside the gallery.

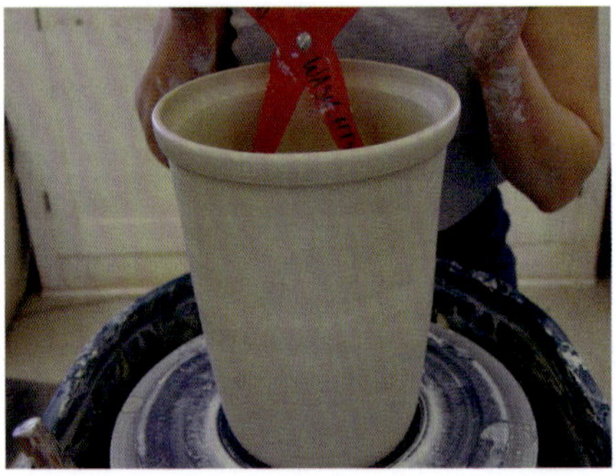

Use another set of calipers to measure about halfway down.

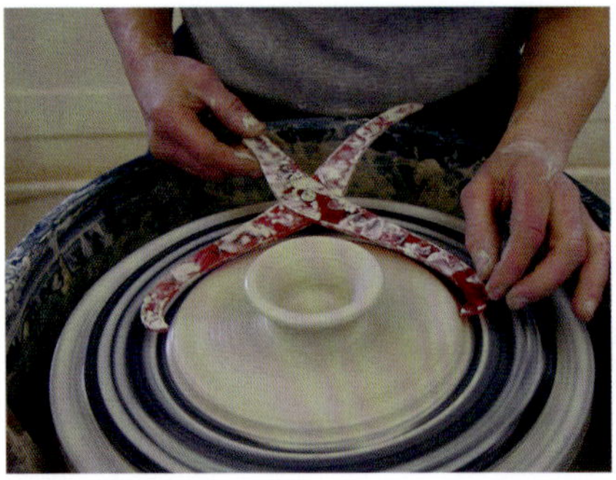

Using 1 to 1½ pounds of clay, make a simple lid, right-side-up, with a knob.

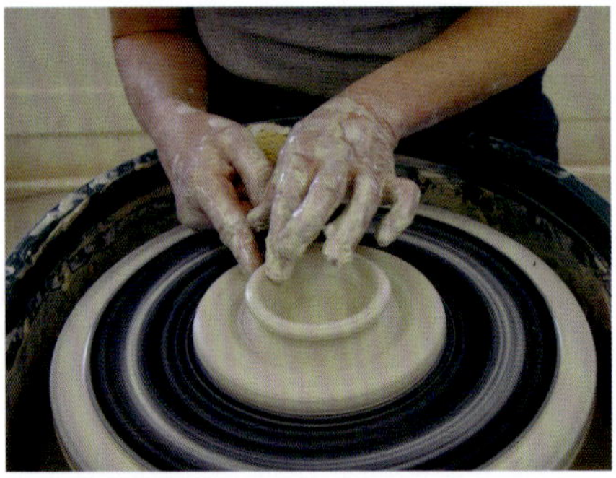

Using 1½ pounds of clay, make the disk that goes inside the crock to weigh down the contents. Throw a wide knob to allow the disk to be fired upside-down so only the knob rim is unglazed.

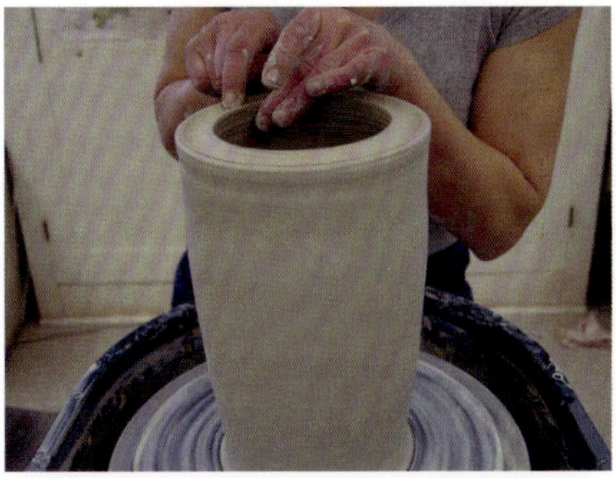

For an airlock rim, leave the second section a bit thick, except for the rim where it joins to the first section. After joining, pull up a couple of times to thin the top of the pot, but leave the rim quite thick.

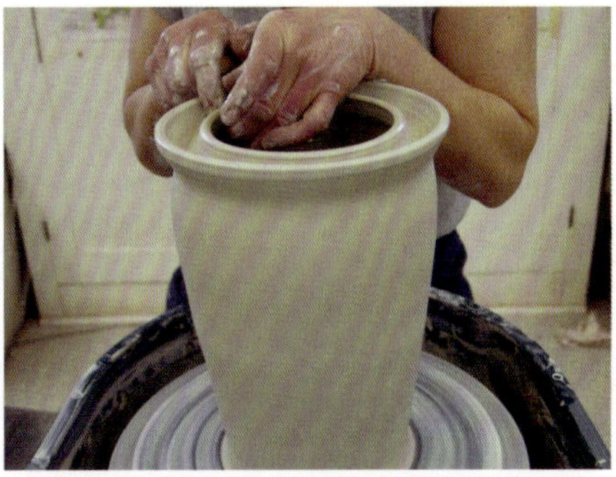

Deepen the groove by pulling up both an inner and an outer rim and finishing both with a chamois. The deeper the groove, the less often the user will have to top it up with water.

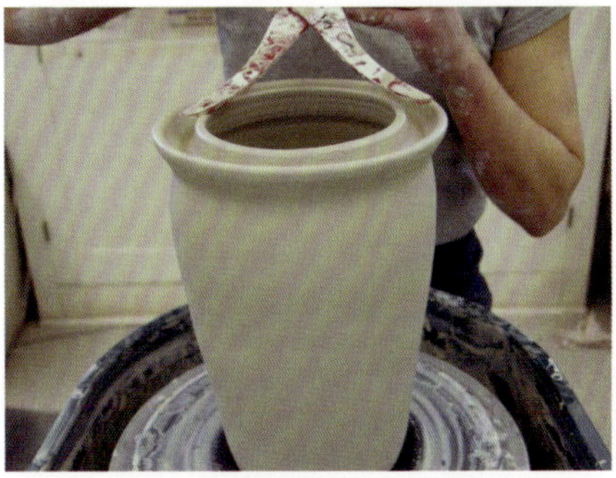

Use the calipers to measure across the channeled rim, taking a measurement about at the center of the groove.

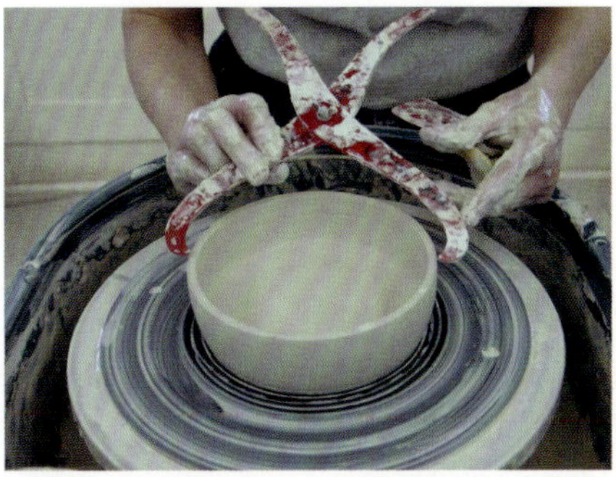

Throw a small bowl to match your caliper measurement. This will be the lid for the airlock rim.

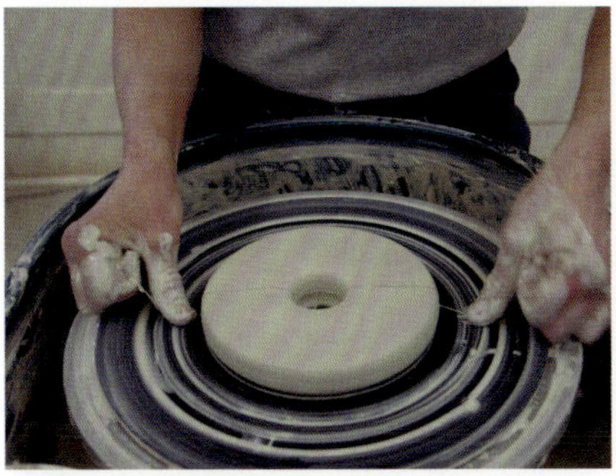

The rim of this jar is narrower than the shoulder of the pot so the weight that goes inside must be two half-disks. The hole in the center allows the user to place the weights in and to remove them.

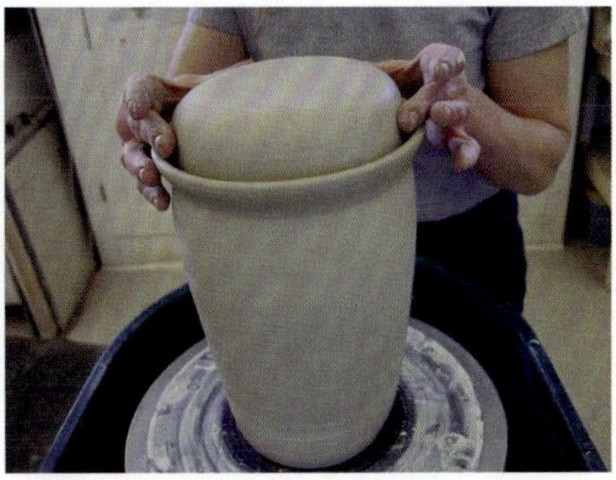

Remove the lid from the bat and trim it lightly. It doesn't need to have a knob on it since it can be grasped from the sides.

RECIPES FOR STORAGE WARE

Making Butter

16 ounces heavy whipping cream
¼ to ½ teaspoon salt

Allow cream to come to room temperature. Pour into the bowl of a stand mixer or food processor, or into a blender jar. Mix on high speed until you see clumps of butter sloshing around in buttermilk. Pour into a colander to drain off the buttermilk. Keep the buttermilk for making pancakes! Cover with very cold water and work butter with your hands to remove the rest of the buttermilk, or return to the blender or food processor with ice water to force out the buttermilk. Or just put the butter in a bowl and fold it with a butter knife to work out the buttermilk. Stir in salt to taste; this will help remove the last of the liquid and help preserve your butter. You will have about 6 ounces of butter and 10 ounces of buttermilk. If you want your butter to be yellow, be sure you get cream from grass-fed cows. Organic cream in spring or summer should come from grass-fed cows.

Flavored Butter

4 ounces fresh butter, salted or unsalted
2 tablespoon fresh herbs—parsley, chives, rosemary, mint, or your favorite herb

Garlic Butter

4 ounces fresh salted butter
3–5 cloves garlic, minced

Honey Butter

4 ounces fresh butter, salted or unsalted
1 tablespoon honey
Optional: pinch of cinnamon, ⅛ teaspoon vanilla extract

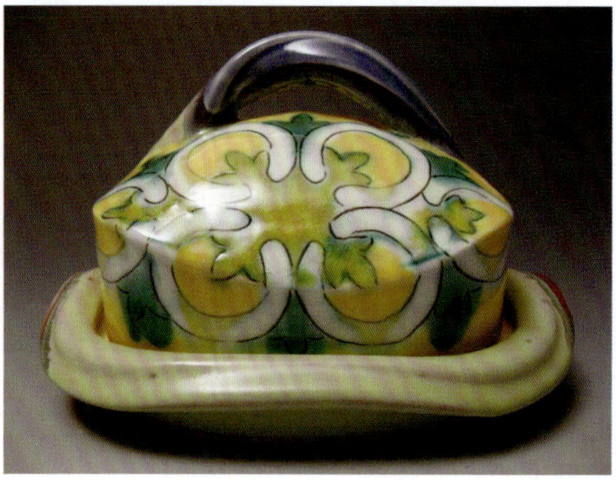

Butter dish by Joan Bruneau, wheel thrown and assembled earthenware with slip, sgraffito decoration and polychrome glazes.
Photo by Joan Bruneau.

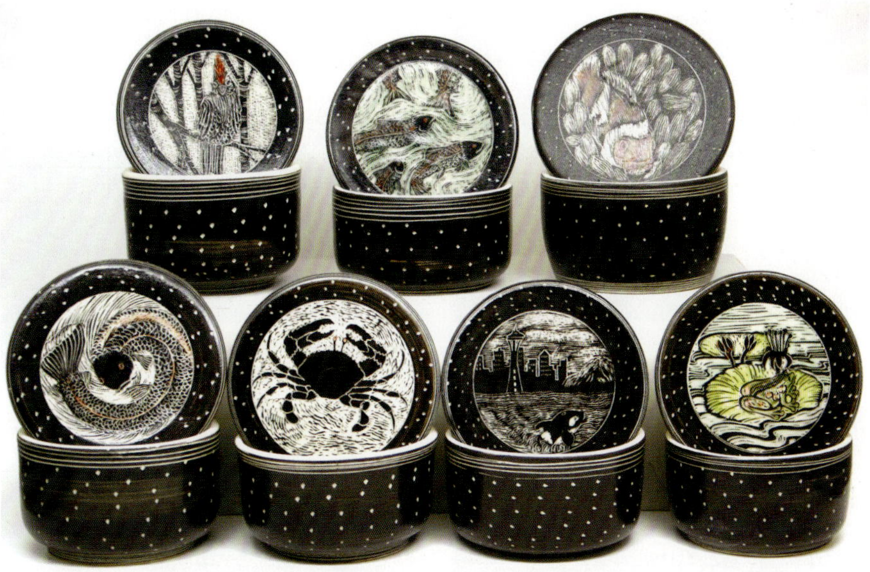

French butter crocks by Gayle Bair, 4½ inches in diameter, oxidation fired to cone 6, white stoneware with black slip and sgraffito decoration. Photo by Gayle Bair

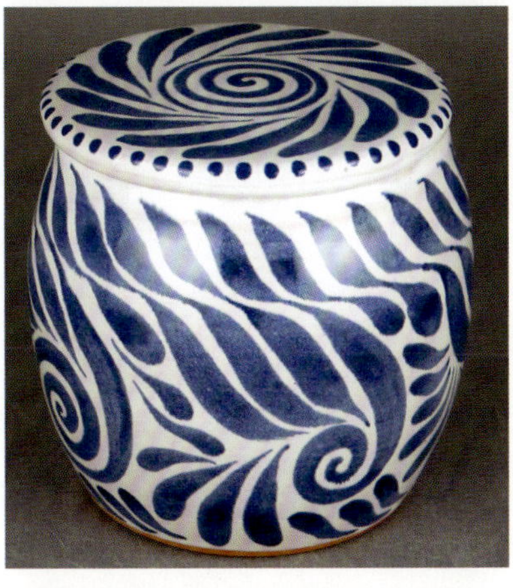

Butter keep by Eleonora Eden, 4 inches in height, earthenware. Eleonora puts holes in the sides of the lid to prevent air pockets from forming as one tries to pack butter into the chamber. This seems to be part of the traditional form that many modern potters don't bother to incorporate. Photos by Eleonora Eden.

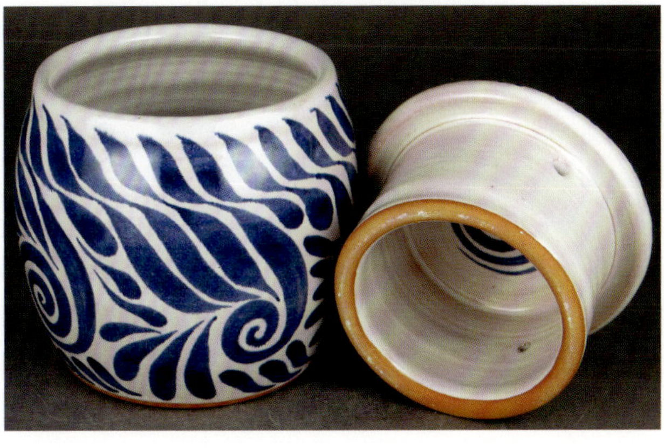

Using a Sauerkraut Crock

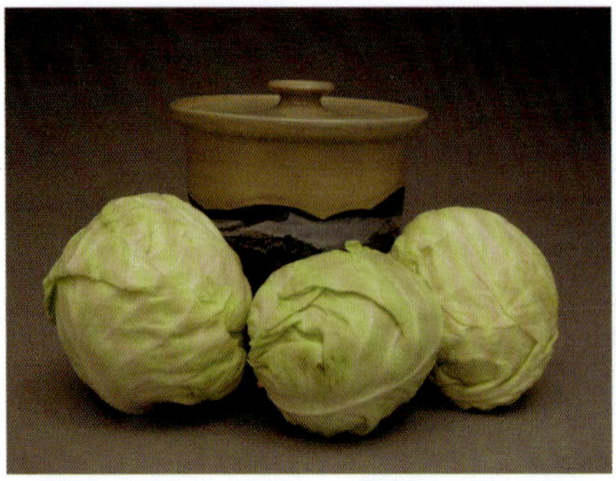

Three cabbages will fill this crock.

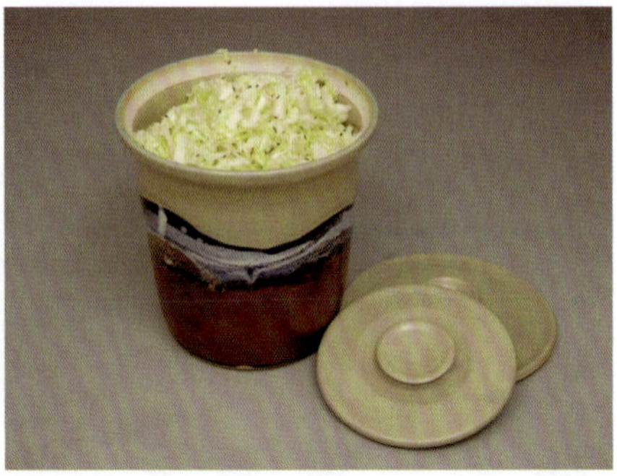

The cabbages shredded, mixed with caraway seeds and salt, and pounded to release juices.

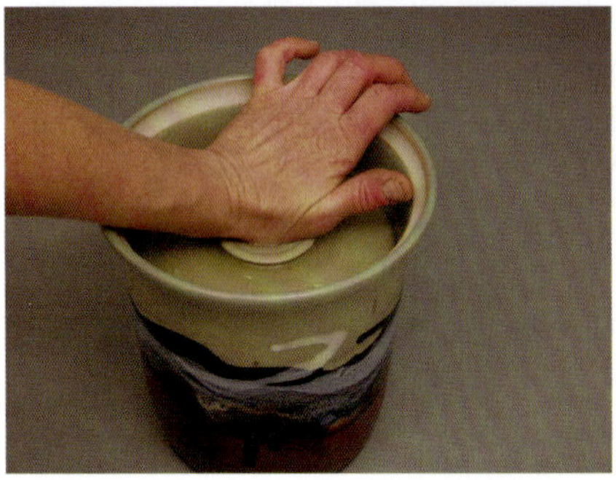

Press on the disk to push shredded cabbage under the brine. Add additional weight to keep the cabbage from pushing up the disk, cover the crock and set aside for several days or weeks.

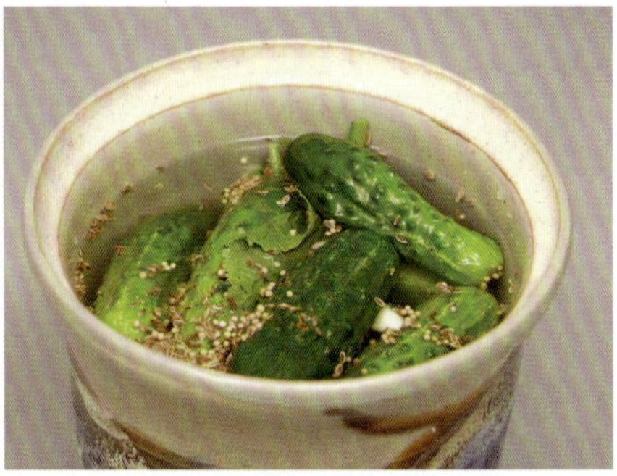

This crock is filled with pickling cucumbers and spices. Brine was added and the disk will be placed on top to hold the cucumbers under the brine, with no need for additional weight.

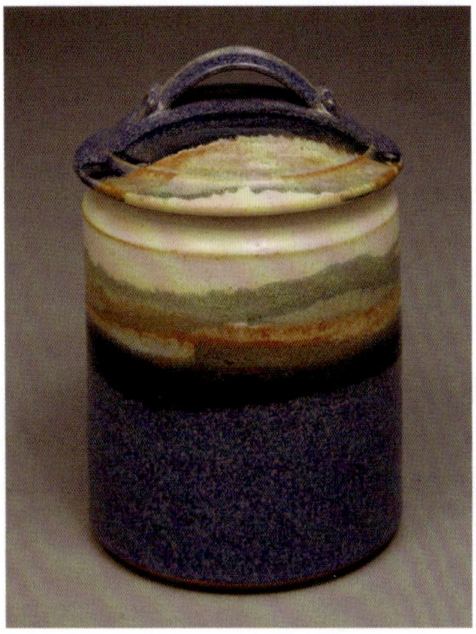

Canister/crock by Catherine Schroeder Abelson, 10 inches in height, stoneware, cone 6 oxidation. This multipurpose lidded jar is equally useful to store cookies or to make sauerkraut in. Photo by Sumi von Dassow

Sauerkraut

One head of cabbage, about 1½ pounds
1 tablespoon non-iodized salt, or sea salt
1 tablespoon caraway, fennel, or anise seeds (optional)

Shred cabbage finely. Place in a metal bowl and massage with your hands or pound with a meat mallet until the cabbage wilts and releases moisture. Pack into crock, pressing down firmly until liquid rises above the shredded cabbage. Place weight on top of shredded cabbage to keep it from floating up out of the brine. For additional weight, use any heavy object or a plastic zipper bag filled with brine (1 tablespoon salt per quart of filtered water, in case the Baggie bursts). Store crock below 80ºF and taste sauerkraut after a few days. Kraut will develop faster at higher temperatures; if kept below 60ºF, it may take a few weeks. When it tastes right, move the kraut to the refrigerator.

Recipe makes one quart; multiply as needed to fill crock. If you don't have enough cabbage to fill your crock, mix in grated or minced turnips, kohlrabi, beets, carrots, onions, leeks, or green onions. Add lemon juice, soy sauce (reduce salt if using soy sauce), crushed red peppers, ginger, or other seasonings if desired. You can be very creative!

Cucumber Pickles

for 1-gallon crock
3–4 pounds pickling cucumbers
6 tablespoons non-iodized salt or sea salt mixed into ½ gallon filtered (non-chlorinated) water
2 tablespoons dill seeds
2 tablespoons mustard seeds (optional) or other seasonings of your choice
Several cloves of garlic
A few horseradish, grape, or cherry leaves to preserve crispness (optional)

Wash cucumbers and remove blossom end. Pack into crock. Add dill and mustard seeds and garlic. Put in a few grape, horseradish, or cherry leaves if desired. Pour enough brine into crock to cover the cucumbers. Place weight on top of cucumbers to keep them from floating out of the brine. Store crock below 80ºF and taste pickles after a few days. Skim mold from surface of brine as needed. Pickles will develop faster at higher temperatures; if kept below 60ºF it may take a few weeks. You may use less salt in cooler temperatures, more if it is warm. When sour enough, store in the refrigerator.

Kim Chi

Kim chi is a recipe that isn't usually measured precisely, and the ingredients can vary greatly. This is a very simple version, omitting the traditional rice paste and salted fish, that will make about a gallon.

5 pounds napa cabbage (about two large heads)
5 green onions, sliced
1 cup chopped leeks
1 cup daikon radish, julienned or grated
½–1 cup carrots, julienned or grated
½ cup salt
1 tablespoon red pepper flakes (or more to taste)
1 tablespoon ginger
1 tablespoon or up to ½ cup garlic, minced
½ cup onion, minced
½ cup fish sauce (omit for vegetarian version)

Quarter cabbages and cut out core. Shred or slice cabbages, rinse, and sprinkle with salt. Mix and allow it to rest for 1½ hours, stirring a few times. Drain and rinse thoroughly. Mix the rest of the ingredients, then mix with the cabbage. Pack into a crock or onggi jar, pressing down until liquid rises above the vegetables. Keep in a cool place for a few days until it tastes good. If you omitted the fish sauce you might have to add filtered water, or simply omit the first step; just mix all ingredients with 4 tablespoons salt, then pack into crocks.

Fermented Summer Herbs

1 bunch of parsley or cilantro, chopped
A few cloves of garlic
Handfuls of sweet basil leaves, oregano leaves, chives and other herbs as available: thyme, dill, rosemary, sage
1 teaspoon salt, more or less

Make in the summer to save the flavors through the winter. Place herbs in food processor until everything is chopped fine. Pack tightly into a small crock, adding salt. You will need a smaller crock than you would think; use one teaspoon of salt per pint and pack in until liquid rises to the top. Cover and set aside in a cool place for several days or weeks.

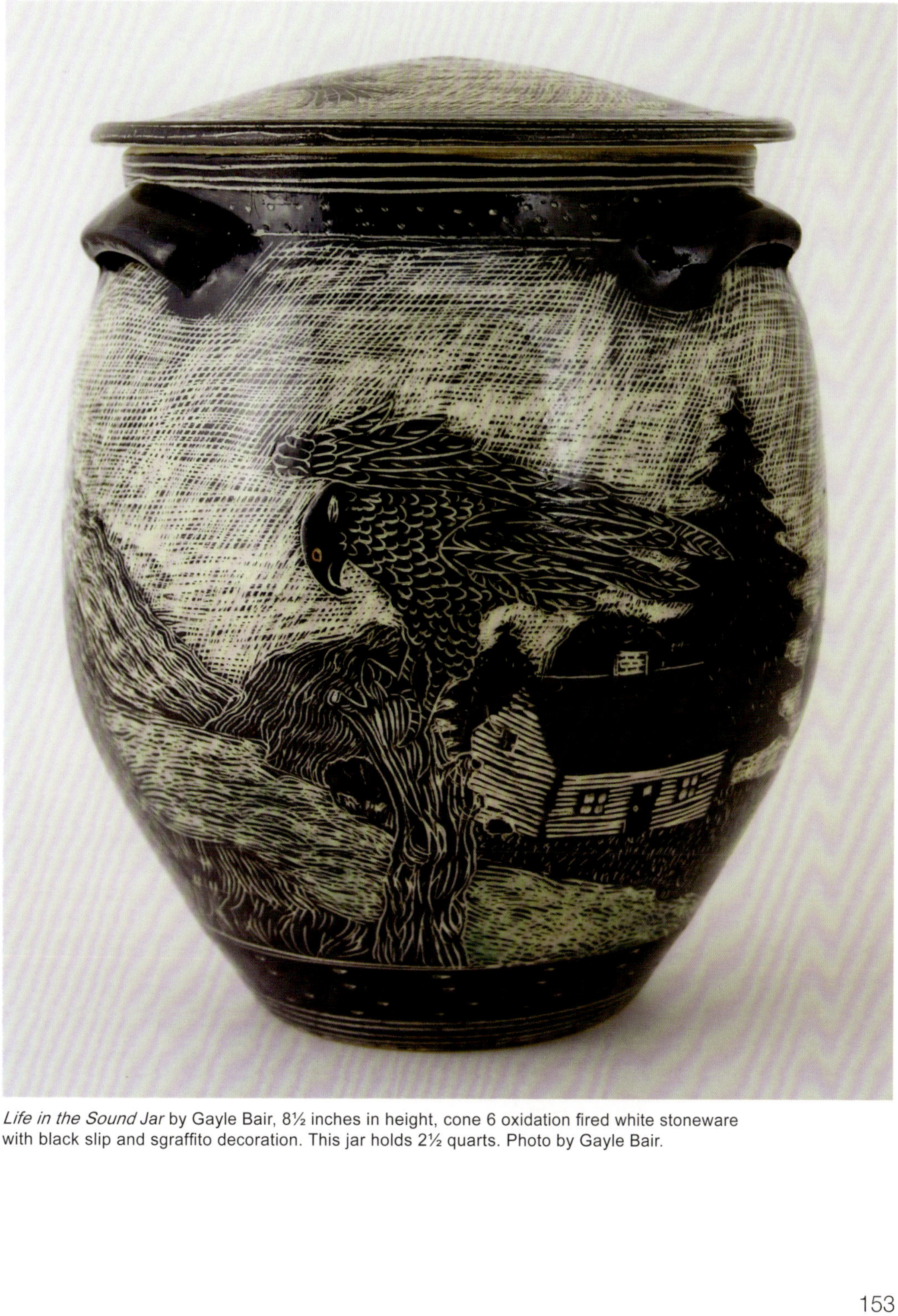

Life in the Sound Jar by Gayle Bair, 8½ inches in height, cone 6 oxidation fired white stoneware with black slip and sgraffito decoration. This jar holds 2½ quarts. Photo by Gayle Bair.

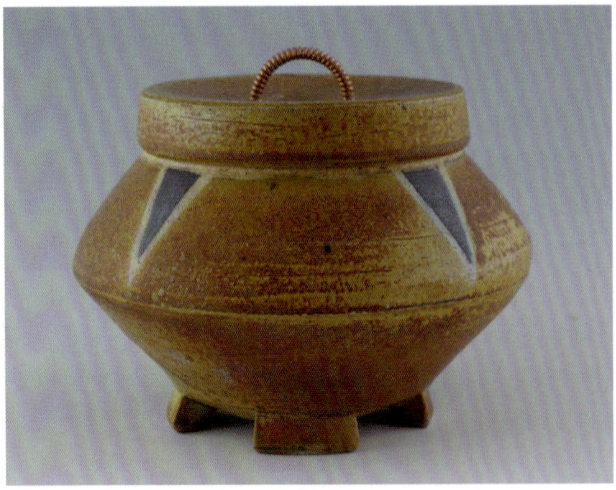

Audreanna's Tea Caddy by Jeff Oestreich, 5 inches in height, soda fired stoneware. In memory of Oestreich's mother, a pianist. The coiled copper handle is a bass string from a piano built in the year of Audreanna's birth. Photo by Jeff Oestreich

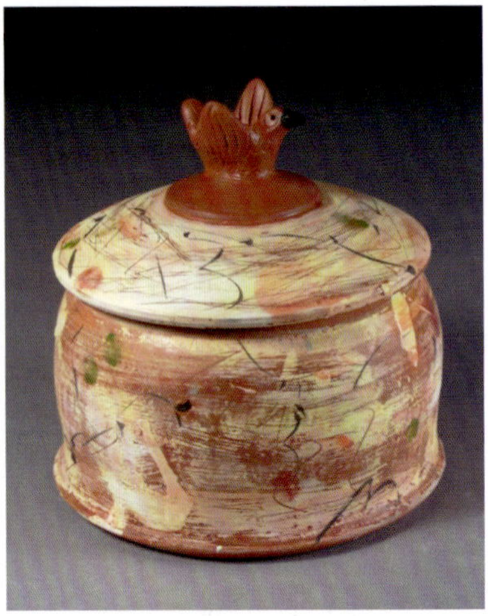

Tea caddy or small storage jar by Dianne Kenney, earthenware, 5½ inches in height. Photo by Dianne Kenney.

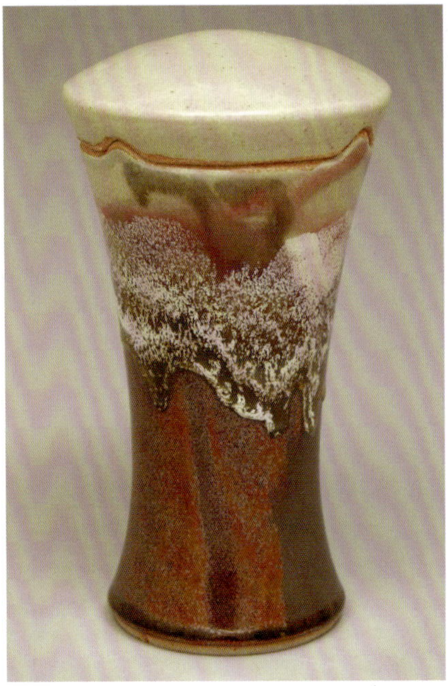

Parsley keeper by Sumi von Dassow, 8 inches in height, reduction fired stoneware. This is another special storage container. Parsley or other herbs are placed standing up in an inch of so of water, to keep them fresher longer. Depending on climate and how often you use parsley, it can be kept on the counter-top or in the refrigerator.

Pickled Cucumbers and Onions

Several peeled firm cucumbers (2 hothouse or 4–5 baby or pickling cucumbers, for a quart-size jar), washed and thinly sliced
1 mild onion, thinly sliced
Seasoned rice vinegar, enough to cover cucumbers
1–2 tablespoons olive oil
1–2 tablespoons chopped fresh parsley (or fresh dill)
Optional: garlic or other spices to taste

Combine ingredients in covered jar. Vinegar needs to cover cucumbers and onions. Refrigerate for several hours before serving.

Red Beet Eggs

2 cups white vinegar
2 cups sugar
1 bunch beets
8 eggs (older eggs are easier to peel)

Wash, peel and slice beets. Pour vinegar and sugar over beets in a saucepan and carefully bring to boil. Simmer beets until tender. Hard boil eggs in water then peel carefully so the whites are not broken or damaged. Placing eggs in ice water aids peeling.

Place eggs in jar then pour beet liquid over the eggs. Place beets in a separate jar to keep them from acquiring an egg flavor. The eggs and beets should be completely covered with liquid. Let cool then refrigerate for 3 days or until the whites turn completely red. Serve in slices or wedges.

Chai Mixture

1 cup loose-leaf black tea
1 tablespoon toasted fennel seed
1 tablespoon cinnamon chips (put a cinnamon stick in a spice grinder and pulse a few time)
16 black peppercorns
16 cloves
16 cardamom pods
1 teaspoon ground ginger

Combine all ingredients. Keep in a covered tea caddy. To make tea, add 1 tablespoon chai mixture to 1 cup boiling water. Cover and let steep for ten minutes. Strain into a cup and add honey and half-and-half or cream to taste.

List of Contributing Artists

Catherine Schroeder Abelson

Gayle Bair
www.claybair.com

Margaret Bohls
www.margaretbohls.com

James Brown

Joan Bruneau
www.joanbruneau.com

Patricia Burns
www.fernhillpottery.net

Jan Cameron
www.janmica.com

Dana Lehrer Danze
danalehrerdanze.com

Elise Delfield
pincupottery.com

Alice DeLisle

Eleonora Eden
www.eleanoraeden.com

Lucy Fagella
lucyfagellapottery.wordpress.com

Adam Field
adamfieldpottery.com

Robin Furuta

Anita Garfein

Lynn Hull

Greg "Kele" Hardy"
potterybykele.com

Lynn Isaacson
www.newprospectpottery.com

Mark Issenberg
lookoutmountain.com

Sarah Jaeger
sarahjaeger.com

Gregory A. Johnson
www.potteryforliving.com

Diane Kenney
dianekenney.net

Fay Krapf
www.faykrapf.com

Robbie Lobell
cookonclay.com

Travis McFlynn

James McLellan

Lorna Meaden
www.lornameadenpottery.com

Judith Motzkin
www.breadpots.com

Farraday Newsome
www.indigostreetpottery.com

Jeff Oestreich
www.oestreichpottery.com

Marcia Tani Paul
maashaclay.wordpress.com

Bill Robbins

Steven Rolf
www.scrolfpotter.com

Lora Rust
lorarust.com

Ellen Shankin
www.ellenshankin.com

Julie Timm
freshmudpottery.com

Sumi von Dassow
www.herwheel.com

Tom Wirt
www.claycoyote.com

Recipe Credits

Note: Recipes without listed credit are from the author's kitchen. Some recipes are listed twice as they can be cooked in the oven or on the stovetop.

Ovenware

Uncovered baking dish

Apple Cake from Robin Kerwin
Apple Crisp, Gluten-free
Blackberry Crisp from Pat Burns
Brownies, Flourless (gluten-free)
Chile Rellenos from Pat Burns
Grilled Tomatoes *by Lucia Zucconi, chef at La Meridiana International School of Ceramics*, for Robbie Lobell
Harvest Season Baked Tomatoes from Catherine Schroeder Abelson
Oven Roasted Brussels Sprouts from Marcia Paul
Rhubarb Crisp from Sarah Jaeger
Roasted Winter Vegetables
Sausage, Peppers and Potatoes from Walter Smethills
Spinach Lasagna
Winter Veggie Cobbler from Elise Delfield

Lidded casserole dish

Baked Ziti from Lora Rust
Boston Baked Beans
Braised Lamb Shanks
Cabbage Rolls from Lili Krakowski
Chicken Enchilada Bake from Marcia Paul
Cholent from Lili Krakowski
Roasted Butternut Squash Soup

Earthenware roaster

Exotic Pot Roast from Bill Robbins
Guinea Fowl in earthenware roaster
Oven-roasted Butternut Squash in earthenware
Salmon in earthenware roaster
Simple Chicken roasted in earthenware from Bill Robbins

Upright chicken roaster

Roasted Chicken and Vegetables

Pie pan

Lemon Meringue Pie
Pie Crust from Eleonora Eden
Pumpkin Pie
100% Whole Wheat Pie Crust

Quiche dish

Onion Quiche from Fay Krapf
Crustless Quiche from Fay Krapf

Loaf pan

Cranberry Bread from Robin Kerwin
Maple Pumpkin Bread from Kirsten Thompson
Meatloaf
Sumi's Sourdough Dark Rye Bread

Bread pot

Judy's Russian Rye from Judith Motzkin

Ramekins

Egg Custard from Alice DeLisle

Garlic roaster

Roasted Garlic

Brie baker

Baked Brie
Baked Brie w/Caramelized onions and herbs from Greg and Donna Johnson
Baked Brie with Kahlua and Pecans from Greg and Donna Johnson

Flameware

Flameware casserole dish

Braised Lamb Shanks
Cabbage Rolls from Lili Krakowski
Cholent from Lili Krakowski
Shrimp Tagine with Vegetables and Preserved Lemons by Emily Swantner. Adapted from Paula Wolfert in *Couscous and Other Good Food from Morocco* via Mourad Lahlou in *Food and Wine* 2009.
Spring Vegetable Risotto *by Lucia Zucconi, chef at La Meridiana International School of Ceramics*, for Robbie Lobell

Micaceous or earthenware soup pot

Green Chile Stew from Jan Cameron
Beef Stew
Basic Clay Pot Beans
Roasted Butternut Squash Soup

Microwave Ware

Bowl

Fruity "packs a wallop of flavor" oatmeal from Gayle Bair

Apple baker

Baked apple

Brie baker

Baked Brie w/Caramelized onions and herbs from Greg and Donna Johnson
Baked Brie with Kahlua and Pecans from Greg and Donna Johnson
Hot Brie or Camembert with Chutney from Dana Lehrer Danze

Serving Ware

Cruet set or salad bowl

Favorite Family Salad from Lora Rust
Mama's Oil and Vinegar Dressing from Lora Rust
Miso Ginger Dressing from Marcia Paul
Summer Herb Salad Dressing

Chip and dip set

Edamame dip
Hummus from Lora Rust
Baba Ghanouj (Eggplant Purée) from Lora Rust
Easiest Guacamole Ever from Lora Rust
Spinach Artichoke dip
Spring Pea Dip from Joan Bruneau
Summer Salsa from Joan Bruneau
Spiced Pumpkin Dip from Kirsten Thompson

Dip chiller

Hot Crab Dip "The real thing" from Greg and Donna Johnson

Cheese bell

Lavender Goat Cheese with Cherries, from Anderson Turner of Lucky Penny Farm
Flavored chevre or cream cheese

Butter dish

Flavored butter
Garlic butter
Honey butter

Food Preparation

Citrus juicer or an egg separator

Lemon Meringue Pie
Unbaked Cheesecake

Food Storage

Tea caddy

Chai mixture

French butter crock

Making butter
Flavored butter
Garlic butter
Honey butter

Sauerkraut crock

Cucumber Pickles
Fermented Summer Herbs
Kim Chi
Pickled Cucumbers and Onions from Gayle Bair
Red Beet Eggs—a Pennsylvania Dutch style recipe from Gayle Bair
Sauerkraut

Suppliers

Aardvark Clay & Supplies
www.aardvarkclay.com
(714) 541-4157
1400 East Pomona St.
Santa Ana, Ca. 92705

Armadillo Clay and Supplies
www.armadilloclay.com/
(512) 385-7311
3307 E 4th St.
Austin, TX 78702

Clayworks Supplies, Inc.
www.clayworkssupplies.com
(410) 235-5998
4625 Falls Road
Baltimore, Md. 21209

Highwater Clays
http://www.highwaterclays.com
(828) 252-6033
600 Riverside Drive
Asheville, NC 28801

Leslie Ceramic Supply
www.leslieceramics.com
(510) 524-7363
1212 San Pablo Ave.
Berkeley, CA 94706
Carries a flameware clay: Toki Flameclay

Industrial Minerals Co.
www.clayimco.com/
(916) 383-2811
7268 Frasinetti Road
Sacramento, CA 95828
See website for distributors. They make Flameclay for Leslie Ceramic Supply

Minnesota Clay
www.mnclay.com/
(800) CLAY-USA (800-252-9872) or locally (763) 432-0875
2960 Niagara Lane
Plymouth, MN 55447
Special mix flameware clay recipe. Requires minimum 1,000 lb purchase.

New Mexico Clay
www.micaclay.com
(505) 881-2350
(800) 781-2529
3300 Girard NE
Albuquerque, New Mexico 87107
White and red micaceous clay, and powdered mica to add to clays and slips. To make micaceous clay, add 20% coarse or fine mica to an earthenware clay body.

Plainsman Clays, Ltd.
www.plainsmanclays.com
(403) 527-8535
702 Wood Street S.E.
Medicine Hat, Alberta, Canada T1A 1E9
See website for list of distributors. Flameware clay in development.

Sheffield Pottery
www.sheffield-pottery.com/
(888) 774-2529 or (413) 229-7700
995 North Main St
P.O.Box 399
Sheffield, MA 01257

Standard Ceramic Supply
www.standardceramic.com/
(412) 276-6333
P.O. Box 16240
Pittsburgh, PA 15242-0240
See website for distributors.

Fulwood Measure
12 Mine Street
Flemington, NJ 08822
(908) 237-0671
http://www.kissimmeeriverpottery.com/fulwood_measure.htm
Measuring tool for duplicating forms.

Norpro 144 Heat Diffuser
Made from two pieces of tin perforated with many small holes, with an air pocket between them. It has a wooden handle. There are many kinds of heat diffusers, but this one is economical and works well with earthenware pottery. Available from Amazon.

Glaze Recipes and Testing

There are thousands of glaze recipes floating around the pottery community. Most are not tested or analyzed for stability and durability. The glazes that follow are tested and/or analyzed with glaze calculation software and, at the time of testing, they were deemed stable; however, materials change. Glazes that were stable at one time may become less stable if their ingredients change. Most of these are "base glazes" meaning they are clear or white, but you can mix your choice of colorants into them to make colored glazes. Just don't use too much colorant—especially in the food contact area. You are safe if you use a clear or white glaze on the inside of ware as a liner glaze, and keep the colored glaze on the outside of the ware.

Note: Test labs (see page 163) can provide more information. See page 16 to assure that the glazes you use are suitable for cookware and serving pieces.

Tony Hansen Glazes

These non-leaching, stable base glaze recipes are printed by courtesy of Tony Hansen, from his website. Go to digitalfire.com/4sight/recipes/index.html for more information about these recipes, for many more recipes, and for a wealth of information about formulating and using glazes.

G1214M Clear Base Glaze

Cone 6

Wollastonite	20 %
Ferro Frit 3134	20
EPK Kaolin	20
Custer Feldspar	20
Silica	20
	100 %

G1214Z Matte Base Glaze

Cone 6

Wollastonite	26.2 %
Ferro Frit 3124	35.0
EPK Kaolin	34.0
Silica	4.9
	100.0 %

G1916M Glossy Base Glaze

Cone 06-04

Ferro Frit 3134	40 %
Ferro Frit 3124	40
EPK Kaolin	15
Silica	5
	100 %

G1947U Transparent Base Glaze

Cone 10 Reduction

Custer Feldspar	27.0 %
EPK Kaolin	20.5
Wollastonite	23.5
Zinc Oxide	2.5
Silica	26.5
	100.0 %

G2571 Silky Matte Base Glaze

Cone 10 Oxidation/Reduction

Wollastonite	5.5 %
Custer Feldspar	28.5
EPK Kaolin	28.0
Dolomite	19.0
Gerstley Borate	4.0
Silica	15.0
	100.0 %

John Hesselberth Glazes

The following recipes are from John Hesselberth, coauthored with Ron Roy of *Mastering Cone 6 Glazes*. They are glazes he tested and found to be stable. See www.frogpondpottery.com for more information.

Potter's Palette Alkaline Green

Cone 04

Ferro Frit 3124	75 %
EPK Kaolin	15
Silica	10
	100 %
Add:	
Bentonite	1 %
Copper Carbonate	3 %
Chromium Oxide	1 %

Charcoal Satin

Cone 6 Oxidation

Ferro Frit 3134	31.0 %
Wollastonite	23.2
EPK Kaolin	31.7
Silica	14.1
	100.0 %
Add:	
Mason Stain 6600	10.0 %
Rutile	6.0 %

Frog Pond Green

Cone 6 Oxidation

Ferro Frit 3124	31.0 %
Wollastonite	23.2
EPK Kaolin	31.7
Silica	14.1
	100.0 %
Add:	
Copper Carbonate	3.5 %
Rutile	5.5%

Floating Blue

Cone 6 Oxidation

Nepheline Syenite	47.3 %
Gerstley Borate	27.0
EPK Kaolin	5.4
Silica	20.3
	100.0 %
Add:	
Cobalt Oxide	1.0 %
Red Iron Oxide	2.0 %
Bentonite	1.0 %
Rutile	4.0 %

Ron Roy Black

Cone 6 Oxidation

Ferro Frit 3134	26 %
Custer Feldspar	22
Talc	5
Whiting	4
EPK Kaolin	17
Silica	26
	100 %
Add:	
Bentonite	2 %
Red Iron Oxide	9 %
Cobalt Carbonate	2 %

Teal Blue

Cone 6 oxidation

Nepheline Syenite	35 %
Whiting	18
Ferro Frit 3134	12
OM4 Ball Clay	5
Silica	30
	100 %
Add:	
Copper Carbonate	4 %
Tin Oxide	8 %

AW Deep Blue

Cone 10 Oxidation or Reduction

Custer Feldspar	28.3 %
Wollastonite	22.6
Gerstley Borate	3.8
EPK Kaolin	18.9
Silica	6.4
	100.0 %
Add:	
Cobalt Carbonate	2.0 %
Bentonite	1.0 %

Hesselberth comments that this is a very stable glaze but it has a somewhat low expansion rate so it may tend to dunt or shiver on some clays. However, if your clay has a low coefficient of thermal expansion, which is desirable for ovenware, this glaze might work well.

Diana Pancioli Glazes

The following glazes are from Diana Pancioli's Glaze Forward project, for which she spent a year developing cone 6 reduction glazes and made them available to other potters. They are available from her website www.dianapancioli.com.

Satin Celadon

Cone 6 Reduction

Nepheline Syenite	34.0 %
Whiting	20.0
Talc	5.0
Ferro Frit3110	2.0
OM4 Ball Clay	19.0
Silica	20.0
	100.0 %
Add:	
Red Iron Oxide	1.5 %
Bentonite	2.0 %

Transparent Gloss

Cone 6 Reduction

Ferro Frit 3195	29 %
Wollastonite	29
Magnesium Carbonate	4
EPK Kaolin	19
Silica	19
	100 %
Add:	
Bentonite	2 %

Satin White

Cone 6 Reduction

Kona F4 Feldspar	38 %
Whiting	20
Talc	5
Ferro Frit 3134	8
EPK Kaolin	18
Silica	11
	100 %
Add:	
Zircopax	8 %
Bentonite	2 %

Dark Blue

Cone 6 Reduction

Kona F-4 Feldspar	41.0 %
Whiting	19.0
Ferro Frit 3110	5.0
EPK Kaolin	10.0
Silica	25.0
	100.0 %
Add:	
Cobalt Carbonate	2.0 %
Red Iron Oxide	1.5 %
Bentonite	2.0 %

Red Terra Sigillata

For sealing earthenware clay

Water	2200 gr
Newman Red Clay (or Redart)	1000 gr
Darvan 7 or 811	30 gr

1. Measure water into a large glass or clear plastic jar with a wide mouth. Add Darvan and stir. Add clay and shake vigorously.
2. Leave undisturbed to settle for three hours. You will see a dark layer of sludge at the bottom of the container. Siphon off the liquid portion above the layer of sludge. Be careful you don't pick up any of the sludge. Discard the bottom layer of sludge.
3. It should be about the right consistency to use right away but if you want it thicker, let it evaporate for a day or two.
4. Apply two or three coats to bone dry ware, allow to dry just until the surface isn't wet, and burnish with fingers, a soft cloth, a nylon stocking, a chamois, a car-polishing mitt, or a plastic grocery bag. Don't touch the wet surface, and make sure your polishing cloth is very clean. For the greatest shine, apply three thin coats, polishing between coats.

Testing Facilities

The test you are most likely to want performed on your pottery is for metal oxide leaching from your glazes. If you are planning to use a glaze with a significant amount of toxic metal oxide inside ware meant for food, get it leach-tested before you commit your entire production to this glaze. If you stick with liner glazes (glazes with no toxic ingredients) inside your ware, then leach-testing is not an issue.

Another test some potters might want performed is a dilatometer test. This tests the clay for expansion. You will only need to worry about this if you are working with flameware clay. Testing labs can test for a whole list of other attributes, such as water absorption, resistance to crazing, freeze-thaw resistance, chipping and impact resistance, thermal shock, metal marking, microwave use, freezer to oven use, and more. Keep in mind these labs are very large industrial facilities, who primarily test for very large industrial producers, and they test for a mind-boggling array of industries other than ceramics—so browsing their websites and finding the test you want can be a bit intimidating.

Listed below are a few labs that perform leach testing; they all perform a wide range of other tests as well. Leach-testing costs around $75–$100 or more per sample, per metal you want tested for, so do everything you can to reduce the number of toxic ingredients in your glazes before you resort to this testing! And once you have sent in your sample and gotten your test results, you'll want some way to evaluate the results. Monona Rossol, an industrial hygienist who specializes in safety issues surrounding art materials, says, "Remember, you need to look at your glaze formulas and pick two or three metals which are the most toxic and/or in the highest concentrations. Only lead and cadmium are regulated, but many other metals are also highly toxic. So once you have the data, I can send you a list of the Maximum Daily Contaminants for potable water which we use as guides. Obviously, if your pot doesn't leach more than would be allowed in a really lousy public water supply, it is probably safe for use." (Rossol can be contacted at http://artscraftstheatersafety.org/). Some potters believe this is too stringent a guideline for glazed pottery, but if your glaze does pass this stringent test, you can definitely breathe a sigh of relief and feel free to use it on anything.

For testing purposes, make plain cups or small bowls lined with the glazes you want tested and don't ask for them back from the lab. These are test pots; make sure you fire them in the same conditions your production work will be fired in. That is, be sure your test pot is fired to the exact cone temperature and firing speed or schedule that you plan to use.

Testing labs occasionally change personnel and practices, not to mention websites and owners, so be sure to contact the lab yourself before sending off a sample to be sure the information below is still accurate. For a list of more testing facilities, see Tony Hansen's Digital Fire website http://digitalfire.com/services/database.php?list=labs

Brandywine Science Center, Inc
204 Line Road
Kennett Square PA 19348
610-444-0850
http://www.bsclab.com/Pottery_Testing.html

Lucideon
http://www.lucideon.com/testing-analysis
Queens Road
Penkhull
Stoke-on-Trent
Staffordshire
ST4 7LQ
United Kingdom
Enquiries +44(0)1782 764428
UK customers 0845 026 0902
Email enquiries@lucideon.com

EMSL Analytical, Inc.
200 Route I 30 North
Connaminson, NJ 08077
856-303-2549 or 800-220-3675
Lab Supervisor, Shannon Kauffman

Galbraith Laboratories
P.O. Box 51610
Knoxville, TN 37950-1610
or
2323 Sycamore Drive
Knoxville, TN 37921-1700
1-877-449-8797
http://www.galbraith.com

Bibliography

Pottery Books

Anderson, Duane, *All That Glitters: The Emergence of Native American Micaceous Art Pottery in Northern New Mexico*, School of American Research Press, Santa Fe, NM, 1999.

Bailey, Michael, *Glazes Cone 6*, A&C Black, London, England, 2001.

Bloomfield, Linda, *Contemporary Tableware,* Bloomsbury Publishing, London, 2013.

Britt, John, *The Complete Guide to High-Fire Glazes, Glazing and Firing at Cone 10*, Lark Books, Asheville, NC, 2004.

French, Neal *The Potter's Directory of Shape and Form*, Krause Publications, Iola, WI, 1998.

Hesselberth, John and Ron Roy, *Mastering Glazes Cone 6*, Frog Pond Pottery, 2002.

Hopper, Robin, *Functional Pottery, Form and Aesthetics in Pots of Purpose,* The American Ceramic Society, Westerville, OH, 2011.

Illian, Clary, *A Potter's Workbook*, University of Iowa Press, Iowa City, IA, 1999.

Obstler, Mimi, *Out of the Earth, Into the Fire,* The American Ceramic Society, Westerville, OH, 2000.

Rhodes, Daniel, *Clay and Glazes for the Potter: 3rd Edition, Revised and Expanded by Robin Hopper,* Krause Publications, Iola, WI, 2000.

Rogers, Phil, *Throwing Pots*, University of Pennsylvania Press, Philadelphia, PA, 2000.

Turner, Anderson, Editor, *Pottery Making Technique: A Pottery Making Illustrated Handbook*, The American Ceramic Society, Westerville, OH, 2004.

Walter, Josie, *Pots in the Kitchen,* Crowood Press, 2002.

Wood, Karen Ann, *Tableware in Clay From Studio and Workshop,* The Crowood Press, Ramsbury, Marlborough, England, 1999.

Woodhead, Steve, *The Teapot Book,* A&C Black, London, England, 2005.

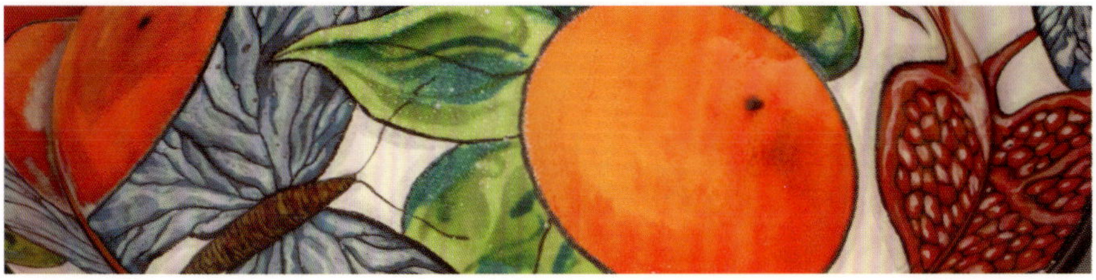

Cooking Books

Albala, Ken and Rosanna Nafziger, *The Lost Art of Real Cooking,* Penguin Group, New York, 2010. This book includes information about fermenting and making sauerkraut, as well as making butter. Albala is a potter as well as a scholar and cook.

Basan, Ghillie, *Tagine, Spicy Stews from Morocco,* Ryland, Peters and Small, New York, 2007.

Basan, Ghillie, *Tagines and Couscous, Delicious Recipes for Moroccan One-pot Cooking,* Ryland, Peters and Small, New York, 2010.

Jacobi, Dana, *The Best of Clay Pot Cooking,* Collins Publishers, San Francisco, 1995.

Katz, Sandor Ellix, *The Art of Fermentation,* Chelsea Green, White River VT, 2012 Complete compendium of fermenting recipes and techniques, including sauerkrauts and dairy products.

Katz, Sandor Ellix, *Wild Fermentation,* Chelsea Green, White River VT, 2003. A much thinner and less comprehensive book that covers the same basic material. Katz has a website with much useful information at http://www.wildfermentation.com/

Woolfert, Paula, *Mediterranean Clay Pot Cooking: Traditional and Modern Recipes to Savor and Share,* John Wiley and Sons, Hoboken, NJ, 2009.

Glaze Software

Glazemaster
www.masteringglazes.com/glazemaster/

Glaze Simulator
www.glazesimulator.com/recWizard.php

Hyperglaze
www.hyperglaze.com/

Insight
digitalfire.com/index.html

Matrix
www.matrix2000.co.nz/Index.cfm

Index

Index